Cocaine

Global histories

"Truly international in its scope, *Cocaine* is the first historical survey of perhaps the most paradoxical of this century's major narcotics. Readers will welcome the balanced attention given to the scientific, medical, commercial, legal and cultural dimensions of the story."

Roy Porter, Wellcome Institute for the History of Medicine

"Cocaine history is back, more sophisticated than ever. *Cocaine: Global Histories* is an important resource for anyone interested in drug history and politics, and an indispensable one for those who would understand cocaine in global context."

David Courtwright, University of North Florida

Originally a medical miracle, cocaine is now a dangerous pariah drug. *Cocaine: Global Histories* examines the rise and fall of this notorious substance. In the nineteenth century it was openly legal and legitimately used by scientists, doctors and pharmaceutical giants alike. This contrasts starkly with the international prohibitionist regimes and underground circuits linked to cocaine today.

Drawing on exciting new global perspectives, *Cocaine* analyses and rethinks the origins of the modern drug cocaine. For the first time, a book brings together the world's leading writers on the history of cocaine. Themes explored include:

- the early manufacture, sale and control of cocaine in the United States;
- Amsterdam's complex cocaine network;
- Japan and the unknown Southeast Asian cocaine industry;
- export of cocaine prohibitions to Peru;
- sex, drugs and race in London.

Cocaine unveils new sources and covert social, cultural and political transformations that shed light on cocaine's hidden history. This volume is essential reading for anyone concerned with the place of drugs in the modern world.

Paul Gootenberg is Professor of History at the State University of New York, Stony Brook, and author of *Between Silver and Guano* (Princeton, 1989) and *Imagining Development* (California, 1993).

Cocaine

Global histories

Edited by Paul Gootenberg

London and New York

First published 1999
by Routledge
2 Park Square, Milton Park, Abingdon, Oxon, OX14 4RN

Simultaneously published in the USA and Canada
by Routledge

270 Madison Ave, New York NY 10016

Routledge is an imprint of the Taylor & Francis Group

Transferred to Digital Printing 2006

Typeset in Baskerville by Routledge

British Library Cataloguing in Publication Data
A catalogue record for this book is available from the British Library

Library of Congress Cataloging in Publication Data
A catalogue record for this book has been requested

ISBN 0–415–19247–1 (hbk)
ISBN 0–415–22001–7 (pbk)

Contents

PART II
European axis, Asian circuits (Germany, Britain, the Netherlands and Java, Japan)

Contributors

Luis Astorga, from the state of Sinaloa (Mexico), is a sociologist and investigator at the *Instituto de Investigaciones Sociales*, UNAM (National University of Mexico). He is the author of two recent books on drugs in Mexico, *Mitología del "narcotraficante" en México* (Plaza y Valdés, 1995) and *El siglo de las drogas* (Espasa-Hoy, 1996). His area of study now is border trafficking since 1900.

H. Richard Friman is Associate Professor of Political Science at Marquette University. He published *NarcoDiplomacy: Exporting the US War on Drugs* (Cornell University Press, 1996) and varied articles on relations between developed countries in the global drug trade. His current research is on immigration, drug control, and social order in the advanced industrial states.

Paul Gootenberg is a Professor of Latin American History at SUNY-Stony Brook. He has authored *Between Silver and Guano* (Princeton University Press, 1989) and *Imagining Development* (University of California Press, 1993), and sundry works on Andean economic, social, and intellectual history. His current project is an archival history of Andean cocaine from 1880–1960.

Steven B. Karch, MD, a forensic pathologist, is Assistant Medical Examiner for the City and County of San Francisco. A recognized medical authority on cocaine, his textbook *The Pathology of Drug Abuse* (CRC Press, 1996) is standard reference in the field. He recently published *A Brief History of Cocaine* (CRC Press, 1998).

Marek Kohn is a British writer, journalist, and cultural historian. His works include *Narcomania: On Heroin* (Faber & Faber, 1987) and *The Dope Girls: The Birth of the British Drug Underground* (Lawrence & Wishart, 1992) and other books. He currently writes on race and bio-technologies.

Marcel de Kort studied at Rotterdam's Erasmus University, where he received a Ph.D. in 1995 with a thesis on the history of Dutch drug policy. At the University of Amsterdam Institute of Criminology he worked on projects on drug trades and law enforcement. He is now a drug policy adviser at the Ministry of Health, Welfare and Sport of the Netherlands.

Ethan Nadelmann taught politics and public policy at Princeton's Wilson School and is the author of *Cops Across Borders* (Penn State Press, 1993). He has edited several recent books on harm reduction and drug policy reform. He is Director of the Lindesmith Center, the New York drug policy institute, an affiliate of the Soros Open Society Institute.

Mary Roldán earned her doctorate in History from Harvard University in 1992 and teaches Latin American History at Cornell. She has worked extensively in Colombia while completing a book on the social history of "*La Violencia*" in Colombia (1946–53) entitled *Hegemony and Violence: Class, Culture and Politics in Twentieth-Century Antioquia.*

Joseph F. Spillane is Assistant Professor of History at the University of Florida at Gainesville, and with their Center for Studies in Criminology and Law. He is the author of *Cocaine: From Medical Marvel to Modern Menace in the United States, 1884–1920* (Johns Hopkins University Press, 1999). Besides the history of United States drug control, his interests span criminal justice and urban public policy.

Foreword

Ethan Nadelmann

During the late 1980s – precisely one decade ago – cocaine became something of a national obsession in the United States. The war on drugs, rhetorically dormant since the Nixon Administration, found a new life in cocaine. TV "news" programs reported day after day on drug enforcement operations, "crack babies," and "cocaine-related" acts of violence. News magazines put it on their covers. President Bush gave a nationally televised speech to the nation on the cocaine threat. Public opinion polls pointed to drugs – notably cocaine – as the "number one" concern of American citizens. Outside of the United States, Colombia reminded some of Chicago during Prohibition, albeit on a much more substantial and deadly scale. Bolivia and Peru were implicated as well as producers and exporters of the raw and semi-refined coca materials used to produce cocaine. Elsewhere, in Europe, Asia, Africa, and beyond, cocaine was largely a non-issue, though some cocaine "scares" were to erupt there, too.

Drug crazes typically come and go, never lasting too long. They usually focus on a single drug, one that either is new or seems new. The rapid spread of crack – a smokeable form of cocaine – was new. Cocaine itself was not, but few Americans knew anything of its history. There were, in effect, few reality checks on depictions or perceptions of cocaine. Anything could be said, and almost anything was, about the drug's unique powers to destroy the bodies and souls of United States citizens and South American nations, or how the problem had emerged. Now the rage about cocaine has mostly passed in the United States, even as cocaine markets expand in other parts of the world.

Drug histories – particularly those of the scholarly caliber exemplified in this volume – rarely reflect well upon either contemporary drug warriors or their predecessors. Drug warriors, and the panics they stimulate, tend to focus on the drugs *per se* as a singular or at least dominant cause of multiple ills. They tend to portray all use of a particular drug as aberrant and destructive. They assume both the necessity of prohibitionist laws and the immorality of using particular drugs. And they rely heavily on simplistic caricatures of participants in drug markets. Drug histories, by contrast, tend to emphasize complexity and nuance: causal relationships become cloudier; political motivations more complicated; and drug-use patterns more diverse and interesting. Both drug use and drug policies are analyzed in terms of the "sets and settings" (the social, cultural, and temporal contexts) in which they occur.

Paul Gootenberg's edited volume is valuable in so many ways. As the first substantial book on global cocaine history, it automatically makes a major contribution to the small but growing interdisciplinary arena of drug history, which has focused (at least as far as "illegal" drugs are concerned) largely on the opiates. The authors have all made valuable use of archives, both virgin and well worn, from around the world. They build responsibly on the extant literature, demonstrating a level of sophistication and insight that heralds a maturation of the field. And Gootenberg's talents are evident in the elegant complementarity of the diverse methodologies and perspectives displayed in the various chapters. It is a shame that no such book (aside from some journalistic attempts) was available a decade ago, when it might have provided at least a modest antidote to the ahistorical tone of political and journalistic commentary on cocaine, the cocaine trade, and the laws prohibiting cocaine. It is a healthy sign that now the drug policy reform movement, indirectly at least, has helped open doors to a new level of intellectual complexity on the origins of today's dilemmas with cocaine.

For example, Joseph Spillane's chapter on cocaine use in the United States between 1880 and 1920 is particularly useful in this regard. Spillane reminds us that cocaine was consumed in a great variety of oral concoctions, some containing modest amounts of fluid extracts of coca and others quite potent concentrations of pure cocaine. His analysis strongly suggests that the first cocaine prohibitions were most effective in suppressing the most benign forms of the drug. Today coca producers in Bolivia and Peru petition international organizations for permission to once again export products containing extracts of coca. Spillane's discussion makes one wonder if low-potency coca-based products might re-emerge as benign but profitable products in international trade.

The history of psychoactive drugs is almost inevitably a history of the regulation and prohibition of particular drugs. Gootenberg and his collaborators are highly sophisticated in their analysis, whether the focus is the political contexts and forces that resulted in cocaine's prohibition in different countries, or the impact of new regulations and prohibitions on drug markets and drug-use patterns. The editor in particular grasps that the emergence of global prohibition regimes is best understood by compiling and weaving together comparative and transnational studies anchored upon serious archival research. A new picture or story of cocaine develops. It is worth noting that no comparable volume has yet analyzed the evolution of opiate controls around the world (and indeed I know of no comparable analysis of the rise of alcohol prohibition in various parts of the world earlier in the twentieth century).

The history of cocaine in the twentieth century has not been pretty. Many millions of people have enjoyed the drug, and many with no regrets. But there is no forgetting the devastation associated with cocaine, particularly among those economically disadvantaged and socially dislocated folk who let cocaine get the better of them. Nor can we ignore the hundreds of thousands incarcerated in jails and prisons, the tens of billions of dollars devoted to the war on cocaine, the devastating violence and corruption generated by the interplay of prohibitionist economics and morals, and the vast waste of human and economic resources devoted to "combating" cocaine. Taken together, the articles in this volume leave the reader with a set of questions worth asking before embarking on the drug crusades of the *next* century: Was all this necessary? Was the emergence of such a comprehensive global cocaine prohibition regime inevitable? Did it prevent a global epidemic of deadly cocaine abuse or did it result in more harm than good? Might coca and cocaine have been "domesticated" into contemporary societies with far fewer negative consequences than have resulted under the current regime? Is a more balanced cocaine regulatory regime possible in the next century? And can we learn anything from this century's experience that might help us avoid comparable disasters with different psychoactive substances in the future?

Ethan Nadelmann
The Lindesmith Center

Acknowledgments

All books are collective but "collections" even more so. So let me first salute the enthusiasm (and remarkable punctuality) of the eight authors gathered here, pioneers of cocaine history all, who first came together from around the globe in May 1997 to conference at the Russell Sage Foundation in New York City. Beyond the pleasure of working together, we've transformed, I believe, into a veritable "working group" of colleagues in this new and hopefully ongoing scholarly project of cocaine history. The symposium from which this book sprang, "From Miracle to Menace: Cocaine in Global and Historical Perspectives," was sponsored and supported by two New York institutions, the Russell Sage Foundation and the Lindesmith Center (an affiliate of the Open Society Institute). The RSF was an exemplary facility for hosting this forum, and I especially thank its intrepid president, Eric Wanner, for adopting a theme that lies slightly off the map of their usual concerns. The "third floor" at the RSF – a more-creative-than-usual clutch of social scientists – made for stimulating *compañeros*, particularly during our memorable (or hard to remember) topical Friday forums. Now on Tenth Avenue, Ethan Nadelmann of the Lindesmith Center, apart from his other busy roles, has warmly encouraged the development of serious "drug history" and has been a stimulating intellectual colleague to boot.

At the RSF, I must still thank Ross Goldstein (who worked a bit as conference assistant), Kim Giamportone and Cecelia Walsh-Russo (of the superb third-floor staff), Cheryl Seleski for upstairs conference support, plus the team of Sara Beckman and Jamie Gray, who bravely attempted to upgrade my technological incompetence. At RSF, Lisa Kahraman gave of herself editorially where others could not. In another time, JoAnn Kawell helped spark my interest in the history of cocaine and also contributed to the conference. Eric Hershberg of the Social Science Research Council's Latin American desk (and now a globalist) has been a friend to advancing drugs as history, as is Bill McAllister, a historian at the University of Virginia who critically read this as a manuscript. A number a perceptive commentators helped in the transformation of draft papers into this polished book: I thank Nancy Tomes and Wolf Schäfer (of the History Department at my home base of SUNY-Stony Brook), Bill Roseberry and Debbie Poole (from Anthropology at the New School for Social Research, a home away from home), Enrique Mayer and Robert Byck, MD (both of Yale: Anthropology and Psychiatry respectively), Ethan Nadelmann (again), John Morgan, MD (CUNY, Pharmacology), and two anonymously frank Routledge readers. I thank our editor, Heather McCallum, and publisher, Routledge (UK), who had the foresight to grab this project and then (with Gillian Kay) carefully see it through to completion – despite a few trying moments along the way. Their copy-editor (Tony Nixon) did the brilliant job of turning these papers into the Queen's (Americanized) English. May cocaine – perhaps the most stimulating substance known – become a stimulus to high scholarship as well as sales. And *gracias* to my wife, Laura Lavín-Sainz de la Peña, who (besides her frequent computer salvation here) never saw anything strange in a historian pursuing guano, her, and then cocaine.

Paul Gootenberg
Brooklyn, NY, 1998

1 Introduction

Cocaine: the hidden histories

Paul Gootenberg

Cocaine, a substance of notoriety today, is certainly no *new* drug or menace on the global scene. From 1860, when first synthesized in a German lab from dried Peruvian coca leaf, to around the turn of the century, openly legal and legitimate cocaine stirred a massive boom among scientists and medical men, consumers and enthusiasts of many ilks, and international traders and manufacturers, including some of the world's leading pharmaceutical firms. Yet almost as rapidly, from 1900 to the 1920s, this early medical and commercial fascination with cocaine collapsed, its prestige replaced step by step until the 1960s by the global prohibitionist regimes and underground cocaine circuits that we know too well today. Indeed, it can be argued that cocaine's first rise and fall in the West as a "heroic" and "modern" drug was a prelude to its construction and current status as a dangerous and pariah one. Yet that birth of cocaine, as we know it, remains its hidden history.

This book, *Cocaine: Global Histories*, brings together fresh efforts to retrieve and rethink these elusive origins of the modern drug, cocaine. It looks from global and interdisciplinary perspectives, by comparing and connecting the key international players and places in the definition of early cocaine – ranging from the remote coca-rich tropical slopes of the Andes to the regulatory politics of the Progressive-era United States, from modernizing European science and medicine to an industrializing imperial Japan. It focuses on a core yet wide open analytical question: How did cocaine suddenly erupt and spread into a global drug and how did that process invert after 1900, leading to its international pariah status and working (or not-so-working) regimes of prohibition? What was it actually like when drugs like cocaine were freely available on the market and in the culture? In a past tense, just how is it that drugs get redefined as socially menacing? How did those broad processes unfold across varying countries, contexts, and cultures?

The national histories pursued this way include the United States and Peru, Britain, Germany, the Netherlands and colonial Java, and Japan, along with essays on the origins of contemporary Colombian and Mexican entanglements with illicit cocaine. A book such as this one should be of interest not only to the small but growing circle of historians of drugs but to any student of history interested in how substances interact with societies and cultures – as well as by the larger social-science community or public critically concerned with drug issues. For along the way, *Cocaine: Global Histories* inevitably bares some tangled roots of our currently troubled relationships with cocaine and evokes new historicized ways of viewing our troubled proscriptive regimes. We also hope it suggests novel and serious ways of doing "drug history" writ large.

Neglect, academic and otherwise, of cocaine history has been active – a forbidden as well as hidden history – for issues of such import could not have been ignored on their own. Still, *Cocaine: Global Histories* marks what can be considered a "third wave" in study of this stimulant. What cocaine's latest historians are attempting here – with their sights on the recovery of fresh primary sources, on the unveiling of covert social, cultural, and political transformations, and on teasing out the drug's internationalist networks – is first and best seen against its historiographic backdrop. Once in mind, this Introduction, turns to what distinguishes and unites this new wave of study and finally to the rich diversity of cases in cocaine's hidden history.

A brief "historiography" of cocaine

The first wave of intellectual and research fascination with cocaine hit shore with the drug itself, and, to an extent, those nineteenth-century networks of researchers, promoters, enthusiasts, and critics remain an object of study here. After a two-decade lag, the dramatic mid-1880s discovery of cocaine's anesthetic properties brought a flood of writings around cocaine's medicinal uses (as a nascent panacea, it had so many), botany, applications, or history (as in colorful renderings of coca's origins in Andean civilizations) – found in the era's pharmacy, medical, or drug trade journals. Each country seen here had its share of cocaine and coca experts, and dilettantes as well, who left a vast documentary record, some of them virtual classics or primary documents of the field. The German-speaking world had its Karl Köller, E. Merck, Sigmund Freud (as is well known), and more critically Louis Lewin, to name a few; the French, Angelo Mariani (promoter of coca-laced Vin Mariani tonic); the British, such distinguished physicians as Dr Robert Christison, pharmacist William Martindale and a world-renowned botanist in Kew Gardens' Richard Spruce. In Peru, one finds the surprising and innovative scientific experiments of doctors Tomás Moreno y Maíz and Alfredo Bignon, unsung agronomists like Manuel Vinelli and the industrial projects of Pedro Paulet and Mario Durand, among others. The Dutch saw colonial horticultural campaigns of Emma Reens and A.W.K. de Jong, and the Japanese their cosmopolitan chemist, Jokichi Takamine. Perhaps the North Americans spawned the richest collection of coca and cocaine literature: from pioneer ethno-botanists such as H.H. Rusby to leading surgeons like William S. Halstead and William Hammond, to pharmaceutical innovators like Parke-Davis's Edward Squibb, and coca devotees such as Dr W. Golden Mortimer with his classic herbalist defense *History of Coca: "The Divine Plant" of the Incas* (1901). Surviving late-nineteenth-century journals are littered with scores of experiments, notes, commentaries, debates, and warnings on coca and cocaine as therapy and tonics, as naïve as they may seem to today's medical science. Hundreds of figures, with multifarious opinions of coca and cocaine, were engaged. The globalizing of such circuits of drug information, personnel, and opinion was both swift and thorough. By the 1890s and early 1900s, however, stronger anti-cocaine passions and politics set in, with its opponents (America's T.D. Crothers or Germany's A. Erlenmeyer are notable examples) having naturally less and less to say about a substance they disdained, battled, or feared. Cocaine became still another "mania" outside a shrinking realm of acceptable medical use. Reformers, of course, wanted it to go away – in thought as well as deed.

The subsequent era, 1920–60, after the onset of cocaine prohibitions (finalized in the vanguard United States by the 1920s, with distinct timing elsewhere), left a long and deep gap in knowledge about cocaine – even, as many have, complained, about its potential dangers.[1] As a criminalized substance driven underground, of discredited scientific prestige, cocaine no longer held legitimate commercial promise. Its dwindling medicinal uses became progressively supplanted by synthetic substitutes like novocaine. Cocaine also made an awkward fit to the new medicalized "addiction" paradigm and research gathering around other drugs. As such it attracted few published studies and no sponsored pharmaceutical research. By the 1930s, cocaine reached its nadir of consumption in the West, seemingly relegated to mythic counter-cultural roles (Hollywood, jazz, the Third Reich). Prospective researchers, say students of pharmacy or history, would have nothing to gain in study of such a marginalized substance. This situation varied only in countries like Peru and Japan that still dragged their feet on the bans, though Peruvians began scrutinizing their native coca use, in newly negative terms, as international organs pressed against it as well by the 1940s. Sometimes, as in the United States of the 1940s, governments actively suppressed findings that could suggest values of either coca or cocaine and made medical research extremely cumbersome. Indeed, it has been noted that until the 1970s scientific knowledge of the drug (and its abuse) lagged seriously behind that of comparable drugs.[2] Moreover, cocaine was to lose much of its juridical and thus historical distinctiveness. Lumped together by American and later international codes with Narcotics – as a stimulant, there are fundamental differences – watchdog and policing agencies (such as the League of Nations' Advisory Committee on Traffic in Opium or the US Federal Bureau of Narcotics – FBN) treated cocaine as a throwaway concern – conflating and losing it in their files and archives along the way. Observations of cocaine that survived were posed in a surveillance or policing discourse or as attempts to bolster the systems of control. Even the scattered users of the 1920s through 1950s, as oral histories now show, regarded cocaine mainly as a drug to mix in with others. Such conflations and gaps are what makes cocaine such a challenging topic for historical researchers today.

Indeed, the noted American drug historian, David F. Musto, has stressed how this long gap in social knowledge about cocaine use, in both popular culture and policy circles, was in part responsible for the frenzy of use when the repressed was to return (as a glamour and recreational drug) in the 1970s.[3] This may be true, and certainly the history of cocaine suffers from these discontinuities. We argue here, however, that it is vital to tease out the lost historical *connections* between the processes of constructing cocaine proscriptions and illicit spaces in the first half of this century and the twin menaces of cocaine and intensified drug warring (driven by cocaine) that finally hit the industrialized world in the second half. At the least, there are analytic analogies to be posed and larger historical assumptions to test about drugs and drug cultures. As readers will see, what transpired in the 1970s can be read as an aftermath of histories and relationships exhumed here.

With the mid-1970s return of cocaine to mass consumption, we became awash in a second wave of cocaine scholarship. Apart from crash government-sponsored medical and social-policy research, for a period (1975–85) we also witnessed a positive resurgence of interest in cocaine's early – and by now wholly forgotten – history. In part, these writers were recollecting as well as collecting the past, in order to help our society (mainly North American) cope with the surprises and shocks dealt by spreading cocaine availability and culture. There were reprints of coca and cocaine classics (Mortimer's *Coca*, for one durable example). Yale's Dr Robert Byck put together an invaluable set of Freud's original "Cocaine papers" and restored Freud's role as a founder of modern psychopharmacology as well as psychoanalysis; a number of quality coca/cocaine "readers" brought to public light sundry writings (pro and con) of the late nineteenth century.[4] We saw coca and cocaine "coffee-table books" (lavishly illustrated *à la* the original Mariani albums) and even user-friendly paeans to cocaine, since the drug was initially reincarnated as a luxury, as if on an historical cycle. Medical and sociological journals of the 1970s reveal dozens of hastily produced review articles, based on recovery and recycling of published pamphlets, research notes, and debates from the first boom.[5]

This second wave was less pronounced in the coca and cocaine-producing regions, though by the 1980s a revalorization and sober anthropology of indigenous coca had begun. But even today, Peru, Bolivia, and Colombia still lack histories of one of their (currently) weightiest commodity exports.[6] Nor was renewed fascination with cocaine reflected in the broader historical work – emanating from concerns with 1960s drug cultures – that returned to dig up and reappraise the origins and development of now shaky American prohibitions systems and values. If greatly useful, most of that scholarship focused on the narcotics, leaving cocaine for footnotes and asides, stuck to institutional or political narratives (rather than hidden social or cultural processes) and rarely reached for transnational relationships in the drug world beyond, save in the traditional ways of diplomatic history.[7] Country histories of drug policies from other points of the globe also helped, in revealing diverging interactions or variations on American designs. All told, opiates (opium, morphine, heroin) won more systematic attention from professional historians, who increasingly brought to bear the sharpest tools of social, medical, or now cultural history.[8] Thus the genealogy left for cocaine history came from that didactic 1970s literature of recollection. We inherited a sort of "great man" (from Marianis, Halsteads, Freuds) or episodic view of the drug's birth (Incas, eye surgery, Sherlock Holmes, Coca-Cola), a narrative narrowly tied to Europe and the United States, and saying little about cocaine's demise and later subterranean transformations. By the late 1980s, public attitudes towards cocaine shifted again, in march with the hardline Reagan years and the turn from high-status cocaine users to sensationalized, *déclassé* scenes of "crack" in the streets – leaving cocaine history orphaned once again.[9]

Cocaine histories: the third wave

This third wave, coming together in this volume, surely carries on from that prior scholarship. But if politically plural, we are also offspring of the Age of Craçk and its related "drug wars," domestic and foreign, and like everyone else in our societies, this affects the questions asked. For example, whether as social-scientifically "futile," actively misguided, or morally tragic, we lean towards skepticism about prohibition as sound drug policy and about the discourse and categories deployed and left by anti-drug crusaders, past and present. We believe it vital (borrowing a phrase) to name the system – prohibitions – so as to explicitly analyze its origins as a system and its systematic, if often unintended, consequences.[10] To confess enabling political contexts in intellectual work is not to say that ours is a political enterprise. None of us are cocaine boosters, if this is at all possible after the horrific social consequences of crack cocaine. What *Cocaine: Global Histories* mostly shares, beyond lost cocaine histories, is converging *methodological* concerns, especially about the historical problem of transitions to prohibitions out of unregulated drug markets and contrasting cultures. We'll begin with our common ground before addressing the book's *diversity* of intellectual styles – a diversifying sign of where drug history is heading.

First, all historians focus here their efforts on cocaine *per se*, and, to some degree, on its natural Andean (and for a few middle decades Javan) raw material, coca. This is a conscious effort to rescue the history, politics, and thinking around cocaine from the better known saga of opiates, to better view cocaine's distinctive path and influences. Such specificity is rare in drug history. Sometimes this genealogy is clear: initial American panics around cocaine, for example, provoked local "cocaine laws" rather than global narcotics acts. But more often the distillation of cocaine issues is not so easy, for the histories of drug users, markets, and prohibition movements intertwine and intersect on many contextual levels. It is not simple, as observers and protagonists actively conflated psychoactive drugs. Isolating *coca*, and the many patent medicines and tonics it spawned in the West, from one of its many alkaloids, cocaine, is also needed and marked by pitfalls, paradoxes, and a politics of its own. For instance, it remains foggy why coca, a light age-old stimulant comparable to coffee, came under prohibitions in the West along with cocaine; alternatively in the Andes, it is intriguing to watch how modern cocaine became valorized over a progressively deplored Indian "vice" coca.

Second, all of us here, whether academic historian or not, have opted to pursue deeply original archival research. We are convinced that new stories lie hiding, in archives around the world, that take us behind and beyond received narratives about cocaine. Thus, each contribution is "substantive" in the historian's sense of filling yawning empirical gaps and for that reason ends with a formal note on the nature of its archival base. In large part, this has been painstaking detectivesque work, for obvious sources on cocaine's history are difficult to locate, use, and piece together. The conflations with opiates and other drugs, and finding a subject that moves so furtively underground and to the margins after 1920, present special challenges. Unlike with opiates, few governments instituted formal cocaine taxes, inspectors, monopolies, or agencies, severely limiting official sources. Other governmental archives – such as the past or overseas papers of the American FBN (precursor to today's DEA) – had to be specially declassified for several contributions here, and most nations are not even so forthcoming about illegal drugs. Still another matter is deciphering at least partial realities from the policing discourse of these kinds of records. Alternatively, corporate drug firms, if key actors here, reactively deny access to controversial papers, though legitimate cocaine was often a leading product before 1910. Thus, the sole pharmaceutical records cracked here are those from conquered nations, Germany and Japan. The global nature of drugs works to fragment materials, though, in collective fashion, links soon emerged across nations, trades, and even cocaine scenes. Taken as a whole, *Cocaine: Global Histories* shows the feasibility of working with fresh sources on the drug, which raise new issues, new questions, and hopefully new perceptions.

Third, in an interpretive sense each contributor soon realized, in separate ways, that cocaine (and its proscription) were often about, embedded in, or meshed with other things, and placed its saga in such wider contexts. This may seem at odds with the goal of isolating a specific genealogy of cocaine, which was our necessary first step. Several of these contextual concerns begin to converge in our conversations and writings. Some have read cocaine into the struggles around colonial spheres; through the lens of transnational political economies; or via nationalisms, scientific, statist, or otherwise. Others place the drug's evolution as part and parcel of national campaigns for regulation and professionalization of pharmacy and pharmaceutical industries. Several essays analyze how the perceptions and prospects of cocaine get entangled with wars, of which our century has seen many – raising the possibility that age-old metaphors about wars against substances are not accidental. The most global contexts invoked were concepts of "modernity," a surely much-used (and often highly *abused*) word these days. Cocaine – one of the first scientific alkaloids developed on a commercial scale – was the most unprecedented and fast-paced of new drugs, and a seeming cure-all for anxiety-ridden industrial societies in rapid transformation.[11] In a Third World context like Peru, motley nineteenth-century dreams of modernizing science and capitalist development became fixated on cocaine, and were slow to shake off. In Britain and other precocious drug scenes, moral panics against cocaine (after 1900) had much to do with defining the boundaries of modern pleasures, and of urban gender, class, and race relations. Closer to our present, in Colombia, cocaine enterprises could violently dissolve and remake the "traditional" social values of soon-to-be famous towns like Medellín.

Fourth, part of this contextual fabric is woven from the multicolored threads of our collective inter-disciplinarity: none of us could define ourselves primarily as "drug historians," if this can or should exist. We count among us a political scientist interested in states and international relations; a forensic pathologist who happens to be a leading medical authority on cocaine; an economic historian of Latin America with an expertise in nineteenth-century commodity trades; a European drug policy adviser with a doctorate in history; a writer from British cultural studies drawn to questions of race and gender; an American social historian and professor of criminology and public policy; another social historian committed to issues of social inequality and violence; and a Latin American sociologist and close observer of Mexico's illusive cultures of drugs.[12] This creative mixture around a single problem leads to eclectic styles of writing and argument – and hopefully lights some new ways ahead in drug history.

Fifth, all of us, to one degree or another, share in what one might label a social, political, or cultural "constructionist" view of drugs. There are many ways to express this still controversial stance. Both miracle or dangerous drugs are made, not born, and borne largely from cultural and political circumstances. A teleological or Whig view of drug control regimes – that they progressively emerged as we became enlightened about the relative health risks of certain substances – is unrealistic. Chemistry and biology are at work, but make risky guides for deducing drug history and its moral outcomes. Definitions of harm to individuals or societies are rarely resolved in the "pharmacocentric" or medical sphere, as testified by our current cultural struggles to reassess (or even invert) the roles of tobacco and marijuana. Drugs are protean and relational things, and cultural magnets for charged meanings. The line between today's licit and socially ingrained drugs and taboo ones was historically drawn.[13] Clearly, constructionist perspectives are apt for looking at transformations in the status of drugs and at the erection of control regimes. They are also, in some sense, a reflection of our times: good for rethinking prohibition and for gently "de-constructing," as it were, our troubled relations with drugs like cocaine.

There are many disciplinary sources to constructionist views of drug regimes, from the most structural to post-structurally inspired. The classical one in Drug Studies is the concept of "set and setting" in drug experience, developed by sociologists like Becker and psychiatrists like Zinberg. That is, the psychological context for drug-taking profoundly impacts a given drug's range of effects, and helps to shape its perceived dangerousness or domesticity. History and national cultures, in an enlarged sense, are arguably social set and settings of the largest kind. Recent trends in social history of medicine have also enhanced constructivism: even germs, it seems, were a theory before they became popularly believed and politically viable "facts." The claims of medical science, that it is objective or asocial, are questionable and ahistorical. The central interpretations of alcohol and *its* prohibition have come to read them as "symbolic crusades" around contested meanings. Anthropology of many schools contributes strongly to constructivism. For example, the field of ethno-botany long pioneered the study of psychoactive substances, including coca, across non-Western cultures, asking how drugs become integrated into socialized and ritualized use. Path-breaking work by historical anthropologists like Sidney Mintz carries such insights back to "complex" class and industrial societies, and shows how power-laden distinctions between licit and non-licit "food-drugs" are themselves culturally and politically made. A "new ethnography" of urban drug users is opening novel vistas here at home.[14] Among symbolic anthropologists, the exploration of structural and symbolic boundaries of "purity" and "danger" is virtually canonic. Today, with the linguistic turn turning up everywhere, scholars must take passionate rhetoric about drugs as potentially constitutive of our punitive-prohibitionist drug regimes. Naturalized notions of "good" and "bad" drugs and narcotics "control" – with their stylized historical and academic discourse – might well be about containing other things and cry out for critical insight.

Sixth and last here, all of us see our task here as part of a "global" history. There are many global stories, however, and care is needed that one-worldism does not become just today's latest academic buzzword. Early cocaine – as much as the later cocaine – was a quintessential cross-boundary experience. All contributors here were deeply impressed by the speed and range with which information, infatuations, commerce, and cultures around cocaine spread, particularly during the boom decades from 1885 to 1905. We came up as a group with remarkable connections between the most far-flung of persons and phenomena. By 1900, cocaine episodes registered in the furthest reaches of the globe. Drugs, as commodities or illicitly, have never respected national borders, which in part is what building prohibition walls is all about, and one reason why their builders also move to internationalize them.[15] Cocaine, with its high value-to-weight ratio, is an especially mobile substance, and once deemed criminal, simple to conceal and transport. Its nascent smuggling networks after 1920 – "traffickers" – or policing circuits – "Narcs" – scrambled to become even more globally dispersed. All said, cocaine's rise and fall from the 1880s to the 1920s coincided with one of the most radical and sustained expansions ever of the international economy – the one that arguably brought the "modern" world to fruition – including the last struggles for colonial spheres and the First World War. Cocaine, then, may be read as the first modern global drug.[16]

There is no one best way to conceive of the global in cocaine or drug history. Our efforts here are, at best, tentative. One way adopted in *Cocaine: Global Histories* is to think in terms of three or four shifting world "networks" of commerce, culture, and consumption of coca and cocaine. These are roughly comparable to transnational "commodity chains" identified in economic sociology, *à la* World Systems theory, though interest in networks as such is now ubiquitous in social science.[17] Such shifting chains are not traditional cross-cultural trade routes but *hierarchical* orderings of supply and processing, with overlapping cultural and political resonances. One of the first chains to appear was from the eastern Andes to Germanic Europe, which facilitated extensive scientific and commercial exchanges from the 1850s to 1900s. Another chain quickly developed between the United States and Peru by the 1890s, driven by popular consumption and informal political orbits of neocolonialism, and, like it, rife with unseen contradictions. These initial networks were displaced, between 1905 and 1925, as readers will see, by the powerful eruption of the Dutch–Javan (and pan-European) coca–cocaine network, a short-lived product of colonialism of the classic kind. This in turn helped spawn, as did advancing League of Nations drug control pacts, an autonomous and imperial Japanese-pan-Asian cocaine circuit of the 1920s to 1940s, destroyed (like remnants of the initial European pole) by the outcomes of the Second World War and the triumph of a global cocaine prohibitions network under United States/UN authority by 1950. It is relevant to note that by the mid-1950s, cold-war routes of clandestine supply turned back to the long-marginalized Andes, though here again shifting commodity chains took hold. These layer our current cocaine trades (which now move via Colombia and Mexico) by geography and power, with specialized niches of supply, manufacture, commerce, and with their hierarchical styles of illicit consumption.

However, let us stress that such networks are still being traced and that efforts here never approached a comprehensive "global" research program. Readers will no doubt discern other types of connections and coincidences, too. But our more transnational approach does contest what has been a standard Eurocentric approach or narrative on cocaine's early history. Yet rather than proclaim any new homogenizing or totalistic approach to global forces and contexts, what reverberates strongest here are the diverse intellectual and methodological styles, analytic levels, and strategies embraced by us as historians and writers. An evocative mix of contrasts and comparisons arises from national cocaine experiences. Like other diversities, this one is well worth preserving, for the perspectives it opens about prohibitory regimes, and forms the core of the book to follow.

Cocaine: cases, countries, contexts

The chapters which follow here, if enmeshed in this global context, focus on the major national histories that converged in the early transformations of cocaine from miracle drug into social menace. We can now turn to the centrality of these cases and to the range of methodological tools and styles brought to the problem of emerging prohibition regimes.

The next two chapters, taken as a whole, hone in on the United States and Andean circuit in early cocaine. The United States, between 1885 and 1900, quickly took the stage as one of the leading consumers, producers, and promoters of early cocaine, for medical as well as popular usage. Coca patent products became so ingrained in our restless culture that our national tonic and symbol (a *de*-cocainized Coca-Cola) still bears its name. Yet in the political paradox Musto diagnoses as the "American disease," our national passion for remedies and drug experiences has instinctively inverted into its opposite: dread, intolerance and prohibitions against drugs.[18] So it was that, after 1900, American progressives pioneered moves to restrict and then ban cocaine; after 1912, United States diplomats spearheaded the drives to expand their policy around the globe, eventually (after the Second World War) pushing to remote coca "source" regions as well. In Chapter 2 to follow, social historian, Joseph F. Spillane, carefully unpacks the strands of the rising reformist coalitions against legal cocaine of the early twentieth century. In good part these crusades concerned larger efforts to reform the business and practice of America's unregulated pharmaceutical industries, and would succeed with the willing participation of retail druggist and later pharmaceutical companies. But an unintended outcome, Spillane shows here, was to drive consumers away from relatively harmless coca products, spawning the longer conditions for criminalized use of "harder" drugs after the restrictive national Harrison Act of 1914.

Peru, ancestral South American homeland of coca, was an active player in the rise of modern cocaine, too. In the half-century following cocaine's synthesis in 1860, underdeveloped Peru supplied most of the world's raw coca leaf; most surprisingly, after 1885 it became a major industrial producer of semi-refined "crude cocaine," for export to the United States and Europe. (Neighboring Bolivia, in contrast, barely exported its raw coca nor made cocaine, despite a wide home market of Aymara "coca chewers," or not until shifts to clandestine trades after the 1950s.) In Chapter 3, Latin American economic historian Paul Gootenberg picks up the story of how transnational relations of Peru and the United States led over time to the construction of prohibitions in Peru. The interesting tale lies in the prolonged lag in Peruvian prohibitions. In the initial boom of the 1890s, Peruvian medical men and entrepreneurs (with much United States interest) invested passionate "modernizing" hopes in cocaine as a national industry and spur to regional development.[19] Later pressures and slumping markets aside, legal Peruvian cocaine interests (of the subtropical Huánuco region) continued to yearn for their imagined development well into the 1940s. In Lima, reluctance with American demands translated into intriguing reformist and statist projects for refined cocaine, and in the 1930s climaxed in an ideological resistance to global anti-cocainism. Gootenberg then unravels the vortex of hidden processes that dramatically and finally, in the late 1940s, criminalized cocaine in Peru – a lost prelude to today's illicit circuits of Andean cocaine.

Chapters 4 through 7 turn to the second grouping in early cocaine: the European axis and Asian networks. As a market for Peruvian materials and the productive leader in early cocaine, Germany remains the nation most associated with licit cocaine. Leading German chemists, medical researchers, and drug firms, such as Merck of Darmstadt, pioneered the science and making of cocaine in the Bismarckian nineteenth century and freely marketed their quality product across the globe. For this reason, after 1910, zealous Anglo-Saxon diplomats and historians viewed the Germans as the most interest-bound obstacle to building their international cocaine controls. Political scientist H. Richard Friman, after intensive archival diggings, contests this model in Chapter 4. A highly autonomous German state, not its disunited and recalcitrant national chemical and drug lobby, actually accelerated the country's entry into global prohibitions after 1920, following wrenching social disruptions of the war, including a local cocaine drug scare (analogous to others erupting in Britain and the United States). In turn, this revisionism lends clues to the global international bargaining around drugs Friman elsewhere labels "NarcoDiplomacy."

Great Britain, which had larger medical, pharmaceutical, and colonial-botanic involvements with early cocaine, is visited by writer Marek Kohn in Chapter 5. Kohn incisively turns a series of London drug "scandals," erupting between 1901 and 1922, into a microcosm of the drug's falling social status and a barometer of the cultural mores implicated in modern cocaine. These episodes provide the rare opportunity to watch cocaine transmogrify into a dreaded cultural and legal menace, and is a glimpse at the birth of a new drug underground. As Kohn recovers tabloid "moral panics" around the drug (especially during the First World War), he shows how cocaine, intimately associated with fast-paced nightclubs, foreigners, and "theater girls," threatened to violate English cultural boundaries modernizing around gender, race, and class. Comparable dynamics were working in other nascent drug cultures, too: for example, the United States, where a once respectable "brainworker's" cocaine swiftly transformed, in public eyes, into the drug of choice for prostitutes, "Negroes," drug fiends, and other hardcore elements after 1900.

In the subsequent two chapters, we turn to cases that straddled Europe and Asia. Germany's neighbor, the Netherlands, was a lesser known and seemingly less autonomous player in global cocaine. In Chapter 6, policy adviser Marcel de Kort examines the medical, professional, entrepreneurial, and diplomatic forces that structured cocaine's changing place in Dutch society, which roughly paralleled the rest of Europe in mounting scorn for and limits on licit cocaine. However, the Netherlands proved distinct in two key areas, which de Kort analyzes here. First, the Dutch in fact cultivated a now-forgotten but then-thriving colonial economy of coca from its South-Asian Javan possessions, efforts that other Europeans (the British and French) had only dabbled in. Indeed, with Amsterdam's giant monopoly NCF factory, by 1910 the Dutch came to dominate (for a decade) world cocaine and coca commerce, and championed various 1920s "cartel" arrangements to keep it afloat in a world of sinking legal demand. Second, even while succumbing with ease by 1930 to external (United States and League) prohibitionist campaigns, the Dutch paradoxically managed to define a distinctive variety of national drug policy, preferring to "medicalize" rather than criminalize their modest domestic problems around drugs like cocaine. The latter stance, suggests de Kort, was analogous to flexible Dutch responses to the drug dilemmas of the 1970s and beyond.

Japan, and its Asian cocaine circuit, is addressed by medical authority Dr Steven Karch in Chapter 7. As cocaine became fenced in by the West after 1912, expansive Japanese industrialists and colonial officials took heed of opportunities and forged a new sphere of cocaine interests – in a process not unlike shifting drug networks today. Trading with Java, borrowing upon

European science and even developing a few Andean links, major Japanese pharmaceutical firms (like Hoshi) were producing significant quantities of cocaine by the 1920s. By the following decade Japan, with military input, had likely made itself into the world's premier producer and marketer of the drug (in Asian and clandestine markets), and began exploiting its own Formosan coca plantations, thus alarming and eluding drug controllers of the League of Nations and United States. All the while, cocaine found no popular or cultural use in Japan, which suffered little modernizing problem of drugs. Karch sketches this now-obscured network and its relation to wider charges of "narcotics peddling" at the postwar Tokyo War Crimes trials, which effectively sealed the fate of Japanese (and, with it, most licit) cocaine.

Cocaine: Global Histories summarizes what we know about intersecting American, Andean European, and Asian circuits, chains, and cultures of cocaine, during its transformation from youthful wonder drug of the 1880s to the global yet still largely dormant drug menace of the 1950s. Cocaine proved such an international phenomena – then as now – that certain missing links, scientific or otherwise, still wait to be connected in France, Bolivia, Italy, Russia, and India, to name beckoning cases.[20] Instead of filling every gap, however, we conclude with two more contemporary histories that constructed their cocaine networks later, fully illicit from the start: Colombia and Mexico. Colombia, if home to scattered indigenous coca cultures, had little contact with cocaine *per se* until the 1970s, when it swiftly transformed into the processing and trans-shipment capital of the new cocaine crisis of the north (tapping flows of illegal coca paste from the jungles of eastern Peru and Bolivia). In Chapter 8, social historian Mary Roldán focuses an urban micro-history on Medellín to track the rise of its entrepreneurial families during the making of the first 1970s "cartel" and their startling impact on the town's motley cultures of poverty and class. Cocaine commerce became a powerful solvent in the modernization of traditional and puritanical society here, and in the intensification of social violence – in ways that raise comparisons to turn-of-the-century London as well as our end-of-the-century South Bronx. Finally, in Chapter 9, Mexican sociologist Luis Astorga sizes up the origins of the latest transformations of cocaine by Mexico's now-notorious northern "drug lords." Mexico, as elsewhere, was introduced to coca and cocaine in the late nineteenth century, without major effect. Astorga traces how the lures of illicit cocaine erupting in the adjacent American market (by the 1980s no dormant threat) mobilized Sinaloa's underworld, which drew on venerable local traditions of drug-growing and border-running, and covertly the Mexican state itself. All this has brought the contradictions of a United States drug war closer and closer to home.

Afterthoughts: towards a new drug history?

The question mark is deliberate, for it is not clear that we need a discrete new field called "drug history" (that draws in a larger body of knowledge about drugs) or whether its future lies in the deeper contextualization that history affords: as drugs *in* history. *Drug history* might focus around potent substances themselves (or their users, producers, and controllers), as "essential," autonomous, active historical agents, transforming of their own societal sets and settings. Whereas *drugs in history* might further integrate drugs into the familiar terrain of historical studies and methods, and into pre-existing fields of society, culture, or power. Whichever direction we go, and at the risk of pretension, we hope this collection about one highly controverted drug – cocaine – promotes this larger debate and further studies, of course.

For numerous reasons, we stand at a turning point for innovating approaches to drugs and history. The intellectual space opened by current debates over decriminalization and "harm reduction" (at least among academics) allows, or calls us, to rethink the origins of prohibition, as does the slipping prestige of our harmful and deadlocked drug wars. In methods, the present explosion of cultural, post-structural, and multi-disciplinary approaches to history has made previously odd or marginalized topics (like drugs) central, as this one long should have been. Already, a new wave of anthropologically inspired and globalist writings are shifting the ground for historians of drugs, who shied away from the methodological frays and advances of historical social sciences since the 1960s.[21]

Drugs and history, briefly put, seems one field where the ongoing contest between structural and post-structural historical thinking might find some creative common ground – and is among the reasons for the *diversity* of approaches found and kept in this volume. To roundly grasp the stories of drugs and their regimes requires an appreciation of *both* the rational 'interests' and irrational 'passions' that met in their making, i.e. their realities *and* their representations, their settings *and* special powers. On one hand, varied structural or sociological intellectual traditions force us to see drugs as "normalized" substances and comparison-prone commodities – released from the emotions (and discourses) that made them taboo to begin with and that so often distort their histories. These are frankly "economistic" gazes: trying to look objectively at the production, commerce, and consumption of drugs (as in statistical fieldwork and guesswork), at the fluid social groups or ethnic constituencies who have taken or produced them (as social history) or in the changing global networks, legal and interest-group politics, and State interests (fiscal, diplomatic, or of social control) that gravitate around drugs. Even some abstract social-science constructs are worth trying and applying here, such as the counter-intuitional insights of economic price theory or sociological theories of moral panics. This is one path to a constructionist drug history: literally, piecing together how drugs and their regimes got built.

Alternatively, interpretive traditions and post-structuralism can also prove indispensable in constructivist drug history, precisely because drugs are *so not* like other commodities and should not be essentialized. Beyond some basic chemistry and highly protean human contexts, we are rarely dealing with a constant, dispassionate, tangible thing called cocaine. Various strands of cultural studies might powerfully de-naturalize the volatile discourse, representation, narratives, or consciousness surrounding our relationships to mind-altering drugs. Cultural sensibilities may tease out the entrenched symbolism, racialist dreads, and gendered fascinations that somehow latch on to inert substances, and that remain impervious to rationalist analysis, or help us unlock the doors to their furtive subterranean cultures. The more subjective tools of discourse analysis can help to defuse militaristic, surveillance, and orientalist languages of alterity and social control that greatly infuse State-bureaucratic and drug control mind-sets.[22] Historical anthropology, as argued above, is indispensable here for its mature expertise in cross-cultural understandings of substances and the charged cultural meanings, pro and con, that people attach to them.

While coming from differing directions, such methods share one goal in common: richly understanding our past and present relationships with drugs. This we hope is the genuinely stimulating substance of this one cocaine-centered volume, *Cocaine: Global Histories*.

Notes

I thank Joseph Spillane in particular for incisive comments on an earlier draft.

1 In the United States, by 1905, many local and state laws had restricted cocaine to "prescription" and sundry controls; in 1906, cocaine came under the Food and Drug Act (to expose use via patent drugs); in 1914, under the Harrison Narcotic Act (a federal revenue bill that *de facto* criminalized cocaine nationally); and 1922, the Narcotic Drugs Import and Export Act, which closed border access. By the (first) 1911–12 Hague Anti-Opium Conference, the United States was placing cocaine on global anti-narcotics agendas, followed by a gamut of Geneva-based regulatory treaties of the 1920s and 1930s. Allied victory brought a postwar 1945–50 *de facto* consolidation of international cocaine prohibitions, culminating in the 1961 UN "Single Convention," – which aimed even at eradication of Andean-source coca. See Jill Jonnes, *Hep-Cats, Narcs, and Pipe Dreams: A History of America's Romance with Illegal Drugs* (New York: Scribner, 1996), ch. 15 on the knowledge gap.

2 Robert Byck, MD, ed., *The Cocaine Papers: Sigmund Freud* (New York: Stonehill Publishing, 1974), two decades ago noted this stalled scientific research; see "Introduction," xxvii, xxxix. For cultural signs, see Michael Starks, *Cocaine Fiends and Reefer Madness: An Illustrated History of Drugs in the Movies* (New York: Cornwall Books, 1982), chs 4–5.

3 David F. Musto, MD, "America's first cocaine epidemic," *Wilson Quarterly* (summer 1989), 59–64; "Opium, cocaine and marihuana in American history," *Scientific American* (July 1991), 40–7; cf., David T. Courtwright, "The rise and fall of cocaine in the United States," in J. Goodman, P. Lovejoy and A. Sherratt, eds, *Consuming Habits: Drugs in History and Anthropology* (London: Routledge, 1995), ch. 10.

4 Byck, *Cocaine Papers* (1974), with sets of contextual documents (Parke, Hammond, Lewin, etc.); George Andrews and D. Solomon, comps., *The Coca Leaf and Cocaine Papers* (New York: Harcourt, Brace, Jovanovitch, 1975), an even wider set; Joel Phillips and R. Wynne, comps., *Cocaine: The Mystique and the Reality* (New York: Avon Books, 1980), from a NIDA bibliography and covering the "fall"; W. Golden Mortimer, *History of Coca: "The Divine Plant" of the Incas* (1901; San Francisco: F.H. Ludlow Library, 1974 reprint). Monographs following this plot include Richard Ashley, *Cocaine: Its History, Uses, and Effects* (New York: St Martins, 1975) or the historical parts of L. Grinspoon and J. Bakalar, *Cocaine: A Drug and its Social Evolution* (New York: Basic Books, 1985). The "coffee-table" book (suggestive on historical cycles) is Joseph Kennedy's *Coca Exotica: The Illustrated History of Cocaine* (New York: Cornwall Books,

1985). And, there were many quickly created "consumer guides," "gourmet coke-books," and the like, as well as (of course) scores of non-historical therapeutic and medical texts. A rich recent attempt to follow cocaine after the fall is Joseph F. Spillane, "Did drug prohibition work? Reflections on the end of the first cocaine experience in the United States, 1910–45," *Journal of Drug Issues* 28 (1998), 517–38.

5 A random sample of dozens: Ronald K. Siegal, "Cocaine and the privileged class: A review of historical and contemporary images," *Advances in Alcohol and Substance Abuse* (1984), 37–49; L. Grinspoon and J. Bakalar, "Coca and cocaine as medicines: An historical review," *Journal of Ethnopharmacology* 3 (1981), 149–51; David Smith and D. Wesson, "Cocaine," *Journal of Ethnopharmacology* 10(4) (1978), 351–60; Carl B. Shultz, "Statutory classification of cocaine as a narcotic: An illogical anachronism," *American Journal of Law and Medicine* 9(2) (1983), 225–45; Nancy A. Eiswirth, D. Smith and D. Wesson, "Current perspectives on cocaine use in America," *Journal of Psychedelic Drugs* 5(2) (1972), 153–7; Edward M. Brecher (and the editors of *Consumer Reports*), *Licit and Illicit Drugs* (Boston: Little, Brown & Co., 1972), 267–307; George Gay, C. Sheppard, D. Inaba and J. Newmeyer, "Cocaine in perspective: 'Gift from the sun god' to 'the rich man's drug,' " *Drug Forum* 2(4) (1973), 409–31; Dennis Helms, T. Lesscault and A. Smith, "Cocaine: Some observations on its history, legal classification, and pharmacology," *Contemporary Drug Problems* 4(2) (1975), 195–216; Michael R. Aldrich and R. Barker, "Historical aspects of cocaine use and abuse," in S.J. Mule, ed., *Cocaine: Chemical, Biological, Clinical, Social, and Treatment Aspects* (Cleveland: CRC Press, 1976), 1–13; Bo Holmstedt and A. Frega, "Sundry episodes in the history of coca and cocaine," *Journal of Ethnopharmacology* 3 (1981), 113–47; Craig Van Dyke and R. Byck, "Cocaine use in man," *Advances in Substance Abuse* 3 (1983), 1–2. And so on.

6 See, for example, on coca: Joan Boldó i Climent, ed., *La Coca Andina: Visión Indígena de una Planta Satanizada* (Mexico: Instituto Indígena Interamericana, 1986); Antonil (Anthony Henman), *Mama Coca* (London: Hassle Free Press, 1978); Catherine J. Allen, *The Hold Life Has: Coca and Cultural Identity in an Andean Community* (Washington, DC: Smithsonian Institution Press, 1988); Deborah Pacini and C. Franquent, *Coca and Cocaine: Effects on People and Policy in Latin America* (Ithaca: Cultural Survival, 1986); William E. Carter and M. Mamani P., *Coca en Bolivia* (La Paz: Librería Ed. Juventud, 1986) (etc.). The sole historian look at coca is recent: Joseph Gagliano, *Coca Prohibition in Peru: The Historical Debates* (Tucson: University of Arizona Press, 1994).

7 David F. Musto, *The American Disease: Origins of Narcotics Control* (New York: Oxford University Press, 1973); Arnold H. Taylor, *American Diplomacy and the Narcotics Traffic* (Durham: Duke University Press, 1969); William Walker III, *Drug Control in the Americas* (Albuquerque: University of New Mexico Press, 1981) and his most historical of collections, *Drug Control Policy: Essays in Historical and Comparative Perspective* (University Park: Penn State Press, 1992); H. Wayne Morgan, *Drugs in America: A Social History, 1800–1900* (Syracuse: Syracuse University Press, 1981). For a needed international perspective, see Antonio Escohotado, *Historia de las drogas* (Madrid: Alianza Editorial, 1989), 3 vols. A creative addition to the Americanist genre is Jonnes, *Hep-Cats, Narcs, and Pipe Dreams* (1996).

8 Some of this work of the 1980s includes David T. Courtwright, *Dark Paradise: Opiate Addiction in America Before 1940* (Cambridge, MA: Harvard University Press, 1982); Virginia Berridge and G. Edwards, *Opium and the People: Opiate Use in Nineteenth-Century England* (London: Yale University Press, 1987); Geoffrey Harnoy, *Opiate Addiction, Morality and Medicine: From Moral Illness to Pathological Disease* (London: Macmillan, 1988); Marek Kohn's suggestive *Narcomania: On Heroin* (London: Faber & Faber, 1985); Desmond Manderson, *From Mr. Sin to Mr. Big: A History of Australian Drug Laws* (Oxford: Oxford University Press, 1992). Much has been done since then.

9 On "crack" itself, there's critical history: Craig Reinarman and H. Levine, eds, *Crack in America: Demon Drugs and Social Justice* (Berkeley: University of California Press, 1997)

or Jimmie Reeves and R. Campbell, *Cracked Coverage: Television News, the Anti-Cocaine Crusade, and the Reagan Legacy* (Durham: Duke University Press, 1994).

10 As in Ethan Nadelmann, "Global prohibition regimes: The evolution of norms in international society," *International Organization* 44(4) (1990), 479–526 or *Cops Across Borders: The Internationalization of U.S. Criminal Law Enforcement* (University Park: Penn State Press, 1993), and Sebastian Scheere, "Emergence of an international prohibition regime: The case of cocaine" (MS, Amsterdam, 1991). For a historical critique of prohibitionist discourse, see Luis Astorga, *El Siglo de las Drogas: Usos, Percepciones, Personajes* (Mexico: Espasa-Hoy, 1996), ch. 1.

11 This idea crystallized in Joseph F. Spillane's superb "Modern drug, modern menace: The legal use and distribution of cocaine in the United States, 1880–1920," (Ph.D. (History), Carnegie Mellon University, 1994); cf. the case of opiates in Kohn's *Narcomania* or cultural climes captured in Tom Lutz's study of "Neurasthenia," *American Nervousness, 1903: An Anecdotal History* (Ithaca: Cornell University Press, 1991). See also Marek Kohn, *Dope Girls: The Birth of the British Drug Underground* (London: Lawrence & Wishart, 1992) and JoAnn Kawell's unpublished "The 'essentially Peruvian' industry: Legal cocaine production in the 19th century" (MS, presented at the "From Miracle to Menace" symposium, New York, 1997) and forthcoming study "Going to the source" (MS, Berkeley, 1997, chs. 9–11) for terms of scientific/developmental modernity in the Andean context. For a critical take on these "modernities," see John C. Burnham, *Bad Habits: Drinking, Smoking, Taking Drugs, Gambling, Sexual Misbehavior, and Swearing in American History* (New York: New York University Press, 1993).

12 At the 1997 Russell Sage "From Miracle to Menace" symposium, this spirit was invigorated with anthropological, history of medicine, and medical perspectives, with the participation of anthropologists Enrique Mayer and William Roseberry, John Morgan and Robert Byck, MDs, and Nancy Tomes, a noted historian of medicine.

13 This is hardly the same as claiming that the publicized harms of drugs like cocaine are purely fictitious or "fabricated." It is to say that then, as now, there were diverse debates on their relative risks and on how to contain them – including less criminalizing and more social solutions.

14 Howard S. Becker, *Outsiders: Studies in the Sociology of Deviance* (New York: Free Press, 1963), chs 3–4; Norman I. Zinberg, MD, *Drug, Set and Setting* (New Haven: Yale University Press, 1984); Sidney W. Mintz, *Sweetness and Power: The Place of Sugar in Modern History* (New York: Viking/Penguin, 1985) or recent *Tasting Food, Tasting Freedom: Excursions into Eating, Culture and the Past* (Boston: Beacon Press, 1996); generally, see Wolfgang Schivelbusch, *Tastes of Paradise: A Social History of Spices, Stimulants, and Intoxicants* (New York: Vintage Press, 1992); Richard Rudgley, *Essential Substances: A Cultural History of Intoxication in Society* (New York: Kadanswa International, 1994); John Mann, *Murder, Magic, and Medicine* (New York: Oxford University Press, 1992), for a heterodox medical perspective; Joseph R. Gusfield, *Contested Meanings: The Construction of Alcohol Problems* (Madison: University of Wisconsin Press, 1996) (and his classic 1963 *Symbolic Crusade*); Erich Goode and N. Ben-Yehuda, *Moral Panics: The Social Construction of Deviance* (Oxford: Blackwell, 1994); and vanguard essays in Goodman et al., *Consuming Habits* (1995). Key ethnographies include Philippe Bourgois, *In Search of Respect: Selling Crack in El Barrio* (Cambridge: Cambridge University Press, 1995) or Dan Waldorf, C. Reinarman and S. Murphy, *Cocaine Changes: The Experience of Using and Quitting* (Philadelphia: Temple University Press, 1991). For synthesis (and a fine recent example) see David Dingelstad, R. Gosden, B. Martin and N. Vakas, "The social construction of drug debates," *Social Science Medicine* 43(12) (1996), 1829–38.

15 For pre-modern globalism of "intoxicants," see Schivelbusch, *Tastes of Paradise* (1992), which broadly suggests that drug commodities were a vital ingredient in the making of European modernity and a world system itself, starting in the fifteenth century. Paul B. Stares, *Global Habit: The Drug Problem in a Borderless World* (Washington, DC:

Brookings Institution, 1996), especially ch. 2, for a survey of postwar drug globalism and timely policy critique. We are aware of possible shortcomings of using national-cultural units to explore global forces: see the suggestions in Immanuel Wallerstein, *Unthinking Social Science: The Limits of Nineteenth-Century Paradigms* (Cambridge: Polity Press/Blackwell, 1991).

16 As tobacco was for the *early modern* age of the seventeenth and eighteenth centuries: see the example set for global drug history by Jordan Goodman, *Tobacco in History: The Cultures of Dependence* (London: Routledge, 1993).

17 Gary Gereffi and M. Korzeniewicz, eds, *Commodity Chains and Global Capitalism* (Greenwood: Greenwood Press, 1994), especially the author's Introduction; a final chapter concerns illicit cocaine in the 1980s. For other models of historical globalism, see Mintz, *Sweetness and Power* (1985) (on powers of consumption); Eric R. Wolf, *Europe and the People Without History* (Berkeley: University of California Press, 1982) (on the spread of commodity/labor networks); or Philip D. Curtin, *Cross-Cultural Trade in World History* (New York: Cambridge University Press, 1984) (on the roles of high-value commerce and "diaspora/mafias"). For latest in "transnationalized" drug history, see H. Richard Friman's comparative lens in *NarcoDiplomacy* (Ithaca: Cornell University Press, 1996), or suppression networks in Nadelmann, *Cops Across Borders* (1993), especially chs 3–5; a recent sketch of global coca exchange is David F. Musto, "International traffic in coca through the early 20th century," *Drug and Alcohol Dependence* 49 (1988), 145–56.

18 Musto, *American Disease* (1973), ch. 1, which in "po-mo" would be spelt "(dis)-ease." On Coca-Cola, see the revealing sketch of origins in drug cultures in Mark Pendergrast's *For God, Country, and Coca-Cola: The Unauthorized History of the World's Most Popular Soft-Drink* (New York: Scribner, 1993), chs 1–4.

19 Kawell's " 'Essentially Peruvian' industry," presented at the same "From Miracle to Menace" symposium, elaborates these nationalist themes for the late nineteenth century, in global relation to European medicine.

20 Graduate students: France is the glaring gap. As far as we could tell, no archival-based work examines the culture that bequeathed influential Vin Mariani and proto-Incan imagery of coca in the West. For clues, check William H. Helfand, "Vin Mariani," *Pharmacy in History* 22(1) (1980), 11–19.

21 Goodman *et al.*, *Consuming Habits* (1995); Rudgley, *Essential Substances* (1994); or Schivelbusch, *Tastes of Paradise* (1992); in part, these writers are inspired by the rediscovery of Europe's own "hidden" drug histories, à la Carlo Ginzburg's haunting *Ecstacies: Deciphering the Witches' Sabbath* (New York: Penguin, 1991) or Piero Camporesi's horrific *Bread of Dreams* (Chicago: University of Chicago Press, 1982).

22 The reference to Albert O. Hirschman's eighteenth-century "passions" and "interests" is deliberate, so themselves infused with Enlightenment drugs like coffee and tobacco (Schivelbusch, *Tastes of Paradise*, 1992). For scientistic moves, see N. Heather, A. Wodack, E. Nadelmann and P. O'Hare, *Psychoactive Drugs & Harm Reduction: From Faith to Science* (London: Whurr Publishers, 1993); for a cultural turn on cocaine, see Kohn, *Dope Girls* (1992). For a literary critique of rationalism in drug history, check Nicolas O. Warner, *Spirits of America: Intoxication in 19th-Century American Literature* (Norman: University of Oklahoma Press, 1997), ch. 1. For a lucid post-manifesto, see Desmond Manderson, "Metamorphosis: Clashing symbols in the social construction of drugs," *The Journal of Drug Issues* 23(4) (1995), 799–816, or the same journal, all of 26(1) (1996), for the gamut of new social-science approaches.

Part I

Amer-Andean connections (the United States, Peru)

2 Making a modern drug

The manufacture, sale, and control of cocaine in the United States, 1880–1920

Joseph F. Spillane

Cocaine made its first appearance in the United States during the 1880s, when physicians first interested themselves in the drug's therapeutic potential. Limited at first to a relatively narrow range of therapeutic use, cocaine's popularity grew far beyond the boundaries of medical practice. By the late 1890s, many observers came to believe that the popular consumption of cocaine posed a serious threat to public health and to public safety. The campaign to control cocaine gradually became part of a broader Progressive-era campaign to regulate the development and distribution of new drug products by the pharmaceutical industry. In the course of the campaign for drug regulation, the cocaine experience served reformers as an object lesson of the dangers inherent in an unregulated drug industry.

Cocaine, like every other drug developed and marketed in the late nineteenth century, reached the consumer from a pharmaceutical industry which operated with few restrictions. No legal authority determined the therapeutic claims companies made for their products, or if they truthfully reported their remedies' ingredients. The chief authority, it seems, was that of the market place. If consumers chose to dose themselves with a particular drug or remedy, then a drug manufacturer would supply it. Cocaine quickly passed the test of consumer appeal – the legal supply of the drug increased roughly 700 percent between 1890 and 1902. By the turn of the century, the dollar values of cocaine sales ranked among the top five products of United States pharmaceutical manufacturers.

As early as the 1890s, a broad coalition of reform-minded groups began efforts to control the supply of cocaine. From the beginning, the anti-cocaine coalition demonstrated a dual set of motives. A primary concern for minimizing the harms generated by widespread availability of cocaine reflected the first set of motives. Groups whose central focus was the reduction of cocaine abuse encompassed the fields of public health, child welfare, social work, and temperance – a list which only begins to suggest the diversity of the reform movement. The second set of interests was shared by those whose primary interest was establishing a basic system of drug regulation. For such groups, cocaine was but one example – albeit a very powerful one – of the need to control the pharmaceutical industry. Organizations such as the American

Medical Association claimed the cocaine experience demonstrated that commercial interests, left uncontrolled, would always win out over "medical science" and public safety.

Working together, this coalition of reform groups produced a series of controls over the capacity of the pharmaceutical industry to deliver cocaine to the consumer. The results of their efforts appear to have been as mixed as their motives. On the most basic level, reformers were able to eliminate medicines and home remedies containing cocaine from the market, and to do so even before passage of the federal Harrison Narcotic Act in 1914 launched national drug prohibition. More importantly, the use of cocaine as a powerful example of pharmaceutical industry indifference to public health helped create the basic structures of drug regulation that influenced the remainder of the twentieth century. In what was essentially a public/private partnership, the American Medical Association and the federal government asserted substantive new powers over new drug development, while state and local governments expanded control over drug retailing.

The advance of drug industry regulation, however, did little to ameliorate the problems brought on by cocaine's overuse. The more serious public health concerns posed by widespread cocaine consumption were never adequately addressed by reformers, whose efforts barely affected levels of use. In fact, regulation of the legal drug industry produced a series of unintended effects that may well have made some aspects of the cocaine problem worse than before. That the results should have proven so disappointing illustrates the perils of these early regulatory efforts, and highlights the problem of unintended results. Whether or not the nation's first experience holds "lessons" for the present day is uncertain, but the Progressive-era efforts at cocaine control do suggest the need for regulation to define goals clearly – and to define the cocaine "problem" in ways that deal more specifically with pharmacological issues – and the powerful influence of political considerations, which may or may not have anything to do with dealing with drugs.

The pharmaceutical industry and cocaine sales

The widespread use of cocaine in the United States may be traced back almost directly to the work of Dr Karl Köller, and his announcement in the fall of 1884 that he had been able to anesthetize the surface of the human eye with a solution of cocaine hydrochloride. Köller's successful experimentation with cocaine as a topical anesthetic was immediately taken up by medical researchers in Europe and the United States, who quickly expanded cocaine's role in surgery. Almost simultaneously, other physicians began exploring possible therapeutic applications for the new drug. Cocaine's stimulant and euphoriant properties particularly intrigued doctors, who employed the drug as a treatment for drug addiction, alcoholism, depression, fatigue, and as a general tonic preparation. Within a year, cocaine was in widespread therapeutic use in Europe and the United States.

The pharmaceutical industry that immediately sought to capitalize on Köller's groundbreaking research included two types of companies – "ethical" and "patent medicine" manufacturers. The ethical firms were smaller in number, but included the largest drug companies in the United States.[1] The "ethical" appellation referred to their claim of serving almost exclusively a medical market, and their voluntary restriction of advertising to physicians and pharmacists. The remainder of the nation's drug manufacturers were firms selling so-called "patent medicines."[2] Patent medicine makers also advertised and sold their product through physicians and pharmacists, but nearly always appealed directly to the public as well.

The two decades following cocaine's introduction into the United States coincided with a remarkable period in the history of the pharmaceutical industry. During these two decades the industry expanded its capacities for research, production, and promotion. The traditional view of the ethical pharmaceutical company's function had been that of a large-scale compounder of medicines. The calling of an ethical firm was to respond to the demands of the medical profession for drug products. The best firms were those that could stock as much of the existing materia medica as possible, in as many forms as individual practitioners might require. In the 1890s, ethical firms such as Parke, Davis led the way in establishing a capacity to conduct their own pharmacological research. Such research promised to generate new drugs, or, in the case of cocaine, further uses for existing drugs. In effect, ethical firms now sought to shape demand, rather than simply responding to demand.

In addition, the development of industrial technology meant that both ethical and patent medicine firms could expand production to unprecedented levels, allowing the industry to respond quickly to interest in new drugs. The desire to capitalize on cocaine almost certainly assisted in this process. In early 1884, before Köller's announcement, cocaine was virtually unavailable in the United States (selling for a dollar per grain), and only Merck in Germany had the capacity to manufacture the drug. By 1887, cocaine was available throughout the United States from many manufacturers, and sold for roughly two cents per grain.

Finally, the popularization of cocaine also coincided with the growth of the pharmaceutical industry's ability to promote drug products. Ethical firms such as Parke, Davis established their own publishing branches, turning out journals, monographs, and favorable reviews of important new drug lines that could be sent to doctors and pharmacists nationwide. The patent medicine industry, which had always been a leader in advertising and promotion, reached what may have been the peak of its capacity. Patent medicine firms not only pitched the efficacy of their remedies, but vigorously challenged the notion that consumers needed any medical help beyond what they could give themselves through their purchase.

Coca products

Any effort to characterize the output of the pharmaceutical industry in this period must take into account the tremendous importance of the coca leaf to many products. Before Köller's experiments with cocaine, coca leaf had achieved only limited popularity in Europe and North America. When researchers popularized cocaine's applications in surgery and general therapeutics, it might easily have been assumed that coca might quickly have become nothing more than the raw material from which to extract cocaine. This did not happen – the popularity of cocaine did little to diminish that of coca. Indeed demand for the coca products of both ethical and patent medicine manufacturers increased over the next two decades.

The most common form in which coca appeared was in fluid extracts. In fact, although the pharmaceutical industry imported many tons of coca leaves from distributors in Peru and Bolivia, almost none of those leaves reached the consumer directly. Instead, the coca was processed into fluid extract. Although the fluid extract of coca was available to the public, and prescribed by physicians, fluid extract of coca reached the public through its use in various ethical preparations and patent medicines.[3]

Most coca products were tonics. The tonic uses of coca derived in part from medical research that suggested that cocaine stimulated (and thus strengthened) both body and brain. By the 1880s, tonics were already the largest therapeutic category of packaged remedies, so the idea of coca as a tonic and stimulant found a ready market. In fact, many of the first generation of coca products combined coca with other common tonic ingredients, such as malt, quinine, damiana, phosphates, and alcohol. Early preparations such as the Lambert Company's Wine of Coca with Peptonate Iron and Extract of Cod Liver Oil suggest that the manufacturing uses of coca followed a traditional product development pattern. Companies with existing lines of tonic preparations found it expedient to add a "coca" version of already popular products, as in the case of Maltine with Coca Wine, or Liebig's Coca Beef Tonic.

Of the array of coca products available, three generalizations may be made: they were nearly all beverages; they contained relatively small doses of cocaine; and they were often promoted in ways that emphasized coca's distinctiveness from cocaine. Typical of the early coca products was the Sutliff and Case Company's Beef, Wine and Coca. Made by combining "an excellent quality of California Wine" with beef extract and fluid extract of coca, the product contained roughly 13 milligrams of cocaine per fluid ounce.[4] Sutliff and Case borrowed heavily from medical uses of coca in touting the uses of their tonic: "It restores a remarkable vigor and buoyancy under extreme physical exertion; or mental overwork, and in that languid condition succeeding acute diseases. Valuable as a calmative in those nervous conditions peculiar to females."[5]

In terms of sales to the public, the only group of coca products to eclipse the coca wine tonics were the soft drinks that contained coca, the most popular and well known being Coca-Cola. John Pemberton, Coca-Cola's creator, was an Atlanta pharmacist who also did some manufacturing for a limited market.

Among Pemberton's products was a coca wine, which he called Peruvian Wine Coca. When the city of Atlanta adopted prohibition in 1886, Pemberton was forced to seek an alternative to Peruvian Wine Coca that would contain no alcohol. The syrup that resulted from his experiments he called Coca-Cola. From the beginning, the product was intended as an extension of the therapeutic uses of coca by the medical profession, albeit through a delicious soda fountain drink.[6]

Coca-Cola, perhaps the most successful product of the nineteenth-century patent medicine industry, came under the direction of Asa G. Candler in 1891, who took sales of the company's soft drink to over one million dollars by 1903. A host of competitors joined Coca-Cola in the coca-beverage business, selling products such as Cafe-Coca, Kos-Kola, Kola-Ade, Celery-Cola, Koca-Nola, Wiseola, Rococola, and Vani-Kola. Nearly all employed a fluid extract of coca in their formula, with the result that none of these soft drinks contained large amounts of cocaine. Few 6-ounce glasses of soft drinks contained more than 5–6 milligrams of cocaine, and most delivered considerably less. A 6-ounce glass of Wiseola, Celery-Cola, or Koca-Nola (three of Coca-Cola's larger competitors, with national markets) probably contained about 2 milligrams of cocaine.[7] Since it was common practice at many soda fountains where these drinks were served to increase the syrup proportion by as much as 100 percent, the typical dose of cocaine may have been somewhat higher.[8]

The discovery of cocaine's therapeutic uses was among the most important developments in late nineteenth-century pharmacology. Yet a survey of wholesale drug catalogs from the 1890s indicates that far more coca products were available than those utilizing cocaine. The promotion of coca revealed a conscious effort to distinguish coca from cocaine, including suggestions that the action of coca was unique. This effort built upon a long tradition of medical thought that defined coca as the "primitive" source of the more modern drug, cocaine. One product of that tradition was a school of thought that argued that coca was far preferable to cocaine, safer to the user, and possessing of a more subtle and complex physiological action. Patent medicine makers embraced this view, emphasizing the traditional aspects of their products (such as "Peruvian Wine Coca") and the pharmacological distinction from cocaine.

Whatever success producers of coca products may have had in establishing a distinct identity, however, began to erode after the turn of the century. Efforts to curtail the promotion and distribution of packaged remedies, sparked by bad publicity over the health risks posed by heavy cocaine use, would demonstrate little regard for the pharmacological distinctions between coca and cocaine.

Cocaine sales

The first generation of packaged remedies that utilized cocaine belonged to somewhat different therapeutic categories than the coca products – further reinforcing the notion that coca and cocaine had distinctive therapeutic applications. Many of the earliest products appearing in wholesale drug catalogs capitalized on cocaine's utility as a topical anesthetic. Toothache drops, hemorrhoid remedies, and corn cures all utilized cocaine, either in the form of an ointment or a solution. In Chicago, one wholesale drug firm introduced its own (short-lived) line of cocaine bandages and gauze.

Another significant therapeutic category, especially among patent medicines, was the various "habit cures" that utilized cocaine. Like the anesthetic products, these cures were initially inspired by the medical use of cocaine in treating alcoholism and opiate addiction. The most common of the cures, though, appear to have been tobacco habit cures, such as Dr Elder's Celebrated Tobacco Specific, Tobacco Bullets, and Wonder Workers. Most were typically assertive in making claims for therapeutic benefit. Elder's Tobacco Specific claimed to be "as certain in its cure as are taxes and death to all."[9]

Cocaine may have appeared most often in lozenges. Purchasers of Elder's Tobacco Specific, for example, were instructed to use between fifteen and twenty of Elder's lozenges per day, over the course of three to five days. Elder's lozenges (manufactured for them by Parke, Davis) contained between 1.5 and 3 milligrams of cocaine per ounce. Following the instructions on the package would therefore ensure a fairly constant, but extremely low, oral dose of cocaine. Manufacturers typically advertised these lozenges as voice and throat aids. Ethical and patent medicine firms alike promoted these products for use by speakers and singers, and for generalized relief of sore throats. Existing records of the cocaine content of such lozenges indicate that these products contained small amounts of cocaine, less than 1 milligram per lozenge.[10]

In the early 1890s, a new generation of cocaine-containing patent medicines emerged that would come to dominate the market in cocaine preparations – the asthma and catarrh cures. These products were designed to relieve the symptoms of asthma or nasal catarrh, a condition that incorporated any irritation of the sinus passages and included everything from hay fever to the common cold. Cocaine's properties as a topical anesthetic, vasoconstrictor, and bronchodilator made the drug apparently ideal for the relief – and even cure – of these common complaints. Not surprisingly then, pharmaceutical companies were eager to exploit this potentially vast market. The catarrh cures were designed to be sprayed into the nose or inhaled; they typically consisted of little more than a cocaine solution, or a powder in which cocaine was mixed with a quantity of sugar of milk (lactose).

The catarrh cures were unlike the first generation of cocaine products in at least two important ways. First, they were promoted in ways that directly conflicted with prevailing medical views. Although physicians had been the first to recommend the use of cocaine for the relief of asthma and catarrh, its use had been largely discredited by the 1890s. As late as 1908 the makers of products such as Az-Ma-Syde, a 1-percent solution of cocaine, promised consumers a great deal for their money:

On a Guarantee We Will Cure ASTHMA or Ask No Pay. We have a cure for asthma that is POSITIVE. We know this to be a fact. It is not an irritat-

ing powder or pastille to be burned, or any of the thousand-and-one remedies that have been the source of such keen disappointment.[11]

The catarrh and asthma cures also distinguished themselves from most
existing products by their higher cocaine content. One ounce of Az-Ma-Syde
contained approximately 290 milligrams of cocaine, while powders such as
Birney's Catarrh Powder usually contained between 500 and 1,200 milligrams of
cocaine per ounce. Here too, however, it is notable that the typical catarrh cure
contained only a small percentage of cocaine; a purchaser snuffing an entire
gram of these powders would receive a dose of roughly 15–40 milligrams of
cocaine.

The final category of cocaine sales were those in which the pure drug itself
was distributed directly to the consumer. It is certainly true that sales of pure
cocaine hydrochloride to the public were part of the legal cocaine market. As
with the packaged remedies, no legal restrictions impeded cocaine's sale to the
general public. It is interesting, then, to observe that pure cocaine sales did not
push other forms of cocaine (including coca) out of the market. Indeed, the direct
sales of cocaine appear to have been a relatively small portion of the early
business in cocaine. As with the catarrh cures, however, it also appears that the
relative popularity of low-potency preparations waned over time, as an
increasing number of recreational users sought out more potent forms of the
drug.

The trend toward pure cocaine sales then, was partly a matter of consumer
choice. This trend would be encouraged, however, by efforts to regulate the
pharmaceutical industry's sale and distribution of cocaine.

The Progressive critique of cocaine selling

Before elaborating the basic themes of the critique of cocaine selling by the drug
industry, it is useful to make some observations concerning the interest groups
who generated most of the criticisms, and who shaped the regulatory response.
Like so many Progressive-era reform efforts, the movement to control cocaine
was the product of a coalition of various private and governmental organizations. Four categories of organizations helped develop ways of controlling the
drug industry's distribution of cocaine.

The most prominent of the reformers were physicians, especially their
professional organizations. Despite the initial enthusiasm within the medical
profession for cocaine and its therapeutic potential, physicians quickly
recognized the potential for ill effects in some users. As early as 1885, medical
journals carried articles that described in great detail cases of cocaine overuse
among patients. Such articles often concluded, as Dr D.R. Brower did in
January 1886, with predictions of "disastrous results" from the indiscriminate use
of cocaine "by the laity." As an example of the perils of an unregulated
pharmaceutical industry, the "cocaine problem" served to promote greater
medical control over drug development and distribution. Foremost among the

organizations promoting this reform ideal was the American Medical Association (AMA), and especially its Committee on Legislation, and the Council on Pharmacy and Chemistry.

Working closely with the professional physicians' organizations were agencies of municipalities, states, and the federal government. Chief among these were boards of health, and boards of pharmacy, most often state level agencies whose chief legal authority lay in their power to license doctors and pharmacists. At the level of federal government, the Bureau of Chemistry, led by its crusading chief, Harvey W. Wiley, oversaw the enforcement of the Food and Drugs Act of 1906. Like the AMA, Wiley and the Bureau of Chemistry believed that commercial interests inevitably trampled scientific standards, and endangered the public health. Thus, their impulse for cocaine control did reflect drug-specific concerns, but also a recognition that the "cocaine story" could usefully promote the construction of a broader regulatory regime.

The efforts of the AMA and the Bureau of Chemistry were supported by a third source of reform initiative, the muckraking journalists. Journalists for such reform-minded magazines as *Everybodys Magazine, Ladies' Home Journal,* and *Cosmopolitan* wrote sensational articles claiming to expose the nefarious and dangerous practices of patent medicine firms. These articles typically confirmed reformers' complaints of an incompatibility between commercial interest and public safety. Journalists featured cocaine prominently, nearly always as part of a broader critique of an unregulated drug industry whose sale of cocaine represented the typical lack of concern of the corporation for the health and well-being of the American citizen. The best known of these writers was Samuel Hopkins Adams, whose series "The great American fraud" in *Collier's Weekly* is considered a classic of the muckraking genre of reporting.

Finally, reform activity came from the vast array of private social-reform organizations, many of which had little in common besides their commitment to eliminating the problems caused by the overuse of cocaine. Such groups included temperance organizations such as the Women's Christian Temperance Union and the New England Watch and Ward Society. The most influential of the private reform groups were social-reform organizations, particularly those with concerns over the nation's children. For groups such as Hull House and the Juvenile Protective Association in Chicago, first-hand experience with cocaine use by young neighborhood residents provided compelling evidence of the drug's degrading and harmful effects. Although these reformers certainly shared other reform groups' characteristic suspicion of commercial interests, their agenda appears to have been primarily concerned with improving the health of a community, rather than achieving broad regulatory control over the drug industry.

Despite the varied interests that motivated their actions, each of these groups worked in fairly close concert to publicize the problems associated with cocaine sales.[12] Three concerns were basic to the critique of legal cocaine sales.

Irresponsible promotion

The first element of the critique of cocaine sales was that the pharmaceutical industry promoted the drug in an unscientific and irresponsible fashion. This argument was not specific to cocaine; rather, it was part of a more general argument that the commercial interest of drug manufacturers in any new product would inevitably lead them to encourage irresponsible and unsafe use. Ethical firms had encountered similar criticisms as far back as the late 1870s, when companies such as Parke, Davis introduced "new remedies" – new products promoted by the drug company itself, whose origin and physiological action was often kept secret, in order to protect the company's investment. Critics pointed out that for ethical firms to advertise drug products in this manner was too much like the marketing practices of patent medicine manufacturers. Patent medicines, advertised directly to the public, were regarded with even greater suspicion.

Reformers singled out for criticism two aspects of drug promotion. The first had to do with the specific therapeutic claims made by manufacturers, which were widely regarded as untested at best, fraudulent at worst. The central concern, however, was the failure of drug makers to reveal the proportion or presence of cocaine in their products. In retrospect, the practices of the pharmaceutical industry appear to provide ample justification for such concerns. Even reputable ethical firms such as Parke, Davis downplayed negative reporting on cocaine, and in some instances continued to reprint old medical studies long after they had ceased to represent mainstream medical opinion. Less common were cases such as that of Ryno's Hay Fever and Catarrh Remedy, in which product advertising recommended repeated and excessive use of high doses of cocaine. Ryno's remedy, which contained nothing but cocaine, was recommended for use in "hay fever, rose cold, influenza, or whenever the nose is 'stuffed-up,' red and sore." Moreover, the circular that accompanied packages of the product indicated that the remedy should be employed "two to ten times a day, or oftener if really necessary." For "chronic catarrh" the cure was to be employed two or three times a day, although Ryno's advertising indicated that "this disease is often very intractable, sometimes requiring several months to cure."[13]

As irresponsible as the Ryno promotion was, the actual composition of the product – as long as it contained cocaine – was irrelevant to many critics of cocaine sales. The product's effect on health and potential for abuse were less important than the manufacturer's failure to identify the presence of cocaine as an ingredient, which alone was enough to demonstrate a lack of scientific credibility and a willful disregard for public health. In fact, neither the government nor private groups made much distinction between various types of products in which cocaine was an ingredient. As Harvey Wiley explained to one manufacturer's attorney, "we don't care about the amount [of cocaine in the product] – the amount makes absolutely no difference."[14] This perspective led to especially hard criticisms of low-potency products. The AMA was especially concerned with Vin Mariani; a subcommittee of the Council on Pharmacy and

Chemistry concluded that Mariani & Co. was guilty of "gross misrepresentations and fraud" and of making untrue therapeutic claims for its wine.[15] The AMA even questioned the veracity of the many endorsements that Mariani distributed, including that of former president, William McKinley ("think of it!" exclaimed the author of the report), suggesting that they might be "fakes."[16]

Public health

In addition to condemning the falsity of therapeutic claims for cocaine, critics of its sale also charged that cocaine harmed the health of consumers and addicted the unsuspecting. Moreover, opponents claimed that cocaine and cocaine products were used primarily for non-medical purposes, and that they were employed to satisfy existing cocaine habits.

The records of the legal importation of cocaine support the claim that medical use accounted for only a small portion of the total supply. At the peak of medical interest in cocaine's therapeutic uses in the early 1890s, the legal supply of cocaine amounted to roughly 1 ton – a decade and a half later, production and importation exceeded 7 tons. Assuming that medical demand remained constant, the proportion of non-medical usage would have far exceeded medical usage.

Whether or not this increase in popularity was matched by a corresponding increase in health problems or cocaine abuse is more difficult to determine. Reformers claimed, of course, that vast numbers of Americans had become slaves to the "cocaine habit" through irresponsible drug industry practice. The *Canadian Pharmaceutical Journal* quoted a statement by the Bureau of Chemistry's Lyman Kebler to the effect that "there were at present [1909] 6,000,000 cocaine victims in the United States" and went on to attribute most of this to "the use of certain proprietary patent medicine preparations … which enjoy a large and unrestricted sale."[17] No historical evidence supports such fantastic numbers, which raises the question of what amount of genuine harm these outlandish claims masked.

How to distinguish between general patterns of use and problematic use (or abuse) of cocaine? Earlier generalizations have tended toward polar extremes. One set of views tends to regard use and abuse as largely interchangeable, while the other suggests that "abuse" is a social and legal construction that disappears in the absence of prohibitionist legislation. The historical evidence reveals a more complicated picture. One the one hand, many (if not most) users appear to have consumed in moderation, experiencing few serious problems. On the other hand, there were also those for whom chronic, heavy cocaine use exacted serious costs. The problems experienced by this minority of users were serious enough to represent a noticeable public-health problem.

The historical phenomenon of cocaine abuse had largely been forgotten when scholars in the 1970s began to look backward to the first cocaine experience. As a result, their accounts tended to downplay the extent to which the widespread legal use of cocaine resulted in health costs to users. Such sentiments might be attributed to the belief at the start of the second experience that cocaine was a generally non-addictive, and therefore safe, substance. Yet even as more serious questions emerged about cocaine's potential for causing harm, little information emerged concerning health costs during the pre-prohibition era. The failure to locate the health costs of cocaine consumption is not due to their nonexistence. Rather, this failure stems from three important features of the scholarship on drug abuse and drug policy. First, the influential drug addiction studies of the 1920s and 1930s were based upon the patterns of opiate use, and stressed the physical elements of addiction and drug-taking. Cocaine, which did not conform to the physical model of addiction, tended to be largely absent from important discussions of drug abuse and addiction. Second, many early studies of chronic cocaine users – remarkably detailed and insightful – were written between 1885 and 1915. Despite their insight, these studies were primarily empirical observations of individual patients that made their way into medical journals (some now long forgotten). The kinds of systematic studies of drug-using populations that generated information for future generations of scholars were the products of the 1920s and beyond, and, as such, revealed few cocaine abusers. Third, when historians did look for cocaine abuse, they tended to look in the wrong places. Over time, several scholars pointed out the glaring absence of cocaine users from treatment institutions and hospitals that housed alcoholics and opiate addicts. This absence is primarily a reflection of popular thought regarding cocaine and its users. Because they tended to "straighten up" fairly quickly when deprived of cocaine, users rarely ended up in long-term confinement; instead, short-term confinement for detoxification in the criminal justice system was the more likely action.

The first cocaine users were predominately physicians and middle-class (and middle-aged) professionals, who tended to begin using cocaine in quasi-therapeutic circumstances, and it was among this group that the first cases of abuse appeared. Able to locate and afford large quantities of cocaine for the relief of depression, melancholy, exhaustion, and overwork, the stories of their disastrous experiences appeared within months of cocaine's introduction. In contrast to the relative stability of the physician-addict using morphine, cocaine abusers found themselves to be front-page news. For those for whom the desire for cocaine overwhelmed all other interests, sensational stories revealed the destruction of their careers, families, and lives.

As the use of cocaine broadened into the general population, the problem of cocaine's overuse was redefined. An immediate source of concern was the so-called "coke drunks" – individuals who may or may not have been addicted, but whose public intoxication seemed to demand some kind of public response. At the extreme were cases of acute negative reactions to cocaine, as well as various kinds of cocaine-inspired hallucinations and psychoses, the bizarre novelty of which added to cocaine's reputation as a destructive drug.

The physical effects of long-term cocaine abuse were also observed to be serious, particularly when contrasted to the experiences of opiate addicts. What was most shocking to turn-of-the-century observers was the physical appearance of some users, as described by one New York physician: "rapid emaciation. The individual is distressed of countenance, is restless, talkative, and secretive, the skin has a pale, yellowish appearance, the eyes are deeply sunken, and the pupils dilated. ..." Nor did it require a doctor's training to recognize these symptoms. In a New York City courthouse, five cocaine users arrested during raids on drug sellers writhed and begged for cocaine while awaiting arraignment. Not knowing what other course to take, a health inspector ordered that the five be given some cocaine to get them through their hearings.[18] Nor was this a phenomenon of social or economic standing, since the therapeutically addicted physicians and professionals of the 1880s displayed the same effects of use that characterized the later "cocaine fiends." The "cocaine fiends" were, however, far more visible and enjoyed fewer resources to draw upon than the well-to-do abusers who had preceded them. Thus, these users became a public issue and a public responsibility. This new public concern helped advance the argument for regulation.

Of all the over-the-counter preparations that contained cocaine, the catarrh cures were condemned as dangerous with the greatest frequency – and not without some justification. As early as the 1890s reports described catarrh cure users compulsively consuming several bottles a day.[19] Case histories of cocaine-addicted patients indicate that many of them began using preparations for asthma and catarrh, although many eventually adopted the use of pure cocaine.

Again, however, reports of cocaine's abuse often made little distinction between various kinds of product. Low-potency soft drinks and coca wines, for example, stood accused of creating cocaine addicts as well. Physicians like W.A. Starnes, administrator of a private sanitarium for drug treatment, claimed that "Cocoa-Cola [sic] is doing more injury to the human race than all other drugs put together."[20]

Despite the absence of any specific, empirically traceable incidents, Samuel Hopkins Adams observed that "there is too much smoke not to indicate some fire." Several possible explanations might account for the connection that nonetheless existed in the public mind. It may have been that observers took the habitual consumption of these soft drinks, which also contained caffeine, as a sign of cocaine addiction.[21] Another possibility is that some soft-drink manufacturers substituted cocaine for coca, to develop a more potent product. Using cocaine in manufacturing may have been more cost-effective, since the price of cocaine per soft drink was less than using a fluid extract of cocaine. The records of the Bureau of Chemistry, however, contain no mention of soft drinks that used cocaine instead of fluid extract of coca, and none were substantially more potent than Coca-Cola. The most likely source of the public's tendency to link soft drinks to cocaine abuse was the informal "doping" of soft drinks with cocaine. Reports from southern states in particular suggested that, in dry counties, the cocaine-laced soft drink sometimes replaced whiskey in saloons.[22]

Dangerous retail sales

The final major criticism of cocaine sales, targeted specifically at patent medicine manufacturers and retail druggists, was that products containing cocaine were especially attractive to segments of the general population thought to be unable to handle their potent ingredient. In particular, sales of cocaine products to Black consumers in the South and urban youth everywhere were both cited as important examples of the dangers of an unregulated drug market. Images of cocaine-induced physical and mental deterioration merged with fears of social predation to become a recurring theme, especially in the various journalistic exposés of cocaine selling.

Images of young children being preyed upon in schoolyards stressed the need to protect the youthful potential consumer. *Hampton's* magazine suggested that in Newark, New Jersey, children as young as 8 years old had used the drug, and Harvey Wiley in *Good Housekeeping* reported that cocaine was being sold by "sweets vendors" to schoolchildren. Despite the popularity of such claims, there is little credible evidence that young children used cocaine to any extent. Reformers could, of course, find compelling stories to bolster their claims that patent medicine with cocaine was widely abused by older youths. A father whose son was using Ryno's Hay Fever and Catarrh Cure wrote to the Bureau of Chemistry concerning the product:

> It is ruining our boys ... I have a son that has been using it and have tried for the last year to break him from it, but no use as long as he can get it and there are others that use it more and are worse than my son. ... I hope that you can give it your earliest attention for there are many here that he is ruining with his drug and the sooner it is stopped the better.[23]

Consider, as well, the case of 16-year-old George Fromme of New York City. George and his friends had begun to use cocaine by chipping in to purchase (legally) catarrh and toothache preparations from local drugstores. Eventually the boys found one druggist willing to sell them cocaine by the ounce (in violation of New York law). According to his mother, George often came home "in a dazed condition" whereupon she was "compelled to roll him around the floor of their home ... to straighten him out."[24]

In other instances, reformers clearly feared the results of widespread use of cocaine among other groups, and they did much to disseminate information that reinforced these negative images. The *New York Medical Journal* reported to its readers that "the debilitated and neurotic take to it readily, and the poorer classes fall easy victims to its charms," while the *Medical News* observed that cocaine had "become alarmingly prevalent" among Southern Blacks.[25]

Concerns with the group identity of cocaine's users were matched by a hostility to the "recreational" or "pleasure-seeking" motives for use. While medically addicted opiate users were widely regarded as having little or no control over their drug use, the cocaine user appeared to be a wholly self-indulgent figure. One physician observed considerable sympathy for "the innocent and ignorant formation" of drug habits, but the:

> vicious user of a drug whose sole excuse is the seeking for new sensations, is a person who does not need protection, but rather restraint by law in order that he may not become a menace to the public weal and a care for public charities.[26]

In 1923, W.C. Fowler, health officer for the District of Columbia, explicitly linked group identity with pleasure-seeking use:

> when you use the word "fiends," I think that can be very properly applied to a great many of the underworld persons who were originally mentally and morally degenerates. ... Many of the addicts began their addiction through a desire to gratify certain sensual pleasures.[27]

The indictment of the pharmaceutical industry's involvement in the cocaine trade drew upon a curious mixture of real and imagined problems. Most striking was the relatively undifferentiated treatment of an array of products encompassing vastly different dosages, forms, and routes of administration. Even the genuine and obvious problems created by the overuse of cocaine were filtered through hyperbolic attacks on the drug business in general. All subsequent efforts at regulation would reflect the basic elements of this critique.

Regulation and its impact

The product of varied interests from the start, the efforts to control the manufacture and distribution of cocaine yielded mixed results. As an object lesson in the dangers of an unregulated drug industry, cocaine served reformers well. The regulation that resulted from these concerns proved remarkably effective in curtailing the legal market in cocaine, virtually eliminating the business in remedies containing the drug. It must be remembered, however, that the efforts to control cocaine were not solely intended as a means of controlling the pharmaceutical industry's ability to develop and distribute new drug products. It must be said that reformers were also motivated by genuine concerns over the abuse of cocaine, and the fear of the public-health burden potentially created by unrestricted sales. As a means of achieving those ends, unfortunately, the regulation of legal cocaine distribution failed. In the end, whether this result can be attributed to mixed motives or unintended consequences, the failure of reformers to achieve their goals illustrates the perils of early cocaine regulation.

Restriction of retail sales

Many of the most significant regulatory efforts aimed at controlling the distribution of cocaine and cocaine preparations focused on retail sales, rather than manufacture. Critics of cocaine selling were naturally critical of retailers, who were the most obvious and immediate part of the drug business. Regulation of retail sales was an expedient choice as well; while reformers found few strong precedents in the law for regulating manufacturers, they did find precedent for governing pharmacists. In particular, state and local boards of health and boards of pharmacy engaged in limiting cocaine sales at retail.

Boards of health were largely a product of the late nineteenth century, although their powers were initially quite limited. The growth of concerns over cocaine, however, coincided with a period in which boards of health exerted broad new authority in regulating threats to public health. Although much of this authority was confined to dealing with infectious diseases, epidemics, and sanitation, some boards of health used their authority to control poisons to limit what kinds of products could be sold within their jurisdiction. In Massachusetts, for example, the state board issued a list of products it said could no longer be sold in the state. State boards of pharmacy were even more critical to the successful control of retail sales. Most dated from the late nineteenth century, and their responsibilities included setting educational requirements for druggists and setting standards of drugstore operation. Using their authority to revoke pharmacists' licenses, pharmacy boards in many states became a primary agency for the control of cocaine and narcotics.

Restrictions on cocaine and cocaine preparations were thus frequently embedded within state pharmacy codes. A 1907 California law, limiting sales of cocaine and opiates to a physician's prescription, made the California State Board of Pharmacy directly responsible for enforcement, and resulted in over fifty arrests of drugstore owners and clerks in the first year. Boards of pharmacy could also serve as legal authority where other efforts had failed. In Chicago, a coalition of public and private organizations, including Hull House, the Juvenile Protective Association, and the juvenile court, turned successfully to the state board of pharmacy to end legal sales of cocaine to minors.

These efforts in Chicago also suggest another aspect of retail sales restrictions – efforts not simply to restrict certain products, but to mandate how cocaine (if it could still be sold) was to be distributed as well. Here, state and cities devised a great many ways of restricting sales to "legitimate" uses. In New Orleans, a city ordinance did not prohibit the sale of cocaine or medicines containing cocaine "in recognized therapeutic doses," but did prohibit the "combination of drugs which may be now or hereafter made, wherein the ingredient cocaine gives such proportions as to make its deliriant, or intoxicating, effect the main reason for their use." Such an ordinance clearly sought to distinguish between legitimate and illegitimate forms of cocaine selling. Its primary failing was the lack of specificity about what exactly separated legitimate sale from illegitimate, a confusion that defendants sought to exploit in court.[28]

Other regulations were more specific in targeting types of cocaine sales associated with illegitimate consumption. These regulations usually prohibited or limited only certain forms of cocaine, or its sale in large amounts. In 1913, the New York State legislature passed the Delahanty Measure, which restricted the stocks of druggists to only 5 ounces at a time. The Measure also banned the sale of flake or crystal cocaine, the form of cocaine that was used for cocaine sniffing. It did not restrict the sale of large crystal cocaine, used in the preparation of cocaine solutions – the form of cocaine used in medical and dental practice.[29] Another New York proposal, the Walker Anti-Cocaine bill, which was strongly supported by the drug lobby, confined druggists to a stock of no more than 1 ounce at a time, and limited the sale of cocaine in solution to 4 percent cocaine (the strength most commonly employed in its use as an anesthetic).

For all the diverse efforts at limiting cocaine distribution at the retail level, however, perhaps the most significant source of change was the active, and voluntary, compliance of countless retailers to limit their sales even in the absence of regulation. This may be explained partly by the extent to which professional-minded retailers shared the anti-cocaine sentiment of the reformers. Cocaine's rise coincided with a remarkable period of growth in the retail drug business in the United States. According to the United States Census, the number of retail druggists increased from 6,139 in 1850, to 27,700 in 1880, and finally to 57,346 in 1900. The large number of pharmacists posed a challenge for pharmacists who sought to professionalize their calling. Professional-minded pharmacists reacted angrily to the assertion that "a patent medicine handed down from the shelf of a drugstore involved no greater consideration than if sold from a wagon by a peddler."[30] Therefore, though pharmacists had an economic interest in cocaine sales, most appear to have concluded that the benefits of good publicity and cultivating a professional image were more important.

A telling indicator of this may be found in the editorial pages of the *National Druggist*, which strongly supported the patent medicine business and criticized most drug regulation. At various times, the journal referred editorially to: the "arrogance and greed of power" demonstrated by the "clique of machine doctors" in control of the American Medical Association; the "insidious, misleading, and deceptive" articles in *Collier's Weekly* and *Ladies' Home Journal* written by "Sissies" and "Miss Nancys"; and the "wild statements" and "irresponsible babbling" of "pseudo-chemist" Harvey Wiley. The editorial page of this very same journal, however, applauded the passage of specific anti-cocaine legislation, and urged druggists to help end the "unholy traffic" in cocaine.[31]

The response of the *National Druggist* was mirrored in many individual decisions made by retail druggists. Journalist Samuel Hopkins Adams wrote several sensational articles about the dangers of cocaine and cocaine-based products, especially the so-called catarrh cures, which were snuffs designed for use in clearing and draining sinuses. Adams reported, however, that sales of these products were reaching the "end of their rope," not because of regulation, but because druggists refused to sell or stock any more of the products. "In store after store of the better class," Adams reported, "even where the law does not forbid the sale of cocaine concoctions, my inquiries for the catarrh snuffs have been met with the curt rejoinder: 'No you can't buy that rotten stuff here.' " Out of twenty drugstores he visited, only one would sell him any.[32]

The control of cocaine products at the retail level owed as much to the voluntary actions of retail druggists as it did to the regulatory efforts of state and federal government. Most efforts to regulate the legal supply of cocaine at the retail level were easily circumvented. That so many druggists appear to have exercised discretion over their sales, even in the absence of legal requirements that they do so, suggests the power of public opinion to place informal limits on legal markets.

Labeling requirements

One of their most important achievements, reformers argued, was the adoption of requirements that manufacturers identify the composition of drug products sold to the public. Reformers' preoccupation with labeling requirements rested in part on their belief that consumers were being duped by unscrupulous drug manufacturers. When the deception merely involved a failure to cure, the harm was serious enough, but critics of the drug industry pointed to the sale of products with unacknowledged quantities of cocaine and opiates as the most serious examples of products by which consumers could unknowingly injure themselves. Using the model of consumer as dupe, Progressive-era reformers hoped that revealing the contents of drug products would shock an ignorant public into shunning those that contained cocaine.

One set of regulations operated on the state level, and typically took the form of requiring manufacturers to indicate the presence of cocaine in what they manufactured. Many states imposed an additional requirement, however, that the packages also bear a label reading "POISON," as fair warning to any who purchased the product. Boxes of Birney's Catarrh Cure sold in New York bore labels reading: "this preparation, containing among other valuable ingredients, a small quantity of COCAINE, is, in accordance with the New York Pharmacy Act, hereby labeled POISON!"[33] In keeping with the reformers' view of the cocaine problem, state labeling laws such as that of New York made no exceptions or distinctions between products. Manufacturers resisted the idea of putting such a label on certain of their products, understandably concerned at the negative impact this would have on sales. Thus, Parke, Davis was forced to consider withdrawing its voice tablets from the New York market, because the poison label required by the 1907 Smith Anti-Cocaine law "would practically render them unsalable."[34]

On the federal level, the Food and Drugs Act of 1906 imposed a national labeling requirement, one which meant that manufacturers were henceforth required to state the presence of cocaine in their products. In fact, Section Eight of the act enumerated which drugs were specifically required to be identified: morphine, opium, cocaine, heroin, alpha or beta eucaine, chloroform, cannabis indica, chloral hydrate, or acetanilid, or any "derivative or preparation of any such substances." Although the Act (administered by Harvey Wiley's Bureau of Chemistry) held out the possibility of dealing with false or misleading claims, initial enforcement focused largely on mis-labeling. The Food and Drugs Act also allowed claims of adulteration of food products, if the food "contained added ingredients which may render such product injurious to health"; cocaine was one such ingredient. Wiley was able to utilize this provision of the legislation to great effect against soft drinks and wines, simply by classifying the beverages as food products. Wiley and the Bureau were joined in their efforts by the work of the AMA's Council on Pharmacy and Chemistry, established in 1905. The Council's purpose was to provide an official stamp of approval for all drug products; a company risked disapproval if it made specific therapeutic claims, failed to disclose ingredients, or advertised directly to the public. Like the Bureau of Chemistry, the Council gave itself additional weight through an active publicity campaign against those drugs that failed their tests.

Although manufacturers of cocaine products faced seemingly formidable opposition, the role of voluntary compliance – as with retail sales – should not be underestimated. Both ethical and patent medicine firms frequently chose to withdraw their products altogether, rather than face compliance with the new acts. Ironically, the most likely to withdraw their products were not the worst offenders (whose clientele of recreational cocaine users was, if anything, going to be aided by having dosages printed on labels) but manufacturers whose sales would be damaged by the public's association of their products with cocaine. Manufacturers of tonics, coca wines, voice tablets, and soft drinks found themselves exposed to the same criticisms and penalties as catarrh cure manufacturers. The public image problem this situation presented for the makers of such products was considerable. Most had extensive lines of products they did not want compromised by negative publicity over a single product. Moreover, the possible advantage of maintaining general customer loyalty carried little weight because few companies derived much business from cocaine seekers.

Maltine Coca Wine, one of a series of tonics sold by the Maltine Company, sold over 10,000 bottles annually. Yet the product was withdrawn in September 1907, in response to growing public scrutiny of patent medicines containing cocaine. Each bottle of Maltine contained only a few milligrams of cocaine, and the precise amounts were too small to be measured. Nevertheless, as the company's attorney explained to the Bureau of Chemistry, the product was withdrawn:

> [s]imply because all these cocaine preparations are getting into such bad odor that the Maltine Company doesn't want anything to do with one ... we thought it advisable to be on the safe side and give up the preparation altogether rather than get mixed up in anything unpleasant.[35]

Other companies chose to retain the products they sold, but in cocaine-free forms. Chief among these were the soft drinks that contained fluid extract of coca. Coca-Cola and most of its soft-drink-producing counterparts voluntarily eliminated the trace amounts of cocaine in their products by switching to "de-cocainized coca leaves" – usually the residue coca from the cocaine manufacturing process – or by eliminating the coca altogether. Even the oldest of all coca products, Vin Mariani, switched to a de-cocainized version for sale in the United States, although the older version could still be purchased in countries around the world.

The model of consumer as dupe was typical of Progressive-era thought. Therefore, when publicity over their ingredients put countless packaged remedies out of business, reformers assumed that the education of the public had been the cause. Historians have continued to assert much the same case. Historian Raymond Brastow, for example, argued that "drugs containing alcohol and narcotics were effectively eliminated when consumers were informed of their presence on the label." This observation may well have been true for products such as Maltine. The problem with such generalizations is that they fail to acknowledge the different consumer base for different cocaine preparations. As we shall see, the regulation of the legal market did not affect all forms of cocaine equally.

Drug regulation as cocaine control

In many respects, efforts to control cocaine through the regulation of the drug industry proved a success. The number of retail outlets for cocaine had been dramatically reduced, although this was largely voluntary, rather than the result of compliance with specific regulations regarding cocaine sales. Great numbers of products containing coca or cocaine had either been driven off the market, been voluntarily removed, or had their formula altered. The American Pharmaceutical Association surveyed 1,108 packaged remedies in 1915 and found that none contained any cocaine. Moreover, the "lessons" of the cocaine experience helped fuel the construction of a basic regulatory apparatus that has operated to the present day. When judged by the standard of its impact on cocaine consumption, however, the results of regulation are decidedly more ambiguous.

Regulation had some unintended effects, the most important of which was that low-potency coca and cocaine products were the ones driven off from the market earliest, while products that posed a more serious public-health risk continued to find their customers. By making little or no distinction between the forms or potency of various preparations, reformers failed to consider (or were unconcerned about) the resistance of certain parts of the drug industry. Specifically, reformers failed to acknowledge that manufacturers had different stakes in the products that they sold. Ethical and patent medicine manufacturers with additional product lines that might be threatened by the bad publicity, or whose products contained relatively little cocaine, or were not dependent on recreational cocaine users for their customer base, readily dropped products altogether.

Makers of high-potency products such as catarrh cures, on the other hand, stubbornly resisted the imposition of restrictions on their enterprise. Many of the catarrh cures were manufactured by firms that made only that one product, which obviously increased their incentive to keep the cures on the market. Not surprisingly, many such manufacturers openly defied what Charles L. Mitchell, maker of Coca-Bola, called "crank legislation." Moreover, since recreational users of cocaine were among their most important consumers, the cocaine content of these products was already well known; indeed, cocaine was their *raison d'être*. Laws that mandated labeling – even poison labels – had little impact on such products.

Nathan Tucker, maker of Tucker's Asthma Specific, defied the Government and reformers for years. In a meeting with Harvey Wiley, Tucker's attorney challenged the notion that the labeling of his products as a "specific" for asthma constituted mislabeling. The attorney challenged Wiley:

[I]f you will send out and bring in twenty-five of the worst cases of asthma I will demonstrate that it is a specific for asthma, and within three minutes from the time of application there will be an absolute and instantaneous relief of each and every one and I do not care of long standing.

Wiley commented sarcastically that "so good a thing ought to be widely published in medical journals." Despite the hostility of reformers, Tucker was able to continue selling his asthma remedy well into the 1920s, simply by complying with the labeling provisions of the Food and Drugs Act. Records of the Bureau of Narcotics indicate that Tucker's use of cocaine in production during 1926, for example, was as high as it had been fifteen years earlier. For Tucker, the efforts at regulation had little effect, other than allowing consumers to determine more easily the relative strength of available cocaine cures by requiring the contents to be labeled.

Another conspicuous failure of regulation was in the control of pure cocaine production. No more than a dozen large chemical and pharmaceutical firms had supplied the drug industry with the cocaine needed to manufacture everything from corn cures to catarrh snuffs. Although the Food and Drugs Act restricted the use of cocaine in packaged remedies, the Act said nothing about the sale of cocaine itself. Indeed, as long as the cocaine met agreed-upon standards for purity, and was properly labeled, there were no federal restrictions on its sale. Even passage of the federal Harrison Act focused more on the retail distribution of cocaine, leaving manufacturers of cocaine relatively untouched. Not until passage of the Jones–Miller Act in 1922 did the federal government enact any serious restrictions on cocaine production. In the interim, the quantities of legally produced cocaine did decline over time, but not nearly so rapidly as the number of legal outlets for its sale.

In the end, it seems clear that the regulation of the drug market accomplished a dramatic reduction in the prevalence of cocaine consumption, as countless Americans were offered new "de-cocainized" forms of Vin Mariani and Coca-Cola. In response, most of these consumers appear to have simply abandoned their use of cocaine – certainly there is no evidence that these users now adopted the use of the pure cocaine still available. In the case of Coca-Cola, for example, caffeine (already present) provided suitable effect. Since purchasers of Coca-Cola, Vin Mariani, and other dilute oral-dosage forms of cocaine accounted for a small share of overall cocaine sales, it is not surprising that general levels of consumption did not decline nearly so rapidly. On the contrary, cocaine consumption was still at peak levels as late as 1910, and there is some evidence that consumption may not have significantly declined until after 1920, by which time most cocaine-containing medicines had already been removed from the market for several years. The market that remained was dominated by sales of pure cocaine, most of which went directly to the public through an increasingly marginalized network of distribution.

The legacies of the "propaganda for reform," as the AMA fashioned it, are numerous. The "success" of reformers in driving out certain products from the market was aided immeasurably by the voluntary actions of countless retail druggists and pharmaceutical manufacturers. Their actions suggest that legal status alone was not enough to protect sales of cocaine, and that negative publicity and professional disapproval limited the availability of many forms of cocaine. In this sense, cocaine control was a movement propelled by concerns specific to the drug, but also embedded in a reform tradition in which industry and the professions looked to regulation to secure a friendly and responsible social order.[36] The great failure of reformers was in making little distinction (pharmacological or otherwise) between various cocaine products, or between cocaine and the coca leaf from which it came. Faced with a vast array of products and forms in which cocaine appeared, reformers sought to restrict access to them all. In the process, legitimate concerns over public health and illegitimate advertising were too often blended with imaginary fears and misleading generalizations.

This approach had a disastrous consequence for cocaine control, since it helped demolish a thriving coca business that presented no great threat to public health, while leaving cocaine production virtually untouched. By driving low-potency cocaine products off the market entirely, the field was left wide open to sale of pure cocaine. Why was the focus off the mark? It may have been, as some have suggested, attributable to ignorance over the differences between various forms of cocaine and coca. Or it may have been, as some claimed at the time, that the control of cocaine could not have been accomplished without restricting all of its forms, including the coca leaf. But ignorance and expediency are only small parts of the answer. What must be considered is that the effort at regulation reflected a dual impulse – one grounded in a concern for limiting cocaine abuse, the other in a desire to control the drug industry more generally. By the standards of the latter interest, no exceptions were possible – any commercial interest in cocaine would inevitably threaten the public interest, if not the public health.

Primary sources: the United States

The most important primary sources for the early history of the American cocaine experience are those that detail the actions of manufacturers and distributors. As a legal enterprise, their activities are documented to a greater degree than those of the subsequent illegal traders in cocaine. Problems of access to surviving company records persist, although firms may soon make their historical records more available to researchers. One hopes this trend will continue. A good starting point for information about companies such as Parke, Davis, and the pharmaceutical industry in general, is the American Institute for the History of Pharmacy (AIHP) located on the campus of the University of Wisconsin, Madison. The AIHP houses a large collection of pharmaceutical journals and company catalogs, as well as the Kremers Reference Files, a unique and eclectic collection of materials documenting the evolution of American pharmaceutical practice. Another prominent source of pharmaceutical company materials is the Lloyd Library and Museum in Cincinnati, OH, which houses many useful items, including an enormous collection of drug company publications, price lists, and catalogs.

Much of what we know regarding the practices of patent medicine manufacturers comes from the records of the United States Food and Drug Administration (Rockville, MD), which include case files of proceedings taken against violators of the Food and Drugs Act, undertaken by the Food and Drug Administration's predecessor, the Bureau of Chemistry.

The medical literature dealing with cocaine during this period is voluminous; the medical journal articles alone would form the basis for an extended study. Many of these publications (including many monographs) are extremely hard to locate. Consequently, the History of Medicine Division of the National Library of Medicine in Bethesda, MD, deserves mention for its remarkable collection of rare published materials.

Finally, the National Archives houses some useful collections, including the United States Public Health Service Records (Record Group 90) and the Records of United States Delegations to the International Opium Commission and Conferences, 1909–1913 (Record Group 43). The latter group includes a remarkable volume of correspondence between Hamilton Wright (a member of the delegation) and representatives of drug manufacturers, wholesalers, and law enforcement.

Notes

1 Many of the leaders of the modern pharmaceutical industry came out of the ranks of the nineteenth-century ethical drug industry, including Squibb, Eli Lilly, Upjohn, Abbott, and Parke, Davis. The distinction between the two categories of drug companies was, not surprisingly, heavily promoted by ethical firms themselves, although I would argue that the similarities often outweighed the differences. [Editor's note: this chapter employs the contemporary name "Parke, Davis" rather than Parke-Davis (or Parke & Davis), the alternative or later usage.]

2 Patent medicines were not actually patented. They were protected by trademark, and were thus often referred to instead as "proprietary" remedies. For consistency, I will

use the terms "patent medicines" and "patent medicine manufacturers," rather than "proprietaries" and "proprietary manufacturers."

3   Most of the coca products made by ethical firms were largely indistinguishable from their patent medicine counterparts – what separated them was the methods by which they were promoted and distributed.

4   The low potency of such products suggests that so-called "cocaine fiends" would have found them to be close to useless. To give some idea of how this cocaine content compared to the amount taken by users, commonly identified at the time as cocaine "addicts," one should note that estimates of the "typical" daily consumption of the cocaine addict ranged from 10–15 grains (roughly 650–975 mg) per day. Although other estimates were higher, even the lower figure would have required the con-sumption of at least 50 ounces of Sutliff's Beef, Wine, and Coca. Even that would likely have not proved very satisfactory, since the dilute oral dose in the wine would have a markedly different action from the intra-nasal route of administration of the cocaine sniffers.

5   Interstate Seizure File 11366-d, Notice of Judgment No. 2213, "Beef, Wine, and Coca," box 272, United States Food and Drug Administration, Rockville, MD [hereafter FDA].

6   In its early advertising, Coca-Cola not only openly acknowledged its coca content, it ardently invoked accepted medical knowledge of coca to make its sales pitch. In 1896, the *National Druggist* (a St Louis publication) ran its first advertisement, entitled "Coca-Cola a triumph over nature," for Coca-Cola:

> It seems to be a law of nature that the more valuable and efficacious a drug is, the nastier and more unpleasant its taste. It is therefore quite a triumph over nature that the Coca-Cola Co. of Atlanta, Ga., have achieved in their success in robbing both coca leaves and the kola nut of the exceedingly nauseous and disagreeable taste while retaining their wonderful medicinal properties, and the power of restoring vitality and raising the spirits of the weary and debili-tated. Not only have they done this, but by some subtle alchemy they have made them the basis of one of the most delightful, cheering, and invigorating of fountain drinks."
>
> (*National Druggist*, July 1896: 214)

7   Although the Coca-Cola formula was a closely guarded secret, most published accounts presumed that Pemberton employed coca in his product, a presumption confirmed in 1993 with the publication of the original formula by Mark Pendergrast. The formula discovered called for the addition of 4 ounces of "F.E. Coco," which despite the misspelling, referred to the fluid extract of coca. See Mark Pendergrast, *For God, Country and Coca-Cola: The Unauthorized History of the Great American Soft Drink and the Company that Makes it* (New York: Scribner, 1993), 421–5.

8   In pursuing a case against Coca-Cola, the Bureau of Chemistry sent agents to various soda fountains to determine whether or not servers filled glasses with more syrup than the company specified in its guidelines. They discovered that many customers asked for and received stronger versions of the drink.

9   Interstate Seizure File 17442-b, Notice of Judgment No. 930, "Dr Elder's Celebrated Tobacco Specific," box 244, FDA.

10   Information regarding the composition of packaged remedies comes from the case files maintained by the Bureau of Chemistry.

11   *Nostrums and Quackery*, 2nd edn (American Medical Association: Chicago, 1912), 551.

12   To a great extent, the activities of these groups overlapped, and each frequently found occasion to work with the other toward common regulatory and reform goals. The AMA, for example, distributed over 100,000 copies of Samuel Hopkins Adams's series. The AMA's Council on Pharmacy and Chemistry, whose approval was

necessary if a manufacturer wished to advertise a product in professional medical journals, counted as members Harvey Wiley and Lyman Kebler (chief of the Bureau of Chemistry's drug division). Wiley himself was something of a muckraking journalist, publishing a regular series in *Cosmopolitan*, and worked closely with various private organizations, including the WCTU.

The close relationship between public and private organizations in seeking to regulate cocaine sales was less indicative of a grand and exceptional conspiracy to deprive consumers of cocaine, than it was of the typical Progressive-era reform mechanism. If private groups such as the AMA, for instance, worked to affect public legislation to their own advantage, they did so no more than countless other interest groups.

13 Interstate Seizure File 9164-a, Notice of Judgment No. 323, "Remedy for Hay Fever and Catarrh," box 230, FDA.
14 Bureau of Chemistry Hearing No. 144, "Nathan Tucker's Asthma Specific" (4 September 1908), BC.
15 The committee pointed to a Mariani circular that claimed that Vin Mariani was "good for" the following conditions: "anemia, winter cough, debility, vocal weakness, la grippe, continued fevers, bronchitis, nervous troubles, muscular weakness, diseases of the aged, malaria, melancholia, overwork, neurasthenia, impotence, malnutrition, depression, heart troubles, wasting diseases, mental overstrain, and in certain cases of protracted convalescence." While mainstream medical opinion at the time of the AMA's report did not support such claims, a review of medical journal articles twenty years earlier would have found claims for each of these therapeutic uses of coca wine.
16 *The Propaganda for Reform in Proprietary Medicines* (Chicago, American Medical Association), 114–18.
17 "Cocaine in the United States," *Canadian Pharmaceutical Journal* 42 (1909), 396.
18 "Cocaine victims in torture," *New York Times* (15 September 1908).
19 See for example: Daniel D. Gilbert, "The cocaine habit from snuff," *Boston Medical and Surgical Journal* 138 (3 February 1898), 119.
20 Interstate Seizure Files 16578-a and 31622-a, Notice of Judgment No. 694, "Alleged drug habit cure," FDA. Starnes may not have been entirely credible – he was later charged with selling drug cures that contained unacknowledged quantities of morphine! Nevertheless, charges of addictiveness were made concerning Coca-Cola by groups such as the WCTU, and from Harvey Wiley, chief of the Bureau of Chemistry.
21 The following report from a Bureau of Chemistry agent in Atlanta was typical:

It was learned in Georgia, as in almost every other place, that coca cola was consumed by people in all walks of life, but most abundantly by office workers and those confined largely to what is frequently called "brain workers." The people in the offices at Atlanta usually drink a glass of coca cola before beginning their work, one during the noon recess, and a number at the completion of the day's duties. We personally saw the beverage consumed by children of four, five and six years of age, and information was also obtained to the effect that the beverage was bought in pitchers, taken home and consumed by the entire family as is frequently done with beer. Soda fountain clerks in many cases referred to persons drinking from eight to ten and twelve glasses of the beverage, which was quite common, as "coca cola fiends."

See report in Seizure File 352, Notice of Judgment No. 1455, "Coca Cola," FDA.
22 Numerous sources suggest that a pinch of cocaine added to either whiskey or a soft drink in saloons was not uncommon. Historian William Ivy Hair's description of New Orleans' working-class and red-light districts suggests that this occurred. See William Ivy Hair, *Carnival of Fury: Robert Charles and the New Orleans Race Riot of 1900* (Baton

Rouge: Louisiana State University Press, 1976). A report from Georgia noted that following alcohol prohibition, saloon-keepers were "not going out of business altogether" but were "putting in soda fountains in connection with their cigar stands and making their places as attractive as possible in order to retain their old customers." See "Prohibition and the soda fountain," *National Druggist* (February 1908), 41.

23 Interstate Seizure File 9164-a, Notice of Judgment No. 323, "Remedy for hay fever and catarrh," box 230, FDA.

24 "Boy cocaine snuffers hunted by the police," *New York Times* (8 January 1907), 3.

25 This does not even begin to take note of the more vitriolic foes of cocaine, such as E.H. Williams, who wrote that cocaine transformed "hitherto inoffensive, law-abiding negroes" into "a constant menace to the community ... sexual desires are increased and perverted, peaceful negroes become quarrelsome, and timid negroes develop a degree of 'Dutch courage' that is sometimes almost incredible." See E.H. Williams, "The drug habit menace in the South," *Medical Record* 85 (1914), 247–9.

26 "Public waking up to cocaine menace," *New York Times* (3 August 1908), 5.

27 *Limiting Production of Habit-Forming Drugs and Raw Materials From Which They Are Made: Hearings Before the Committee on Foreign Affairs*, 67th Cong., 4th sess. (1923), 55–6.

28 W.J. O'Connor, Inspector of Police to Dr Hamilton Wright (22 June 1909), *Records of the United States Delegations to the International Opium Commission and Conferences, 1909–13*, Record Group 43, National Archives.

29 "New York to have drastic cocaine law," *Pharmaceutical Era* (February 1913), 96.

30 *Southern Pharmaceutical Journal* (August 1909), 611–12.

31 "Druggists take the initiative in prosecuting vendors of habit-forming drugs," *National Druggist* 40 (May 1910), 203–4.

32 Samuel Hopkins Adams, *The Great American Fraud* (Chicago: American Medical Association Press, 1912), 177–8.

33 L.F. Kebler, *Habit-Forming Agents: Their Indiscriminate Sale and Use a Menace to Public Welfare*, US Department of Agriculture, Farmer's Bulletin 393 (Washington: Government Printing Office, 1910), 10.

34 O.W. Smith to Parke, Davis and Company (4 December 1909), box 20, Parke, Davis and Company Collection [hereafter PDC], Burton Historical Collection, Detroit Public Library. In an earlier memorandum, the company's Detroit counsel had been asked if cocaine laws "would affect all preparations containing cocaine including" those products "which would not be used by cocaine habitués?" Counsel Woodruff's discouraging reply suggested that they would. Memorandum, Norvell to Counsel Woodruff (30 September 1909), and Woodruff to Norvell (31 September 1909), box 20, PDC.

35 Bureau of Chemistry Hearing No. 64, "Maltine Coca Wine" (12 November 1907).

36 This is an aspect of reform movements that has been well described by historians, starting with Gabriel Kolko's *The Triumph of Conservatism* (New York: The Free Press, 1963) and James Weinstein's *The Corporate Ideal in the Liberal State 1900–1918* (New York: Beacon Press, 1968). Histories of cocaine generally focus on the drug control movement in isolation, which ignores the extent to which anti-cocaine interests had stakes in much broader reform and regulatory issues.

3 Reluctance or resistance?

Constructing cocaine (prohibitions) in Peru, 1910–50

Paul Gootenberg

Peru is widely, famously known today as the source of more than half of the world's coca and cocaine paste for *illicit* markets to the north; it is also recognized, in historical terms, as ancestral homeland of Andean coca leaf, of traditional use since remote pre-Inca times. Hidden in this story however is a crucial middle and transitional period: the seven decades, from the 1880s to the 1950s, when Peru was for the world market the leading if now-forgotten producer of fully *licit* and legal cocaine.

This chapter explores aspects of the slow Peruvian embrace of cocaine prohibitions during the era 1910–50. It focuses mainly on the politics of that process, though its transnational context (in Peru's close yet ambivalent ties with the United States in the history of cocaine) and its context in the regional political economy of cocaine (in the subtropical province of Huánuco) are also carefully drawn. The key fact here is that Peru lagged over four decades (from 1910 to 1950) in disparaging and criminalizing cocaine, a long pause in which the heroic, nationalist, or modernizing repute of Peruvian cocaine, produced in the late nineteenth century, lived on in new, old, and revealing forms. Peru's belated joining after World War II with the American anti-cocaine crusade also left a suggestive mark on the birth of today's illicit world networks of cocaine.

The chapter begins by tracing the roots of Peru's legal cocaine industry in the prior half-century, 1880–1930, and its complex relation with the United States and other global networks. The next section is a close recounting of a remarkable middle era, the 1930s, when Peru, through the vocal campaigning of Carlos Paz Soldán, came closest to actually contesting the global tide of anti-cocainism. The third and final section examines over the decade, 1940–50, the global and local factors that changed, and had to change, for Peru to make cocaine a pariah and illicit drug, here at its source of supply. Was Peru a resistant or merely reluctant partner in that portentous shift? Were cocaine prohibitions a United States export or a nationally constructed regime? Whatever the answers, the Peruvian legacies are here to stay.

Political economies of national cocaine (1880–1930)

In early 1885, an urgent cable reached American consular posts across the Andes: in the wake of recent medical discoveries, the world was entering its first coca–cocaine frenzy, and the flexing United States – from ambitious pharmaceutical firms like Parke-Davis to the United States Navy – were not to be left behind. Would full information be sent to assure quality Peruvian coca for growing demands in the United States?[1] The same year, an obscure Atlanta pharmacist was unknowingly concocting a formula that would buoy desires for coca for decades to come, shaping its politics along the way. Even that quintessential American, "Mark Twain," fantasized of cashing in on the coca craze, by spreading plantations across the globe. A few years later, in Peru, its national economy and state still in shambles from the myriad calamities of the passing nineteenth century (the guano export bust, the disastrous 1879–81 Pacific War with Chile), a fragile government in Lima convened a blue-ribbon panel of its best medical-scientific minds, led by Dr José Casimiro Ulloa, to present an official "Informe Sobre la Coca." Their task was to define what Peru might do to exploit this new worldly fascination with their age-old Andean herb. Among their most enthused recommendations: the modernizing production and large-scale commercial export of "cocaína bruta" – legal crude cocaine – made in Peru.[2]

From Peru, this initial historical cycle of turning Andean coca into modern cocaine was also the transformation of a *national* white hope of the 1890s into a 1920s *regional* problem of dashed frustrations (of the eastern producer province of Huánuco). It is also the story of a liberal hope – of a rejuvenating, innovative, outward-looking private-sector drive, which by the 1920s would mutate into statist and inward dreams of official rescue, guidance, and control through public monopolies of national coca and cocaine. During both phases and conceptions, however, changing international market conditions, and an evolving United States politics of cocaine, became stumbling blocks to Peruvian "imagining of development."[3]

By the turn of the century, Peruvian coca producers, industrialists, doctors, chemists, and merchants had indeed achieved the remarkable: by 1900, Peru was not only the world's largest exporter of raw coca (supplying almost a million kilos a year to world markets from its eastern tropical "montaña" regions), but also at its peak in 1900–5, the world's leading maker of cocaine itself. That year, Peru sold nearly 10,000 kilos, or 10 metric tons, of "crude cocaine" (sulfates of cocaine, of 85–94 percent purity), mainly to Germany, the United States, and France. During this decade-long boom of the 1890s to 1900s, coming with Peru's politically formative, modern "República Aristocrática," earnings from coca and cocaine ranked among the top five national exports, with crude cocaine a growing share of profits. What gave cocaine added luster was its close fit with national modernization ideals: it applied modern science (some of it home-grown) to a uniquely "Peruvian" crop, Andean coca. Epitomizing what economic historian Rosemary Thorp has defined as the rise (and fall) of an "autonomous" Peruvian development effort, crude cocaine was especially laudable for the minimal demands it placed on scarce public infrastructure and direction.[4] No wonder liberal industrialist spokesman Alejandro Garland lauded cocaine as "that essentially Peruvian industry."

The origins of this boom are still murky. Coca leaf sales begin to accelerate by the mid-1880s (from all of the recuperating ports of the country) and the national medical and business press soon brimmed with notices and tips about its products. By 1885 – the year of the first coca–cocaine price bubble – Peruvian businessmen had not only identified with coca as a "national" good (boasting, for example, that Peruvian doctor Tomás Moreno y Maíz had discovered its anesthetic properties long before any German scientist), but called for widespread Amazonian colonization and nearby *factories* to make it an eminently Peruvian industry.[5] By the early 1890s, on the heels of the Ulloa Commission, an enterprising expatriate chemist, "Arnaldo" Kitz, possibly working for German firms, had made his way to remote Amazonian Pozuzo, a legendary lost 1850s colony of Austrian peasants, and established there a crude cocaine factory. Kitz applied the "Bignon formula" of processing invented in Lima itself in the 1880s, by local druggist and medical researcher, Alfredo Bignon, and soon in use by other urban pharmacy producers, notably Meyer & Hafemanns. By one account, Kitz must have saved the desperate Pozuzo community from ruin, for the manufactory alone employed twenty to thirty workers around 1897, before moving to Huánuco, the next pole of the national industry. United States consuls convened with Kitz in the early 1890s to discuss price and supply conditions.[6]

Indeed by 1890 – a precocious date – Peru was exporting more than 1,000 kilos of crude cocaine sulfates; by the mid-1890s production quadrupled and at least seven substantial factories were running, three around Huánuco, the others in Lima-Callao. Economists of the 1890s such as José Rodríguez celebrated the boom, pushing liberal tariff incentives to keep it moving fast ahead; Peruvian inventors evaluated and innovated on technologies in use. In 1905, then-Finance Minister, Garland, spoke glowingly of Peru's model industry and noted some twenty-three manufacturers; Peru enjoyed a natural – rather than a forced or protectionist – monopoly here, as foreign attempts to "acclimatize" the Andean coca plant had all failed (or so he believed). "This novel and so essentially Peruvian industry," already at 7,000 or more kilos, "satisfied world demands in this realm. If no one can possibly predict the range of importance it will reach ... we affirm its grand future." In 1906, Minister of Promotion (*Fomento*), Cisneros, counted some twenty-one factories (most of likely modest size), ranging from the capital Lima and Otuzco province of northern Libertad to Abancay and the old Incan capital of Cuzco in the south. He found Peruvian producers of coca-laced syrups, wines, even flavored beers and chocolates; a subgroup of the ministry was working on coca-driven jungle "colonization" projects. The ministry's gazette published technical schemes to encourage and upgrade cocaine processing, like that of Peru's leading civil engineer, Pedro Paulet, in 1903.[7] Major export houses – names like W.R. Grace and Schroeder – profitably plied both products abroad. Banks such as the Banco del Perú y Londres supplied factories with commercial legitimacy and funds. In 1901, the United States for its part imported 863,252 kilos of coca and 461 kilos of cocaine, mainly through the ports of Callao (Lima) and northern Salaverry.

By 1905, however, the profile of this industry was changing, along with the unbounded national expectations. Even before Kitz's passing in 1896, the trade began to consolidate ever more around central-east Huánuco, a coca supply zone to Peruvian mining regions, renowned for the high-alkaloid leaf grown in its adjacent tropical *montaña* (Amazonian foothills of the Andes). The key figure here was Don Augusto Durand. Durand was the Huánuco region's weightiest *caudillo* and modernizing landowner, and a legendary national politician, inveterate insurrectionist, founder and leader of the opposition Liberal party, diplomat and owner of the Lima daily *La Prensa* to boot. Durand may have picked up interest in modern cocaine while touring Europe and the United States in the early 1890s. He centered his burgeoning factory and farm operations on an extensive Derrepente-zone *hacienda* named "Éxito" (aptly enough meaning "success"), which kept his extended family clan going strong years after his controverted political assassination in 1923. Durand was joined here by a coterie of mainly Croatian-immigrant, small factory owners, ex-miners with such unlikely Peruvian surnames as Nesanovich, Plejo, Marinovich, and the Spaniard, José Más. Their raw coca leaf supplies were met from intensified commerce and clientelistic ties with the area's dispersed and ethnically dominated small-holder peasantry, planting and harvesting coca in their time-honored ways. Durand forged deal after deal to consolidate Peru's cocaine export trade, even going abroad in attempts to form large-scale seller "trusts" against slumping prices.[8] Durand controlled regional exports and articulated this *Huanuqueño* agro-industrial oligarchy to national politics and the Peruvian state itself, a mantle later assumed in the 1920s by his heir apparent, Andrés Avelino Soberón.

After 1905, there is a subtle shift of mood in national cocaine promotional and technical literature. A stream of technical works by writers such as Bües, Ravines, Pozzi-Escot, Hohagen, Mario Durand (a son), Manuel Vinelli (an aspiring chemist from Huánuco), and others sound pessimism, calling for drastic measures to upgrade primitive coca cultivation and drying methods as well as cocaine chemistry. By 1910, they increasingly call for Government guidance in these transformations – for example, for scientific refining of cocaine sulfates into more valuable, more marketable, and purer end-product, cocaine hydrochloride.[9] This at a time when relative national interest in *montaña* coca was falling, eclipsed by the wildly profitable but short-lived scramble for wild rubber in nearby Amazonian terrain, something the Durands pursued as well. As yet the "crisis" of Peru's national cocaine after 1910 was not related to its evolving disrepute in the West, though Peruvians had heard about the fuss over "cocainomía," notably in widely read reports of their prolific commercial attaché in New York, Edmundo Higginson.[10] Rather, the crisis had to do with unexpected and sudden losses of world market shares: due to Dutch market competition and the shifting "political economy" of North American drug control.

The Dutch, as the British and French, had toyed on colonial Java with plantings of borrowed strains of Huánuco leaf since the late nineteenth century. But the meteoric rise of top-quality modern *plantation*-grown coca came between 1907 and 1914. By 1914, Dutch exports surpassed Peru's peak of one million kilograms, equal to the entire world demand of 10 metric tons of cocaine, in Amsterdam, via newly efficient ecgonine-extraction methods! The Dutch (as de Kort shows in Chapter 6) had built a vertically controlled industry right in the geographic core of world medicinal demand; after licit demands steadily fell after 1920, it was the Dutch who organized defensive European buyer cartels around cocaine, further limiting Peru's market share.[11] Ignoring warning signs of Dutch initiatives, perhaps for their excessive belief in the innate "Peruvianness" of coca, the Peruvians had lost out, in a manner strikingly similar to the earlier saga of chinchona (once *Peru* bark) and the coeval bust in Amazonian wild rubber. In any case, scale economies, productivity boosts or improvement in Peruvian coca strains and processing methods would, at best, have proved difficult, given the rudimentary fact that coca here was an entrenched small-holder crop, predominantly in the hands of a traditional and socially marginal Andean peasantry. By the 1920s, most Andean coca production quickly returned to its roots for the national Indian market.

Another irony was that Peruvian merchants and cocaine makers had sought salvation in Europe as the closer United States market tightened after 1905. To make a complex story short and simple here, United States policy, even before the anti-cocaine "scares" and restrictions of the 1910s, had discriminated against Peruvian crude cocaine. The aim, starting with the 1896 national tariff, was to favor domestic American cocaine producers, like Parke-Davis, Mallinckrodt and (New Jersey) Merck, by excluding all foreign cocaines and easing duties on raw coca. Such protectionism, which likely helped consolidate a smaller club of big firms in this field, became functional to or merged into United States drug control strategy after the 1914 Harrison Act. Not only was it far simpler for United States treasury officials to monitor a clutch of highly co-operative corporations (rather than scores of patent medicine men or thousands of dentists), but, after 1922, the Jones–Miller Narcotic Drugs Import and Export Act institutionalized this controlled structure of trade, by permitting only easily monitored bulk imports of coca. By then, Peruvian sales had fallen dramatically, to less than 200,000 kilos a year of coca, which even competed here with Java. Furthermore, by the 1920s, the new United States Narcotics Bureau (precursor of the FBN: the Federal Bureau of Narcotics) had found a cozy active corporate "intermediary" in this process: Maywood Chemical Company of New Jersey, sole makers of a famous coca product called "Merchandise No. 5." This was the *de*-cocainized flavoring of coca used in North America's booming soft-drink symbol, Coca-Cola: their coca needs (more than half of United States imports) came not from Huánuco, but from northern Trujillo, in a local and lasting compact with the powerful merchant family of Alfredo Pinillos.[12] In remarkable ways, Maywood, whose coca came under strict almost ritual supervision by the

FBN, became a vital actor and meddler in United States policy on Peruvian cocaine.

In any case, by the 1920s, Peruvian cocaine (and coca as well) had lost most of its earlier markets, and with it the earlier luster. The long-term problem was how to confront receding global cocaine demands – chronic after 1910 – due to limiting international conventions and falling "legal" consumption. Peruvian advocates later condemned these market conditions as a United States "embargo" against their product, though they arose from a mix of adversities. The bottom line was that Peru's exports of crude cocaine fell from almost 34,000 kilos (34 tons) between 1904–8 to less than 22 tons over the next four years, 1908–12. In the 1920s, averages would fall below a single ton a year (300–800 kilos), worth less than 100,000 *soles*, though the League of Nations had set world licit needs at some 6 tons.[13] The trends in prices (save for a post-World War I blip) and coca exporting (save for steady Maywood) were just as dismal.

Given such a depressing global picture, what can be said about the regional political economy of Peru's struggling producers of legal cocaine? Here, helping sparse local documentation are a series of detailed United States reports of the time, such as "Reports on coca," as the United States began a long watch on the Peruvian industry. (One graphic report, from 1931, is testimony by the Embassy's Chief-Consul William C. Burdett, dispatched to far-off Huánuco for a first-hand look.)

By the late 1920s, the Peruvian crude cocaine industry had shrunken into an overwhelmingly *regionalized* force: reduced to greater Huánuco (some six to eight small factories) and a pair of active factories in northern Trujillo and its Otuzco interior. All exports were nominally controlled and centralized through Lima's port of Callao and Salaverry in the north, under registration with Peru's Department of Public Health. Coca export for Maywood and Coca-Cola formed a separate northern circuit, of the Pinillos clan, who on occasion had their own cocaine factory going, too. Coca cultivation and colonization for domestic traditional use (so-called Indian "chewing") was actually spreading fastest in the southern tropical lowlands of Cuzco province (especially La Convención); coca for export, after 1912, had only receded. Despite various proposals for reform, coca cultivation remained a largely age-old form of peasant agriculture, in the hands of (for want of better terms) "Indians," albeit, as custom, commercially savvy, active jungle colonizers. Coca, a fairly resilient plant for its zones, was plagued by soil depletion and endemic insect plagues. Coca dominated but a few of Huánuco's nearby hot-watered valleys – as a "sea of green" – and was also planted among crops most everywhere in the central "Eyebrow of the Jungle." "About half," went the cliché, of Peru's population (upland, Quechua-speaking, poor) used coca leaves on a daily basis, consuming about eight million pounds annually.

Peru's small factories, facing cloudy market prospects after 1910, had never made the long exhorted technological jump to cocaine hydrochloride refining, still relying on the nationally approved Bignon mechanical crushing method from the 1880s (sometimes called the Kitz formula). This leached out, by mixing in sulfites, kerosine, and soda ash, a basically craft product, ranging from 82–94 percent purity. As early as 1909–11, observers lamented these way "out-of-date" Peruvian methods.[14] Everything was done by hand, using local artisan materials (such as wooden tubs and piping) bereft of modern chemical industrial inputs. Peruvian "brute" or "crude" was in many ways akin to today's hastily prepared clandestine jungle "pasta básica" of cocaine and was rarely used for direct human consumption. Paradoxically, Peru imported its tiny medicinal needs for hydrochlorides from Europe.

To say the industry was "regional," "rudimentary," or "small" (labs employed off and on about three to five workers each) is not to say it lacked influence. For example, in both areas the industry, through municipal taxes, was a major prop to road-building, schools, and other local services. Especially around Huánuco, dozens of farmers and planters encircled the cocaine processors, who were akin to regional "gamonales" (Peruvian for rural strongmen). Both zones hosted influential cocaine magnates – would-be modernizers who dominated the commercial action. In Trujillo this man was Teofilio S. Vergil – respected citizen, merchant, self-proclaimed "*Caballero* widely connected in commercial circles of the north" (in company ads) whose factory, opened in 1914, boasted sixteen employees and could potentially process 800 kilos a year in the 1920s, i.e. the full national export tab, give or take. The other northern base of highland Otuzco was controlled by the Martín Ayllon family over several generations, and was said to enjoy half that capacity (400 kilos) – "if a market presents itself," in the consul's precise words.[15] From time to time, smaller labs show up in the north, too.

Huánuco was dominated by two concerns: the "Negociación" (family corporation) of Augusto Durand, his extensive heirs, relatives, and other hosts after his 1923 killing. Its manager, Alfredo Mastrekado, ran an array of coca farms in Derrapente and nearby Chinchao and Monzón districts as well (around Tingo María, now known as the capital of Peruvian cocaine during the 1980s). In 1926, the "Éxito" factory capacity was still listed at 1,000 kilos a year, though they were clearly not using much of this, and in the next decade would diversify out into surer and profitable ventures like raising domestic tea. The second, highly dedicated and now rising star of Huánuco (opening his factory upon the short-lived World War I boom, buying out the last of the Croatians), was Andrés Avelino Soberón, who would strive singlehandedly to reconstitute the Huánuco cocaine industry over the next three decades. Most of his market contacts were German, notably Lima's A. Dammert & Sons, who shipped their crude cocaine to overseas wholesalers in Hamburg and Darmstadt, home of the original Merck. Soberón, who also owned small mines and other area properties, somehow managed to get wealthier along the way, despite the continuing world and regional slump in cocaine. His enthusiastic goal for his "Huánuco"-brand factory was 400 kilos a year and of all producers he was by far the most active and visible. Indeed, the factory itself was located in a prime block of Huánuco city real estate, and the family, like Durand's before them, forged vital political connections, mainly with the nascent "APRA" party, which took hold in outlying zones such as Huánuco. Soberón advertized widely and proudly, garnered prizes (for cocaine quality) at foreign exhibitions, and by the 1930s was energetically hoping to break into the off-limits United States market – provoking the concerns of the FBN and thus the embassy's Huánuco tour. His factory employed eight in 1932, but output ranged wildly, from 1 kilo to 30 daily, depending on order or demand. Around these two magnates worked a seemingly intermittent and primitive clutch of other tiny (if usually) Government-licensed export factories. Business guides list anywhere from six to ten establishments operating in Huánuco from the 1920s through 1940s, apart from coca export houses, with a high flux in ownership (the Lafosse, Ibérico, and Rodríguez, or later Ofanides, Mori, and Baroli establishments). These were likely the shells of factories, at best seasonal operations of larger *montaña* coca planters, such as the Radas of Monzón.[16] By the 1930s, the Croatians had abandoned this field.

' Of remarkable note here was a *Japanese* foothold in the zone, with distinct imperial overtones, linking Peru for a time to an emerging and much distrusted (by drug agencies) Asian network of cocaine. Run by Peruvian *Nisei* Masao Sawada, or Saito, this site was variously called the "Negociación Japonesa," Tulumayo property, or "Pampayacu" farm-factory. It dated to a huge purchase of *montaña* forest and *cocales* in 1917, negotiated with Durand, by no less than agents of Hoshi Pharmaceuticals! This territory soon expanded to nearly 3,000 square kilometers lying between Tingo María and deep-jungle Pucallpa, which even provoked press coverage and official suspicion in the United States. By the mid-1920s, there were intermittent if notable direct shipments of Huánuco crude cocaine and coca to Japan, some two-fifths of local product (on a par with German shares), consigned for Osaka drug firms by Lima's branch of Nonomiya Shoten.[17] By the 1930s, when these lands became embroiled in a bitter and highly politicized land dispute, exports had dwindled, for the Japanese had achieved relative self-sufficiency with their newer colonial coca plantations in Formosa. One intriguing question is the knowledge the Japanese possibly extracted about coca or cocaine from Huánuco's long hands-on experience. This enclave of foreign investment abruptly ended with its expropriation (and expulsions of local Nisei) in 1937, on the brink of war in the Pacific.

United States officials in Peru, schooled in anti-"narcotics" doctrine by the late 1920s, already took a dim view of Soberón's type of business activities, though he and the others of course saw them as wholly legitimate and honorable ones. Indeed, in the early 1930s, there had been some fines or closures of factories for alleged drug contraband, north in Trujillo. But in 1932 the Americans studiously determined "no grounds for suspecting Mr Soberón of complicity in illicit traffic in narcotics," though at the same time they saw no reason to trust his integrity alone: "The local standard of business ethics sanctions violations of any laws of any kind." Our consul duly informed and warned Soberón that unsolicited exports of cocaine to the United States (even the customary business samples) were a serious illegal offense, but by the late 1930s he'd be hoping again, in the gathering war climate, to sway prospective American buyers and officials. Peru's domestic narcotics bureau, the Sección de

Control de Narcóticos in the Public Health Ministry, erected bit-by-bit after 1922 sanitary laws, was not very big or strong, dedicated mainly to inspecting local pharmacies and hunting down Chinese "opium dens." But they characteristically made Huánuco seem too remote for control in its occasional "no-thank-you's" (funneled via Peru's Foreign Ministry) to inquiring League or United States officials. In fact, the zone was linked by decent and improved roads to Cerro de Pasco and on to Lima and was compact enough for control – until, that is, late-1940s repression scattered cocaine into forbidding jungle zones. Factories practiced forms of self-regulation through regional tax agencies, the prefects, and the locally run, medical "Juntas de Farmacia," likely oiled by regional sovereigns like Soberón. After his voyage to the Huallaga – the now infamous river flows through Huánuco town – Consul Burdett, in a telling note, deemed the danger "more potential than actual" from this long-suffering region. But with a "remunerative demand for crude cocaine in the United States, or the development in Peru of methods for producing salts of cocaine in shape for consumption, the control machinery in Peru would be a most unsatisfactory barrier to illicit trade."[18] By the 1930s depression, however, voices were raised again for industrializing Peru's national cocaine, but for very different motives than his presumed criminal ones.

To close here, we need to briefly sum up Peru's response to the system of global cocaine controls and restrictions being jerry-built by the United States and the League during those two decades, 1910–30. Peruvian diplomatic and élite opinion, while fully aware of those campaigns and institutions, made the move to stay apart, in a passive form of international resistance. It was the United States (for reasons that still beg clarification) that took the aggressive global lead after 1910 against cocaine, along with other "narcotics." They noted and pointedly protested to Peru and Bolivia at the time their conspicuous absence from early anti-drug negotiations at the Hague (1912–13) and beyond. Peru's "real interest" took the blame. By late 1920, the fledgling American anti-drug bureaucracy had already defined and found "illicit" supplies of cocaine within United States borders (some 75 percent of the drug, they claimed), but rarely traced it to Andean sources. Rather, contraband drug was invariably read, in official pronouncements and routines, as leakage from competing European or Japanese pharmaceutical firms; American manufacturers, in their complacent working compact with narcotics officials, were never possible suspects. In any case by the early 1930s, for equally complex reasons, earlier recreational cocaine use seems to dry up in the United States. Indeed, in their triumphal discourse of the 1930s, the FBN then deemed domestic illicit cocaine "so small as to be without significance," measured in ounces, and a useful exemplar of what hardline exclusionary policies could do.[19] In the United States, Peru's cocaine was simply out of sight.

Despite this sense of security, United States officials in Peru and the FBN did do one thing in the 1920s: they began to watch Peruvian coca and cocaine ever more closely, in what might be called a narcotics "gaze." By the mid-1920s, American foreign anti-drug intelligence had begun, independent of fanciful

League statistical and treaty crusades. Every few years, extensively researched "Reports on coca" were submitted to Washington; Peruvian legislation and production collated; local opinion plumbed. Indeed, by the early 1930s, I venture that the FBN and State Department possessed a greater local knowledge than the League about cocaine, and likely surpassed even the capacity of the Peruvian state itself in these matters.[20] Still, United States officials took no visible steps to pressure Peruvian policies or attitudes about cocaine, though, on occasion, the local agents of Maywood in Lima (*anti-cocaine* because it might hinder or complicate their flow of Peruvian coca supplies) would suggest or act out that role. As the Consul had said, Peru's crude cocaine remained but a "potential" peril to the United States.

While the United States focused its gaze, the League of Nations built its fictitious "maze" around Andean cocaine. Throughout the 1920s and 1930s, the League's "Opium Advisory Committee" (the OAC) and allied bodies convened dozens of meetings and formal conventions, spawned hundreds of volumes of debates and statistics around global narcotics, and yet never seemed to get a handle on cocaine and coca, despite some specific attempts. For example, "Subcommittee C" of the 1924 Geneva Conference on Narcotics worked out primitive coca-eradication projects; "Coca report" forms were mimeographed and mailed throughout the 1930s. Peru soon left the League (for other reasons) and kept a studied distance until World War II. To be sure, letters and invitations arrived monthly to Lima, shelved by Foreign Affairs or forwarded to the Health Department. Nominally, Peru was a member of the Hague anti-drug Convention, inadvertently it seems for having signed on to the Versailles armistice in 1919. But only twice over those next two decades did the Peruvians bother to send crude statistics to Geneva. In every yearly session, League drug officialdom noted the glaring absence of reports on Andean coca and cocaine, and publicly implored Peruvian participation. (Maybe they should have known better, for when nationalist *Bolivians* actively participated, as in 1924, they took the occasion to loudly denounce the anti-coca prejudices of the League.)[21]

So undeterred, the League simply went on its way and built its maze of restrictive devices, a byzantine imaginary world of controlling statistics, quotas, supervisory bodies, and "legitimate" world needs. Again, it was as if the Andes produced no cocaine. Only Dutch colonial coca and medicinal cocaine was directly affected, though indirectly League campaigns helped define shrinking world markets, or, indeed, the concepts of legitimate and illicit drugs themselves. On occasion, United States and other hardline critics used this reality gap to embarrass the powerless League: as in an aptly titled 1928 broadside from Geneva "Strange omissions: Crude cocaine."[22] But it wasn't so strange so long as Peru played its studied absentee role. And Peruvian suspicions weren't so odd either, given their long dashed hopes in modernizing cocaine.

Peru's national cocaine debate (1929–39)

The 1930s became a crossroads for all these trends – of decayed regional industries, hopes for cocaine modernization, and distance from big-power anti-cocainism – and years of fiery political debate over prospects for national cocaine. The galvanizing figure in these controversies, Carlos Enrique Paz Soldán, opened the debate with a nationalist salvo of late 1929: a call for Peruvian resistance to advancing global controls through a new national "monopoly" of coca and modern cocaine. This controversy had wide implications, but paradoxically was to be the last pause before Peru's move to prohibitions in the coming decade.

Dr Carlos Enrique Paz Soldán was scion of one of Lima's most distinguished intellectual families. A cosmopolitan medical figure, he served in Washington during the 1920s and 1930s as Sub-Director of the Pan-American Sanitary Union, where he left his mark as a prominent regional spokesman against the racist Anglo-Saxon "eugenics" movement. In Peru, Paz Soldán is celebrated as founder of the activist "Instituto de Medicina Social" at San Marcos University (and later Dean of Medicine) and editor of its reforming journal, *La Reforma Médica*.[23] He seems to have been an early sympathizer with the new "APRA" movement (Alianza Popular Revolucionaria Americana), the northern-based, left-wing, anti-imperialist party of Víctor Raúl Haya de la Torre that would convulse Peruvian politics until the 1960s. Paz Soldán was moved to invest his considerable energies into questions of coca and cocaine by two events – a 1929 coca monopoly proposed to Congress by Dr Carlos Ricketts (to free Peruvian Indians of their age-old "vice") and by personal ties to the international drug reformer, Carlos Pagador. But the stamp he put on this problem was clearly and idiosyncratically his own.

Paz Soldán's campaign was above all a Peruvian challenge, or even alternative, to the influences of the consolidating global prohibitions regime. He reversed the standard formulas of drug control. Whereas the West increasingly saw cocaine as a "menace" emanating from uncontrolled drug surpluses of places like Peru, Paz Soldán looked on cocaine as a savior, from local perils caused by global prohibitions and shrinking licit demand for the drug. Here, the State was a solution, rather than American-style compacts of the market. And at last, this was a call for Peru to take an activist stand, on cocaine, and the global system itself.

Paz Soldán plied his thesis in scores of articles in the 1930s, from medical pamphlets and editorials in his *Reforma Médica* to public polemics and debates in the daily press. The opening shot, in Peru's intellectual *Mercurio Peruano* was his 1929 manifesto "The medical and social problem of coca in Peru."[24] While anti-coca in the rising *indigenista* sense (the national pro-Indian rights movement that began by the 1910s to view coca "addiction" as a mass social problem), it also turns that discourse around. Peru, Paz Soldán contends, suffers from a growing national "toximonía" (poisoning), a "cocamanía" of the "degenerating Indian race," drawn to an excess of coca harvests wasting in the *montaña*. There was also growing cocaine abuse in the West following World War I, derived from an expansive Japanese cocaine industry. But the most intriguing move here is a reversal of causality: the *reason* for ever more Peruvians addicted to coca lay in how the Peruvian coca industry had progressively lost its healthy and natural outlet – in modern cocaine exports to the outside world. Paz Soldán struggles to perfect this thesis with statistical precision as the decade progressed. But at heart the argument is about Peruvian interests and reasons of State: cocaine markets cut year after year by international conventions, which Peru had never participated in. Peru's dramatically falling share of world cocaine (by then *one-twentieth* of the peak at the turn of the century) is broadly correlated to each new prohibition regime since 1912. Those conventions themselves are portrayed, not without reason, as clubs for industrial nations to protect their pharmaceutical interests, at the expense of poor weaker countries like Peru. Thus, a League "quota system" was dragging down Peru's industry, oppressing her natives and her languishing regional economies. "The coca producers of Peru, without organization or solid bases of defense, are clandestinely exploited by the giant international trusts."[25]

The emphatic solution and centerpiece for Peru was an all-encompassing "Estanco": "The Peruvian Monopoly of Cocaine would be a type of Chamber of Commerce and at the same time an organ capable of regulating production, controlling consumption, and working decisively around the whole of the problem." What Paz Soldán envisioned, visualized in roughly hewn flow charts, was a gigantic articulating drug administration, with four corporate sections and functions. In his nationalist political lingo, invariably capitalized, this is dubbed "LA FRENTE NACIONAL DE LA INDUSTRIA COCALERA DEL PERÚ" or the "National Alliance of the Peruvian Coca Industry." Its first bureau was for "technical and chemical studies" – to establish new State factories of refined salts of cocaine (hydrochloride) and even diversify into profitable medical substitutes like novocaine. The second bureau was aimed at "indigenous cocainism"; it would mount studies and campaigns, using Peru's expanded cocaine revenues, to "redeem the indigenous population," that is to eradicate the coca habit. The third bureau was to specialize in "propaganda, education, and toxic aid," for prevention of other forms of modern (presumably non-indigenous) drug abuse and addiction. The fourth bureau was devoted to "administration, statistics, consumption, prices, and international conventions" – which, besides managing the larger enterprise, would set the terms by which Peruvian cocaine would assertively recapture world medicinal markets.[26] The first step was wrestling back Latin American cocaine markets from the Germans, and then the world.

Paz Soldán's dream of an expanded, State-regulated, modernized industry is refined and repeated over the next decade, in writings that verge on an extended polemic. By 1934 he was responding to new developments. In a series in his *Reforma Médica*, Paz Soldán deplores "the ruin of the Peruvian coca industry, by the international blockade of markets, inexorably fulfilling itself" – an attack against the new 1931 Geneva Accord, which unknowing Peruvian diplomats hastily sign in 1932. With one act, Peru's 8,000 tons of coca leaf will now silently finish off the Peruvian Indian. As "producer of coca par excellence, Peru feels

the duty to exploit its native plant." The path beyond harmful restrictions are "giant manufactories of pure cocaine," a road to "equality with German, French, Dutch, Swiss, Italian manufacturers." "PERU SHOULD ENJOY MODERN FACTORIES IN ITS OWN TERRITORY TRANSFORMING THE NATIVE AND ABUNDANT COCA OF ANDEAN VALLEYS INTO NOBLE PRODUCTS OF MEDICINE AND INDUSTRY [his caps]."[27] Peru's signing of the Geneva pact was the "RIP" of a time-honored industry, with dire implications of Indian "racial degeneration" and "spiritual death" at home. The argument would not always make sense.

What of possible meanings to Paz Soldán's crusade? His was a mixture of motley notions and intellectual trends. His professional passions lay in the international "social medicine" movement, which sought to fuse public-health policy with progressive political action. He also reflected the anti-imperialist resistance and messianic statism of the rebellious Peruvian APRA party. His ideas meshed with growing pro-industrial sentiments in Peru, gaining momentum with the economic dislocations of the depression, and with international "corporatism," attractive across the 1930s political spectrum. The marriage of science and control is revealing. The notion of forming monopolies for drug control had been endorsed by the League itself in the 1920s (against United States opposition) for the specific case of opium. An admiration for scientific and pure cocaine, combined with disgust for backwards Indian coca (now a pathology) was a medicalized form of Peru's intensifying national schizophrenia around coca.[28] While removed from prior cocaine promoters, or even Huánuco producers, he seemed to express in exaggerated terms their long-felt hopes of modernization. But Paz Soldán's intellectual and political influences extend forward, too – into the 1940s "Andeanist" school of social medicine developed by his younger scientific colleague, Dr Carlos Monge, who in remarkable ways would challenge UN stances and policies towards coca by the early 1950s. It may have affected the creation of ENACO (the Peruvian state coca monopoly founded in the 1950s), with its special euphemistic branch for "*industrialization* of coca." Yet beyond its intellectual content, Paz Soldán's manifesto ignited real repercussions at the time: covert diplomatic ones, national political ones, and others linking the League politics of Geneva to cocaine politics in Lima.

First, United States archives reveal astonishing *covert* international activity sparked by Paz Soldán's efforts. In September 1930, the *New York Herald* reports "League drug crusader believed slain by poison." This tale was the mysterious case of Spanish diplomat, Antonio Pagador, who, during a private mission to Chile, was felled by drug traffickers while taking his daily glass of milk. The State Department and FBN held a deeper version of events, linked to Peruvian cocaine monopoly schemes of the 1930s. Pagador, a major player in League anti-drug politics, was at the time of his death in talks for "installation of a plant in Lima, Peru, for the manufacture of cocaine out of coca leaves under the auspices of the Peruvian government." "The project appealed [to me]" wrote his collaborator, Purdue Professor of Chemistry, R. Norris Shreve, as "a means for the controllable manufacture of this essential local anesthetic."[29] The hope was to curtail over time both native coca use and coca exports to the West. In fact, Schieffelin Drug of New York (an ex-importer) was to become exclusive "world agent" for the Peruvian monopoly of cocaine hydrochloride. To a disillusioned Shreve, Pagador was murdered by agents of the British, German, or Swiss pharmaceutical firms, from whom "illegal traffic in cocaine originates." The FBN was sure that professional "traffickers" had murdered him instead. No matter: the truth was that some plan did have the secret blessing of the League and that negotiations in Lima had advanced by 1930 to even selecting a factory site. Then, in the familiar Peruvian ways, a sudden shift in Government (the depression collapse of President Augusto Leguía's 11-year *Oncenio* regime) doomed the project, as did Pagador's unsolved death. Rumors spread that Pagador had just grasped that the scheme was a fraud, a front for "illicit traffic" and "washed his hands of it," adding more suspects to the lists.

Pagador's project had other links, for example, to Paz Soldán himself, who dedicated his first 1929 essays to his inspiring friend, affectionately dubbed the "Don Quijote" of drug control. From another angle, representatives of Maywood Chemical (which about this time seriously toyed with making cocaine in Lima, until halted by angry American authorities) would try to get Peruvians talking to the League again, over the next few years, "to protect their legitimate sale of coca." This had none of the allure of a State monopoly. The State Department opposed all along the Pagador mission: on the simple grounds that industrialized cocaine would never legally enter the United States.[30] Here was the crucial obstacle to Peru's one coveted scheme of control.

Second, Paz Soldán's initiative, seized by others, actually reverberated openly across Peruvian society as the 1930s depression deepened. It was to mobilize, for the first and last time, the range of agrarian and regional actors associated with national cocaine. Amid the depression, when all employment or revenues seemed worthy, the cocaine campaign was embraced by echelons of the Peruvian state itself, not only for its statism but from skepticism of multilateral accords. Parts of the imagined "National Alliance" emerged: even businessmen joined the ranks. In May 1933, Don Teofilo Vergil, the solid merchant-citizen of Trujillo, began campaigning in his local newspaper, *La Industria*, for "national industry" – his cocaine factory – against the "monopolies" and "restrictions" of the League. His speeches found their way to the Lima press, and then under watchful FBN eyes in Washington. In 1934, Paz Soldán began agitating specifically against the new Geneva Accord. The new Peruvian president, Oscar Benavides, responded, if only to stem the contagion. In 1935, Peru's official *Boletín de Agricultura y Ganadería* publishes a long technical piece, "La coca en el Perú," by agronomist C. Bües (a coca authority since the 1910s), which frames coca's secular decline, besides highly local soil difficulties, in familiar global terms. A partisan now of Paz Soldán, Bües notes how Japanese interest in Peruvian leaf was foiled by the inability of coca farmers to meet modern quality demands.[31]

But 1936 would be the banner year for mobilizing around Peruvian cocaine, sparked by rumors of impending new Geneva talks on illicit traffic. Paz Soldán's triumph of public relations was to convince Peru's powerful *Sociedad Nacional Agraria* (SNA, the main lobby for coastal sugar and cotton) to adopt the "coca question" in the name of Peru's landed interests. In 1936, the SNA sponsored publication of a thirty-five-page report, appendixes and all: *La Coca Peruana: Memorandum Sobre su Situación Actual*, penned by none other than Paz Soldán. It was his usual stuff, in respectable garb, with all the *Aprista* "national alliance" rhetoric carefully edited out, befitting Peru's landed class. The pamphlet decried "unjust international pacts" and lauded coca as "Peru's special gift to the world." In painstaking detail, it laid out agrarian conditions in the three suffering regional economies invested in coca and cocaine. It surveyed world markets for refined cocaine and ended in an emotive call for Peru's unequivocal "denunciation" of the 1931 Geneva Convention.[32] Echoes of this report would make it to Geneva and back again.

First, *La Vida Agrícola*, Peru's leading private agricultural journal, took up the cause. A dramatic editorial of March 1936 is simply called: "Coca imperiled." Endorsing the SNA's new "petition" to the Ministry of Health, they take to task a national policy of "endangering" coca and cocaine by international pacts. "We hope this opportunity is not lost. The dangers threatening coca are hardly new. Disgracefully, until now Peru has not paid this problem serious attention ... beyond defense of obvious rights as the millennial grower of coca." *La Vida Agrícola* argued that impending world quotas on licit cocaine would inflict "a serious blow to critical regions of the country."[33] Peru's passive politics of resistance from the 1910s and 1920s now looked obsolete.

By March of 1936 the protests forced President Benavides himself to issue yet another clarifying decree. It called for "remedying this situation and defining clearly the action of the State towards one of the most autochthonous of Peruvian industries." A national "study commission" was established, its members drawn from the Health and Finance Ministries, the SNA, and representatives of the coca and cocaine industries. They were to prepare both a new "defense of the national interests" for Geneva and new restrictions on native coca use. Throughout the year, the Lima press kept pressures up with feature selections from Paz Soldán.[34] The ultimate fate of this commission remains a mystery, but the SNA soon appointed its pair of delegates. Vergil launched a new round of protests from the north, reprinted in Lima's leading dailies, before arriving in person to the capital as regional delegate. He spoke of a "50 percent" loss of coca crops to his home provinces of Trujillo and Otuzco, pledging to win back markets "displaced by the foreign boycott."[35]

These events were monitored with alarm by the United States Embassy in Lima – though non-intervention remained their style. In a June 1936 secret memo, "Subject: Approaching narcotics conference interests Peru," officials zeroed in on Paz Soldán's argument and its contagious national appeal. Peru, they believed, was soon to follow nationalist Bolivia on coca; Peru was "awakening" as Turkey had in defense of opium, when it established morphine factories against the West's wishes. Peru's Foreign Minister was in talks with Bolivia about a common front on the issue. Peru might move to occupy a vacant seat on the Opium Advisory Committee. The Peruvian Congress has voted to "demand" a larger export share from the League and was planning a delegation "ensuring that future Conventions shall not be detrimental to Peru's coca growers."[36] The prospective Peruvian delegate – Enrique Trujillo Bravo – had his credentials and views dissected. Two follow-up reports, overflowing with translated press clippings, assess this threat. As cocaine exports withered, Peru's doubts grew about signing on to the Geneva Conference, "without having taken part in the discussions, and without insisting on her rights as the oldest coca producer in the world." In short, if a brand of drug protectionism had initially driven American cocaine control policy, they watched a new kind erupting in Peru. Meanwhile, Paz Soldán himself journeyed to Washington, bringing his spirited message on Peruvian coca to delegates of the 1936 Pan-American Sanitary Congress.[37]

Some of the year's pronouncements read more ambivalently – besides revealing Peru's widening mental split around national (indigenous) coca use and exportable modern cocaine. They suggest, vitally, that external forces were not the sole foes of the Paz Soldán monopoly scheme: so were the local Peruvian owners and operators of private cocaine factories. For example, the ubiquitous voice of cocaine-king Andrés Avelino Soberón is conspicuously silent during this debate, though he shared (as did much of Huánuco) Paz Soldán's affinity for *Aprista* politics. Some pointed to an earlier 1930s outcry by Huánuco growers that foiled the original Ricketts's plan for a monopoly on coca. According to one source, owners coveted "intervention" "to reconquer the export market," but in no sense a nationalization. Typically, calls for bigger Peruvian "export quotas" come with vague warnings to "restrict consumption of narcotics" at home. In another twist, Peru's free-market mouthpiece, *El Comercio*, is heard quoting statist Paz Soldán verbatim in its 1936 editorials. Peru, as Mexico had, must take its place in the League "to assert the rights of Peru for a larger exportation of cocaine. Peru is vitally interested."[38] Strangely, few Peruvians doubted this campaign's larger premise: that a substantial licit cocaine market was somewhere out there beckoning for Peruvian action, during the stagnant world economy of the 1930s.

The 1936 Geneva "Illicit Traffic" talks were doomed from the start. The League of Nations, hit by bigger defections, was fading into irrelevance as clashing industrialized nations geared up for war – which including obtaining larger medicinal stocks. The conflict-ridden meeting stalled, taking no steps on limitation of "raw materials" or drug "traffic." In fact, coca had been quietly dropped from League agendas almost two years before and no stab was made at specific "quotas," as Peruvians had feared.[39] It was another noble failure. Paz Soldán would gloat as even the United States refused to sign on. League records show the lonely Peruvian observer sitting quietly through the sessions. But Peru still sent no data on cocaine, save for a list of eight "Licensed Factories" and notes on opium dens. In two years, the OAC would add Peru to its ranks (in name), but the impact was nil, as the organization fell into paralysis.

The paradox-filled climax of this larger Paz Soldán controversy actually came when Geneva visited Lima: the 1938 tour of OAC General Secretary, Eric Ekstrand, to Latin America. A "PR" junket for a troubled League – ringing with upbeat reports of co-operation – narcotics was a diversion to drum up desperate support in the Americas.[40] But Ekstrand's tour ends on one ironic note: his dramatic open public debate with none other than Carlos Enrique Paz Soldán.

Ekstrand arrived in May of 1938, with opportunities to meet with a range of top officials (from Public Health to Foreign Affairs), pressing for formal signing of the 1925 and 1936 accords. "Much stress was laid on the advantages, from the standpoint of active cooperation with the League of Nations, of arranging for all important documents," what Peru had never done. He met with the head of the SNA, "an important centre of information ... not itself in any way responsible for the views expressed by authors whose works it published" – i.e. Paz Soldán. He delivered a calming speech on drug control at San Marcos University, Paz Soldán's home turf. Paz Soldán wrote welcoming the visit: the League can now clarify the questions, though Peru will ultimately heed "its own reality."[41] The mission was amply covered by Peru's Foreign Ministry (as well as United States officials), vaunting the latest models of drug control, offering up tidbits of drug data. They would publish Ekstrand's first-hand League response to Paz Soldán himself: "Memoria del director: sobre el libro 'la coca Peruana.' "

Ekstrand's tone is conciliatory. Yet he makes it equally clear that the legal premise of Paz Soldán's decade-long polemic, that League conventions set drug "export quotas," was "in error." There was no reason then for Peruvian officials to view cocaine in conflictive terms. Ekstrand volunteers that "Some of the measures suggested by Sr. Paz Soldán ... are well in line with existing informal conventions regarding opium [monopolies]," while adamantly denying League "plan of limits on the legitimate trade of coca." In Peru, it made sense to make virtues out of long League failures. "Once this misunderstanding is relieved, Sr. Paz Soldán will realize that his country can freely at any time become a manufacturer," for however much cocaine the market can bear. The global drug market was hardly some "conspiracy of industrialized nations" but a "free competition among competing world factories." Ekstrand even suggests emulation of the Turkish way, known in Peru as the "*Frente Nacional de la Industria de la Coca* ... the modern factory making all end-products of coca, under direction of the State." There was no need "to crusade for justice: it was already assured by existing international conventions."[42] Similar themes rang out at his San Marcos address.

In the wake, across Peru, everyone swiftly seemed to back down from 1930s debates over cocaine, all sides claiming victories. The SNA distanced itself from Paz Soldán and boasted *it* had "stopped" international forces from strangling the nation's cocaine. Ekstrand waxed over his reception in Lima, though returning empty-handed. Within Peru's Foreign Ministry, a sea change is seen in a confidential 1938 memo of A. Jochamonwitz, the new technical delegate to the League. He assesses the long (if baneful) shadow of Paz Soldán over debates of the 1930s. "As one sees," Peru "has deliberately placed itself apart from the debate against Narcotics," at the expense of national interests, which now will be actively "defended." But the policy recommended would have made much sense to Paz Soldán: Peru's "industrial backwardness is the source of our moral and material damage" not the League, and coca a brilliant focal point for Peruvian scientific research and technology. "This marvelous plant makes an open field for study ... and with the preparation of pure medical substances, will return its production to its old splendor."[43] Meanwhile, Paz Soldán himself retreated, in his next writings, farther and forever from industrialized cocaine, into strident racialist discourses against the Japanese and Peru's own "Slavery of Indian cocaism" (1939).[44]

Others hardly backed down: a technical survey of 1938, "Making of cocaine in Huánuco," swiftly embraced and spread the good news of open markets, urging productivity on all fronts, including "great factories, that not only make the more or less impure variety as now, but that make and sell hydrochloride of cocaine." Cocaine's difficulties lay at home, not abroad, ending on a bucolic trope of a "small laboratory" on "every hacienda," all under the happy guise of "Government Control."[45] In Lima, a new "Cóndor" factory opened that year – stimulated by the war of words – and with a technical capacity for making higher-grade cocaine from shipped-in Huánuco leaf. As the world war approached, reviving global cocaine, forward-looking Peruvian chemists would literally equate "cocaine" with a grander "industrial problem of Peru" – the now painful fact of Peru's national backwardness, dependent on aging technologies, still "selling primary materials to buy products made from the same." They must no longer forfeit opportunities for finished cocaine, at the cost of national manufacturers, workers, and peasants alike. Paradoxically, this enthusiasm of the 1930s proved to be but a pause, or reflection, on a larger process underway: Peru's embrace of the international regime in the decade of the 1940s.

From global war to wars on cocaine (1939–50)

World War II truly set the stage, by irrevocably shifting the global political and commercial contexts shaping Peruvian cocaine. In its wake, with dramatic speed (1947–50), legal factories were outlawed and hounded, coca came under monopoly and a strict United Nations' gaze, and the State finally established its factory for cocaine hydrochloride, with none of the hopes, scale, or *élan* of the 1930s. Peru became an active member of international anti-drug forums, as United States and Peruvian policing came together. Not accidentally, we also see the first scandalous international coke "busts" and remote rumblings of the clandestine cocaine of the 1960s.

The Second World War marked the decisive turning point in prospects for Peruvian cocaine. In the fullest sense, the war for the first time brought South America, long neglected in the Western informal sphere, into more direct and intensified relations with the United States, a process historians feel in the sheer weight of wartime documentation. The war also saw Peru, for the first time, begin to participate systematically in, and even emulate, American drug control schemes – though such timing hardly proves that restrictive structures were foisted upon a reluctant Peru. But resistance and reluctance had finally begun to wane.

In global strategic terms, the Peruvian search for alternative market spheres – implied in the 1930s debate – died on impact on 7 December 1941 as Axis markets closed for good. In fact, starting in 1938, Soberón and his cohorts visibly redoubled efforts to place their wares abroad, in Germany, Japan, and the United States.[46] War meant that the sole alternative world coca circuit – flowing from Java, Formosa, Japan – was cut off from the West and by 1945 physically demolished. This was followed by the postwar United States occupations of the last two industrial world cocaine producers and sellers, and Allied officials put restructuring and restricting of narcotics along American lines high on their list of reforms. There could no longer be a licit cocaine network autonomous of United States designs, which even the Soviets endorsed. Only the Americans emerged with a substantial cocaine capacity, geared to downsizing world medicinal demand, and still excluding Peruvian cocaine.

During the fighting itself, cocaine became a curious strategic commodity: the one in United States–Peru relations that would not bear a name. Cocaine was essential for battle and the war's horrible new civilian casualty fronts, and exports to the Allies quickly tripled to over 3,000 kilos by 1943. However, unlike cacao, barbasco (an insecticide), cotton, cinchona, and other strategic goods, cocaine was never recognized by any overt bilateral price or quantity pact (via the American War Commodities Board) though understandings of supply are evident. In 1942, Peru's Finance Minister, in a heroic gesture, sought this legitimate status for cocaine, but was strongly rebuffed by Washington, for allegedly delinquent drug behavior. There are signs of a deeper manipulative politics at work here, managed by the perennial and legendary FBN chief, Harry J. Anslinger, and Coca-Cola, to keep the status quo with Peruvian cocaine. For example, Anslinger opposed Peruvian moves to opium poppies by threatening to cut Peru from his war-powers stash of morphine and cocaine hydrochloride. From 1938–42, Anslinger also backed Maywood's pilot projects (in Puerto Rico and Hawaii) to raise coca domestically, to avert wartime shortages.[47] Yet, in a convoluted deal, the secret experiments were terminated on the pledge that Peru abandon poppies and assure steady ampler supplies of coca to Maywood. Coca-Cola's memorable campaign raising GI morale on every front helped double imports of its special Peruvian leaf in the war years, aided by a patriotic 50 percent cut in duties. In 1948, coke (for a decade) replaced natural leaf in its formula, tipping the scales of Peruvian coca politics in uncharted ways. The resounding fact, however, is that even amid these emergency years, the half-century exclusionary trade structure around Peruvian cocaine was strictly upheld by the United States – even if this meant covert State Department-brokered diversions of Soberón's bulging surplus to England and Russia.[48]

Greater integration with the north meant heightened surveillance, spying, and collaboration – namely, on stocks of cocaine readied for the Allies or its foes. It was during the conflict that the United States took its first hard look at "illicit" commerce from Peru, first estimated at "one-third" of local product. Beyond such politicized guessing was the way the concept of the *illicit* seems to form in the global contest itself. It was first articulated in terms of economic warfare: possible suspect shipments to Germany and Japan, in the idioms and methods of war itself. Merchant "loyalties" are checked, with ours the legal ones. The dilemma for Peruvian producers like Soberón, of course, was that Hamburg and Osaka had long been their only dependable markets. According to United States *and* Peruvian officials, all this was contraband now, to be halted. In the years leading to conflict, Peru cracks down on non-nationals involved with coca and cocaine: the dramatic expropriation of Japanese Tulumayo property in 1937, a police raid on two Germans with a home lab in Lima's posh Miraflores section in 1939, the summary expulsions of the Nisei of Huánuco.[49] Concepts of the "illicit" stuck and expanded, until by war's end they acquired definite meanings blurred before, ones infused with the mentality of intelligence and secret wars. From 1939–42, intelligence reports multiply (especially from the British) of impending cocaine shipments, dubbed "smuggling," through Spain, Argentina, and Switzerland, neutrals everyone knew were fueling the Nazis. There were intercepts that verged on "drug busts," the captured cocaine a valued booty. Strategic collaboration grows with the United States: a potent example was the 1942 accord that created (out of the confiscated Japanese property) the Tingo María Tropical Agricultural Station, the largest of the Americas, geared to a range of war commodities, save for coca. Drawing more land-hungry colonists down the Huallaga valley, the station put United States agents smack in the middle of coca country.[50]

This subterranean activity, in discernible ways, fueled new kinds of restrictions on cocaine. This was a movement to de-medicalize the drug and enhance its special or criminalized status. Domestic wartime scarcities, rationing, and thefts of medicines were probable factors. And for the first time direct and sometimes blunt admonitions from the FBN, FBI, State, and local embassy are heard around lax Peruvian drug controls. In Peru, the national police get more involved: 1943 marks the first major cocaine "busts" in Peruvian history, involving among others Huánuco's legendary first trafficker, Anatolio Gómez. Not surprisingly, "cops" quickly began speaking a similar universal language, unlike the slower officials at Peru's Foreign Ministry. In 1939, new controls are set on the Lima Cóndor factory; in 1940, new licenses for cocaine factories are suspended and existing ones scrutinized; in 1941, strict transit controls go into effect for cocaine throughout the country and "*tráfico ilícito*" is juridically defined; in 1942 and 1943, official notices broach a possible monopoly; and, in 1944, the government at last begins trials of pharmaceutical cocaine in their Lima (Department of Health) lab. Somehow, in their close struggle with the Nazis, the British get involved. Throughout 1942 a buzz of diplomatic notes pass about a novel British scheme to limit Peruvian production by tracking and rationing imported supplies of soda ash, used in refining crude cocaine (a "precursor chemical," in today's lingo). Wartime bred modernization, globalization, and control.

Another effect was intensified Peruvian anti-cocainism, with its complex relation to scientific cocaine. It was as if the two sides of Paz Soldán himself split into warring camps, as his own 1940s writings turned radically anti-coca. On one side, with scientific ties with the United States, was the new San Marcos Institute of Andean Biology, founded by his colleague, Dr Carlos Monge. State-sponsored by 1940, the Institute promoted in its charter scientifically tolerant study of Andean coca, and thus worried American officials. Monge would head the postwar Peruvian team with the UN's influential 1948–50 Commission of Enquiry on the Coca Leaf, defining the national and rational dissenting voice on coca against global eradication fervor.[51] In the other direction, Dr Luís Saenz published his 1938 landmark *La Coca: Estudio Médico-social de la Gran Toximanía Peruana*, which, as its title amply suggests, reduced coca use in all forms to an alkaloid poisoning of the Indian nation. The war-era begot the well-known dismal anti-coca "science" of Carlos Gutiérrez-Noriega, which in its golden age of the 1940s negatively conflated the national politics of coca and cocaine, drawing American praise. Peru's national "coca debate" took off. Small steps were taken: the banning of coca chewing in prisons, where, incidentally, Gutiérrez-Noriega had found his "sample" *coquero* population. In 1943, Dr Carlos Ricketts and Saenz founded Peru's home-grown "Anti-Cocainism League," the country's first formal *anti*-coca lobby. They would stridently battle coca and cocaine far and wide into the cold war, accusing foes (including Peruvian governments) of foot-dragging for their "cocaine-mafia" and "communist" pals.

Finally, after 1938, Peru begins to work with the League Opium Advisory Committee, by 1940 a shell of itself in its Princeton exile. That year, Peru formally announced to the League expanded export production and, in 1944, Peruvian coca/cocaine statistics are prepared and mailed, in an act of Allied solidarity. In this, there are subtle signs that Anslinger (working through Maywood officials again) was pressuring Peru.[52] It was ironic that Peru basically joined League efforts when it effectively ceased to exist, and Peruvian officials continued toying with their League-sanctioned "control" principle: the cocaine monopoly of the State. Yet Maywood throughout the war worked to subvert this idea, as the Allies required their free market in coca and Merchandise No. 5, which monopolies of any sort would impede. Anslinger's association with Maywood made them sound very official to Peruvian ears, but we can't say for sure why a "strategic" cocaine monopoly wasn't established now, while Peru truly enjoyed a licit cocaine monopoly with the West. In any case, a cocaine menace wasn't much on Anslinger's agenda, as the United States market (by his accounts) saw *no* illicit cocaine between 1935 and 1945. The tension between drug control and liberal markets has long been around.

At war's end, legal cocaine arrived at its last crossroads, as Peru faced the United States head-on in the global scene. European firms began importing little crude cocaine, leaving modernizing hopes no outlet, though Peru's capacity to produce (and stock) had expanded in the war. The UN swiftly assumed and revitalized efforts at international drug control, operational by 1947 in the new

"Commission on Narcotic Drugs," with Peru as a founding and permanent sitting member. This time, as anxieties spread of another postwar drug "epidemic," the United States exerted a far steadier and visible hand with the UN. That effectively translated into even lower definitions of global "medicinal and scientific needs" (by the 1950s under 2,000 kilos worldwide), a numbers game that earlier critics saw as inflated by now bygone German and Japanese players.[53] The "licit" zone shrank dramatically. And for the first time a serious campaign began that spoke of coca itself as "raw material" of drug control; efforts so easily deflected in the mid-1920s and 1930s in forums of great powers alone. Peru found itself curiously within the apparatus of control.

It may be that the years 1945–7 saw first inklings of true "contraband" trade from Peru. This at least is the official United States version, as told in a series of detailed reports prepared in the late 1940s for the FBN. From their vantage, illicit cocaine was a clear supply-driven export – i.e. of surpluses from the war, or from unscrupulous and unregulated industrialists scrounging for buyers. Cocaine became increasingly branded as "Peruvian in origins." In such trades, it was Cubans who acquired a taste for cocaine during the war, snuck in by Peruvian diplomatic pouch; by the late 1940s, Cuban mobsters and a host of wealthy Latins were enjoying and plying "coke." In fact, amounts confiscated in the United States between 1944–6 rose from a mere 2 to 28 ounces before skyrocketing (in 1940s terms) to 210 ounces in 1948, by now all earmarked from "Callao." Smuggling rings recruited seamen from the frequent Grace shipping line, largely for a burgeoning market in Harlem, though by 1949 cocaine could show up far and wide. The reports also allege that an *unlicenced* processing sector (eight of eighteen known factories) had sprung up in the Peruvian jungle, with full knowledge of corrupt Peruvian authorities.[54] Peru's cocaine – in American eyes – had at last erupted into an active menace. A tempting "White Goddess" of the Andes, as *Time* would dub it in 1949.

What seems so clear from the United States, however, looks murkier from Peru. The transition to prohibitions and illicit cocaine is obscured not only by its remote and informal economies but by Peru's partisan coca politics: of the postwar transition from the leftist APRA-affiliated government of José Luis Bustamante to cold-warrior General Manuel Odría, who seized power by *coup* in 1948, currying American favor and investors. While both regimes were seemingly committed to coca reform, the acceleration to events is dramatic.[55] Within the year, Odría's troops laid all the foundations needed for a full Peruvian regime of cocaine prohibition.

The momentum is hard to miss, even at the simplest level of executive decrees. *Supreme Resolution* (Peru), April 1947: stricter factory transit controls instituted. Each factory must lie within a 2-kilometer radius of "chief towns"; they must also modernize by installing "a small laboratory operated by a pharmaceutical chemist responsible for control of production ... with appropriate statistical data" [UN translations]. *Resolution*, July 1947: Peruvian state convenes inter-ministerial panel "to study question of the industrialization of coca and problems connected with its commerce and Peru's international obligations."[56] A monopoly is endorsed. December 1947: *Decree-law* establishes crude cocaine monopoly. June 1948: the Peruvian state reserves "exclusive rights to manufacture, export, and sell cocaine and its salts and derivatives," authorizing a factory under the Ministry of Public Health. August: local coca taxes assumed by central-government control board. March 1949: *penal code* on drug production and trafficking drastically revised, in accord with international norms. Simultaneously, all existing licenses for legal manufacture are revoked. April: Peru appoints a "Chief of the Department of Narcotics," to be directly responsible to the UN. June: a Peruvian Coca *Estanco* (monopoly) is declared. August: the monopoly assumes sole export rights. September to October 1949: National Commission formed for comprehensive study of coca and collaboration with then-visiting UN Commission of Enquiry. January 1950: juridical and medical conditions of "addicts" defined. July 1950: remnant private contracts canceled; proceeds from "industrialization of coca" and crude cocaine exports will go into new "narcotics control" organs as well as "addict treatment" programs. The institution building, if weaker in practice, was a frenetic effort to envelop cocaine in a working sphere of illegality.

Paralleling this legal campaign was a series of processes and events that linked Peru to global regimes. The UN's "Commission of Enquiry on the Coca Leaf," actually requested by Peru in 1947 during its momentous national coca debate (between public scientists like Gutiérrez-Noriega and Monge) spent a year in bureaucratic preparations before arriving in Peru in September 1949, for its three-month study tour. It also dealt with anti-*cocaine* initiatives and was monitored and massaged by the FBN's Anslinger, who was to be disappointed by their compromise "coca as social problem" conclusions. Anslinger pressured for Howard B. Fonda, a Borroughs–Wellcome executive and friend, as Commission Chief, who sent back frequent "Dear Harry" letters replete with intelligence tips against "illegal" cocaine labs. At home, Anslinger backed up the Commission (and decidedly angered the Navy) by banning NIH research projects on the physiology of coca, then under study as a possible aid to high-altitude jet pilots. The full Commission, and its extensive published report of 1950, marks a much-noted watershed in defining coca discourse, both nationally and globally, especially with its moves to put coca eradication on the international agenda. As the process closed, Monge's internationally publicized "Réplica" of the Peruvian Delegation dramatically objected to the UN's preconceived rush to negative judgment. Yet apart from a call for *further* scientific study of coca and "Andean man," it did not oppose the report in any substantive way.

The year before, in March of 1948, Peru had also invited a more specific UN "Mission of Experts for the Re-Organization of the Narcotics Administration in Peru," strictly about cocaine control.[57] Much of their month-long work focused on creating and advising an autonomous narcotics squad for the national police, headed by Carlos Ávalos. Though the mission sealed the fate of legal private cocaine manufacturing, it once again offered moral ratification of a monopoly model from multilateral institutions. Peruvian officials relished their expert Recommendation 7: "Crude Cocaine – Advises that careful consideration be given to setting up a state monopoly for the manufacture of crude cocaine. We have established such a factory [Peru reports in 1950] and have gone a step further by also establishing a coca monopoly." In gratitude, Peruvian authorities began compiling genuine official statistics and reports for UN consumption, making their 48-page missive of 1950 a mine of data and perspectives on the problem. The Peruvian state had in fact been firm enough to reach into remote Huánuco after all, though the only other "annual report" for the decade (1955) gets thin again. Whatever, the UN had emerged a far more real player in coca and cocaine than the League had ever been.[58]

Behind such official moves lay a thorny underworld (visible in scores of FBN cables) of intersections and intrigues between United States narcotics agencies and agents of Peru. Close informal contacts swiftly transformed into institutionally embedded relations: once cocaine was defined as a policing matter, internationalizing cops saw eye-to-eye. By the middle of 1949, New York's FBN District Commissioner Garland Williams began churning out reports linking events in Peru to the streets of Harlem. His ace agent, James C. Ryan, is dispatched that August on a Latin American tour, warmly received by his Peruvian counterparts, notably Ávalos of Narcotics. In Washington, Ambassador Berckemeyer is generous as is Mier y Terán, chief of the PIP, Peru's repressive home version of the FBI. International "sting" operations are set; witnesses culled; extraditions arranged. Throughout the year of this 1949 cocaine scare, Anslinger takes anonymous tips from United States nationals in Peru, denouncing suspicious "cocaine labs" in Pucallpa, Trujillo, and elsewhere.[59] The strangest notes are from a mysterious, illiterate, and angry "Frank of Lima" – who it turns out is with the nascent CIA. Later, Anslinger would claim in his dramatic 1953 book, *The Traffic in Narcotics*, how his brave efforts stopped a late-1940s cocaine flood at the gates.[60] DEA papers reveal a different truth: a few cordial diplomatic meetings, tardy press releases on "co-operation," and, mainly, a slew of denunciations about Peru and Cuba for a hungry press. Such claims are poor at weighing American pull.

On a more sober level, the mix of "external" and "internal" causes, short-term and inexorable factors in Peru's final move to proscription remain difficult to sort out. Vital are the murky politics of Odría and *Aprismo*, which Anslinger himself purposely muddled and meddled in. Bustamante's progressive government (1945–8) worked from an implicit political alliance with Peru's long-feared APRA party, and began the drive to coca controls before the *coup* of October 1948. One can speculate why: because of APRA's Paz Soldán-style coca indigenism, and with rising national fervor for postwar industrialism, so clear in the first decrees to modernize the aging factories. Harder to calculate is the impact of APRA strongholds in Huánuco and Trujillo, the country's sole cocaine zones. Odría's free-market junta was unabashedly pro-American, coming in the wake of the startling APRA-inspired naval revolts of 1948. It is easy (and likely right) to read anti-narcotics measures as one of Odría's attempts to impress the United States as the cold war began to send its chill across Latin America. His militant moves also reflect the naturally enhanced status of police and soldiers throughout a militarized state. But soon enough, all sides get mired in scandals around cocaine.

The climax comes in a little-known yet crucial episode of mid-1949. General Odría accuses APRA, in fact its revered exiled leader Víctor Raúl Haya de la Torre himself, of involvement with cocaine. With Anslinger's data, Haya and his family are linked to the then notorious "Balarezo gang," just rounded up in New York, Havana, and Callao in July and August of 1949. Odría dramatically charges that APRA used cocaine monies and cocaine-corrupted naval officers for arms to stage their aborted revolution of 1948. Scandalizing headlines and accusations fly throughout the hemisphere. APRA exiles in Cuba vehemently deny the charges and counter-attack – naming names – stating that Odría's regime is rife with traffickers and officials on the take. The connection here, Eduardo Balarezo, was a *Huanuqueño* and local archives do suggest business with drugs.[61] Odría was scheming to discredit APRA (which during the war began to attract liberal American sympathies) just as Anslinger was hoping to capitalize on a foreign drug conspiracy. Meanwhile, a sensible Ambassador Teitelman in Lima strongly warns the State Department against Anslinger's accusations: as undermining of diplomatic efforts and associating the United States with a repressive dictatorship, and ends up reining in the FBN chief.[62] We'll never know the truth of this episode nor its weight in pushing Peru to proscriptions. But Odría knew to combine his military operations against APRA with a new war against cocaine.

The highly publicized international "busts" of July to September 1949 were part of this shift and a preview of the 1970s. "Smash 'biggest' dope ring here" screamed the New York *Daily Mirror* of 20 August 1949, in stories that continue: "Seize leader in city, Peru jails 80 (dope smuggling boss suspect seized here; tied to Peru revolt)." The *New York Times* and *Time* also blared about the cocaine invasion, in the first of such American coke "dope scares" since the 1910s. Organized with informers and inter-agency "stings" in New York in early 1949, the sensational arrests of August caught 83 in all, in New York and Peru, in the first round alone. Balarezo's simple sailor gang was broken, but just as fast other lanes and circuits pop up, through Cuba and Panama, and soon going airborne.[63] A parade of "Narcos" and joint United States–Peruvian campaigns against the likes of "Chino" Morales and wily Mexican white-slaver and dealer, Margarita "La Cubana," marked the early 1950s. Reports mount of clandestine labs from 1950 on, even from Chile and the Amazon. Soon, denounced labs and couriers dot the anarchic map of Bolivia (whose *ancien régime* collapsed in revolution in 1952), along with notorious feminine outlaws like Bolivia's own Blanca Ibáñez de Sánchez. By the mid-1950s Peruvian cocaine *per se* drops off the FBN radar, but what stuck was this general notion of the Andes as the "source" of illicit cocaine.

Quickly and reflexively such illicit networks seemed to mushroom and spread from the politics of prohibition. Officially, cocaine had "disappeared" after United States prohibitions of the 1920s, though it was still surviving licitly elsewhere. The year 1950, a year after the final suppression of Huánuco and

Trujillo factories, is the year of the "trafficker." Massive Peruvian sweeps (beyond the Balarezo group) tally some 75 more arrests and prosecutions, creating in effect a new class of international entrepreneur and criminality, so far as South American cocaine was concerned. The following year saw thirty-five more Peruvian cocaine trials before falling back to usual levels. Among these new criminals, notably, were a number of local chemists (with makeshift labs) as well as previous owners of highly respectable cocaine businesses, now deemed outlaws. For example, Andrés Avelino Soberón – since 1917 Huánuco's would-be modernizing patriarch, belated champion of the Allies – was sentenced to six months' time and fined 10,000 *soles* in 1950, though the year before, in May 1949, under Odría's pressures, he had voluntarily folded his factory. Two sons of the northern cocaine magnate, Martín Ayllon, were jailed for keeping 44 kilos of crude cocaine on their Sacasmanca (Otuzco) estate. Other more mobster-like characters, Gustavo Prados and Orestes Rodríguez, were linked to formerly legal factories.[64] There are politics behind these arrests and also real evidence of trafficking. In contrast, those ex-industrialists who escaped this fate had mainly switched into the auto parts trades of Huánuco or Trujillo (the Durand and Vergil clans, for example) – not a bad choice, given jeep and truck sales for the Huallaga development and coca boom of the 1960s. The global impact of these dispersing and entrenching cocaine networks would be felt a decade later, when an alarmed United States moved to convene no less than three Inter-American "Coca Consultative Congresses" (1960, 1962, 1964) to refocus cocaine containment and police operations, all under the guise of coca.[65] Scores of Latin American agents were specially trained, to no avail. FBN statistics began to tell the early-1960s upward trend in captured Andean cocaine – a prelude to the 1970s "Colombian connection," based on export-processing of traditional crude Peruvian *pasta básica*.

One last thread: what would happen to the long-vaunted and recurring Peruvian dream of a government monopoly to supersede private and licit cocaine? The forced modernization (by chemistry) decrees of 1947 accomplished little, but by late 1950 the State monopoly was officially on line, endorsed by the UN and Article IV of the 1931 Geneva Manufacturing Convention. Peru was finally making genuine crystal cocaine hydrochloride, in a run-down government shop, the "Fiscal Laboratories for the Industrialization of Coca," which it could legally export around the globe. The Americans swiftly sent inspectors in, with dire concerns about security risks and leakage. By 1955, business prospects were reported annually by the parent Peruvian *Estanco de Coca* (ENACO). They weren't very good, given a yearly market of only 500–600 kilos, about a fifth of World War II sales, or 5 percent of turn-of-the-century exports.[66] Without a legal United States market, the factory was a risky and losing proposition throughout the 1950s, saddled with "vast problems" of undercapitalization, antiquated technology, and unsold stock. Understandably, it was a flawed solution to Peruvian "drug control," with few modernizing (alternative or legal) linkage effects for peasant coca growers, by now spreading out into the wilds of the Huallaga. UN teams of the late 1950s and early 1960s urged its continued upgrade and expansion, despite sluggish markets. It was a far cry from the gleaming beacon of scientific, economic, and national modernity so vividly imagined in the 1930s by Peruvian dissidents – perhaps to a global system of proscription itself.

Concluding on cocaine

This chapter has taken a long look, from the 1890s to the 1950s, at the rise and fall of the unknown *licit* period of the Peruvian cocaine export industry. Legal cocaine arose in Peru invested with grand hopes as a national modernizing force, though by 1910, caught in economic and political contradictions of the American sphere, such hopes seemed in vain. In spite of this, cocaine slogged on, as a depressed regional staple of Huánuco, and enough to spark in the 1930s a dynamic and telling national debate about Peru's policy *vis-à-vis* the spread of global prohibitions. Whether from basic insight or self-interest, Peruvians were long reluctant to simply suppress their valorized national cocaine. But World War II and its aftermaths tipped the scales against alternatives to United States stances, and with their help Peru created, at breakneck speed, its own regime of criminalized cocaine. Vestiges of early developmental ideas marked both the debates of the 1930s and the final thrust of Peruvian prohibitions.

Peru is not just another "case" in the history of cocaine, both for its ancestral ties to the coca bush and because twenty years after the cycle ending here, a new boom in *illicit* cocaine, made in Peru, would haunt North Americans for decades to come. One must wonder if Peru's historical reluctance to denigrate and proscribe cocaine could have made a real alternative to United States prohibition models, and if that could have made any difference to the havoc eventually wreaked in the 1970s with illicit cocaine. But it is worth considering that, here at least, prohibitions were neither easy nor natural to construct.

The "chicken or egg" question of which came first – the illicit trade or the prohibitions – may be more fertile than most of its kind. For one thing, a clearer picture emerges here of how illegal and menacing drug trades become themselves actually delimited, defined, or "invented" over the long haul. And now there is good evidence on how the Peruvian crackdowns of 1947–50 were not just the end of a long licit era of Peruvian industry, but the beginnings, literally, of today's endless war with Andean cocaine.

Primary sources: Peru

The sources used for this chapter are part of a book project that will draw a historical picture of Peruvian cocaine and its politics from the ground up (and in global context), using new primary documents. In fact, there's no other choice: secondary works on the subject simply do not exist. Even Andean *coca* still has a scant written history.[67]

Older published materials lend clues here: useful examples are historical travelogues (Anglo-Saxon, or say of Peru's *Sociedad Geográfica de Lima*); promotional or technical articles from Peruvian institutions (like *Boletín* of the turn-of-the-century *Ministerio de Fomento*); reports on cocaine research or medicinal applications (in early medical journals like *El Monitor Médico*). For instance, much of the information about Paz Soldán in the 1930s comes from essays in his own journal of social medicine, *La Reforma Médica* (Lima). These can be consulted in medical or research libraries in the United States, e.g. the New York Academy of Medicine. A few commercial journals – such as New York's *Oil, Drug & Chemical Reporter* – carried regular data or observations on Peruvian raw materials, not always reliable. If systematically used, print sources provide a good start.

At the United States National Archives, FBN (Federal Bureau of Narcotics, later FBNDD) and State Department records together provide rich new sources, perhaps the best in global terms. Dr Steven Karch (of this volume) kindly recommended pursuing and declassifying Record Group 170 of the DEA – their historical papers on overseas subjects. The many boxes in RG 170 section 0660 concern Peru (and a few, Bolivia), and are a goldmine of data, intelligence reports, and political observations about coca and cocaine gathered by the FBN from approximately 1930–60. Parallel and related to these are State Department foreign records, nicely organized by topic under the "Decimal File" system (RG 59, DF Peru/Narcotics, 823.114) or motley LOTs files. The historian must judge the accuracy of such reports and wade through their anti-drug mentality and exaggerations. For the pre-1930 period, reports from on-site United States consuls/officials (on microfilm) are sparse about cocaine, though a few gems are found. The National Archives also hold materials from international drug conferences (in RG 23) and few historians have mined the League of Nation's and UN's voluminous historical volumes on drug control (though Peru avoided both). Private American pharmaceutical firms that dealt with Peru (Stepan Chemical for Maywood or New Jersey Merck) remain closed to researchers.

In Peru itself, a major disappointment remains the central government: no single Peruvian ministry kept systematic or "official" data on cocaine – not Agriculture, Development, Finance, Public Health (nominally in charge of drug supervision from the 1920s to the 1950s), or even Foreign Affairs (whose archive is mostly unrevealing). After 1955, "ENACO," the new national coca monopoly, offers statistics. It may be that key archives "disappeared" (forever) into the vaults of Peruvian police or national intelligence after 1950. Newspapers, except scarce local ones (like *El Huallaga*) are rarely helpful. A relevant pamphlet, magazine, or medical literature exists, even a trove of theses on coca and cocaine, at Lima's San Marcos School of Medicine. But compensating for gaps at the level of the State are local archives. I have mainly used the fine one in Huánuco, the quiet town above today's coca-rich Huallaga valley. There, one can piece together, using public Prefectural, Municipal or local Health documents, or private notarial (*Protocoles*) records and wills, the roles of family cocaine interests like those of Durand and Soberón. In addition, some locals still vividly recall the days of licit cocaine and gladly provide oral history to complement written documents. All said, working in Peru on cocaine is intrinsically and intriguingly detectivesque.

Notes

I thank the SSRC, Lindesmith Center (OSI), and Russell Sage Foundation for research support; Joe Spillane (his critique); and Steven Karch and JoAnn Kawell (for sundry source advice).

1 Record Group 59 (General Records of the Department of State), M155, vol. 2, Consular Despatches, Callao, H.M. *Brent* to S.S. *Hunter*, "Reply to circular regarding

difficulty experienced in obtaining coca leaves," 10 February 1885; Mark Pendergrast, *For God, Country, and Coca-Cola: The Unauthorized History of the Great American Soft Drink and the Company that Makes it* (New York: Scribner, 1993), ch. 2; Mark Twain, "The turning-point in my life," in J. Strausbaugh, D. Blaise, eds, *The Drug User: Documents 1840–1960* (New York: Blast Books, 1991), 148–50.

2 José Ulloa, M. Colunga and J. de los Ríos, "Informe sobre la coca," 31 October 1888, especially "Medios para fomentar el consumo y exportación de la coca," *La Crónica Médica* (Lima) 6(6) (1889), 27–31; precursors in a wave of 1850s–60s coca studies (M.A. Fuentes, Moreno y Maíz, etc.) or Luis Esteves, *Apuntes Para la Historia Económica del Perú* (Lima: Imp. Huallaga, 1882), 73–5, on "scientific" uses. JoAnn Kawell has explored nineteenth-century Peruvian networks around coca/cocaine: "The 'essentially Peruvian' industry: Legal cocaine production in the 19th century," (MS, presented at the "From Miracle to Menace" symposium, New York, 1997).

3 Paul Gootenberg, *Imagining Development: Economic Ideas in Peru's "Fictitious Prosperity" of Guano* (Berkeley: University of California Press, 1993), for ideas in historical perspective.

4 T. Rosemary Thorp and Geoffrey Bertram, *Peru, 1890–1977: Growth and Policy in an Open Economy* (London: Macmillan, 1978), ch. 2.

5 Mariano Albornoz, *Breves Apuntes Sobre las Regiones Amazónicas* (Lima: Imp. El Progreso, 1885), 36–7; for Tomás Moreno y Maíz, "Recherches chimiques et physiologiques sur l'erythoxlyum coca du Pérou et la cocaine" (Paris: L. Leclerc, 1868); Charles Renoz, *Le Pérou: Histoire-Description Physique et Politique. Productions-Commerce. Immigration et Colonisation* (Brussels: P. Wensenbruch, 1897), 65–7, 161.

6 On Kitz: Augusto E. Tamayo, *Informe Sobre las Colonias de Oxapampa y Pozuzo y los Ríos Palcazu y Pichis* (Lima: Min.de Fomento, 1904), 111–12; M155, vol. 13 (United States Consuls, Callao), "On the subject of cocaine," 26 February 1891. H. Richard Friman (Chapter 4) has found some trail on Kitz in German company papers.

7 Alejandro Garland, *Las Industrias en el Perú* (Lima: Imp.del Estado, 1896), 29; José Rodríguez, *Estudios Económicos-Financieros y Ojeada Sobre la Hacienda Pública del Perú* (Lima: Imp. Gil, 1895), 470–1; A. Garland, *El Perú en 1906* (Lima: Imp. Industria, 1907), 180–2, 213 (and other writings); Pedro Paulet, "Industrias: La Cocaína," *Boletín del Ministerio de Fomento* 1(9) (September 1903), 25–42.

8 José Varallanos, *Historia de Huánuco* (Buenos Aires: Imp. López, 1959), 588–90 and ongoing research in Huánuco regional archives (ARH) ("Protocoles"); or "Augusto Durand: Su personalidad – su vida," *La República* (Lima, 1923), an obituary that celebrates "el más grande de los productores de este alcoloide en el mundo." "El gran *Trust* de cocaína," *El Huallaga* (Huánuco), 17 October 1911.

9 For cocaine studies: Alfredo Rabines, "The production of cocaine in Peru," *Peru Today* (Lima) 3 (September 1911), 31–3 (originally "The Engineer," London); C. Bües, *La Coca: Apuntes Sobre la Planta, Beneficio, Enfermidades y Aplicación* (Lima: Min. de Fomento, 1911); E.M.M. Pozzi-Escot, "Recherches sur l'industrie de la cocaine au Pérou," *Bolletin des Sciences Pharmacologiques* (Paris) 20 (1913), 608–17 (originally *L'agronomie tropicale*, 1913); A. Martín Lynch, "Factores que determinan la riqueza de cocaína de las hojas de cocaína," *La Riqueza Agrícola* (Lima) 7(10) (1912), 388–90; Mario Durand, "Coca: dos palabras," *El Huallaga* (all of October 1916); Manuel Vinelli, "Contribución al estudio de la coca" (Ph.D. thesis, Ciencias Naturales: San Marcos University, 1918).

10 For Higginson reports on cocaine: "Memoria que presenta el Consul-general del Perú en NuevaYork," *Boletín de Relaciones Exteriores del Perú* I(V) (1905), 72–3, 186–7; (1906), 186–7; (1912), 110–11. These were reprinted in Peruvian journals such as *Boletín de Fomento* (1903), *La Riqueza Agrícola* (1913) and even Huánuco's *El Huallaga* (1911).

11 Peruvian view in: M.A. Derteano, "Informe que presenta el Consul sobre la coca de la isla de Java," *Boletín de Relaciones Exteriores* 15 (1918), 347–58 (originally 1914, Hong

Kong), or Higginson, "Memoria del Consul-General del Perú en Nueva York," ibid. (1912), 111–12. League of Nations (LN), Advisory Committee on Traffic in Opium, OC 445, "Coca Producers Association," Amsterdam, November 1925. See Karch and de Kort chapters, this volume, on Dutch networks.

12 This paragraph is a brutal summary of my earlier study of the genesis of United States cocaine policy: based on United States records such as the 63rd Congress, "Memo as to importation of coca leaves and cocaine in the continental US" (Washington, DC: Government Printing Office, 1914) or United States National Archives, RG 170 (DEA/FBN, Overseas Papers), box 19, "Drugs/beverages" "Decocainized coca leaves" (1916–30s); box 20, "Coca leaves," etc.

13 For long-term statistics, see Jorge Hohagan, *Sumario de Informaciones Sobre Exportación del Perú* (Lima: Casa de Moneda, 1927), 76–85; or Carlos Enrique Paz Soldán, *La Coca Peruana: Memorandum Sobre su Situación Actual* (Lima: Sociedad Nacional Agraria, 1936), Graph B, "Exportación de cocaína bruta, 1904–1933."

14 See Rabines, "Cocaine" (1911), for laments (or Higginson, "Memoria" 1909); Hahogan, "Cocaine," in *Sumario* (1927), 83–4, for productivity and markets. The following section (besides cited Peru technical studies) is from United States surveys: RG 170 (DEA/FBN), "Narcotics factories," Consul G. Makinson, "Opium and coca industry in Peru," May 1927; RG 59, Dec.File, 800.114, "Producers of refined cocaine in Peru," 8 November 1928, with Health Ministry memo, S. Lorente, "Productores de cocaína," 28 May 1927; and Dec.File 823.114 Peru/Narcotics, W.C. Burdett, "Manufacture of the derivatives of the coca leaf in Peru," 22 April 1932 and "Shipment of cocaine from Peru," 6 May 1932.

15 RG 59, Dec.File 823.114, "Manufacture of derivatives of coca leaf," 1932; also, Dec.File 811.114, n16/418, Guyant, "Exportation of coca leaves from Peru during the past five years," 6 February 1924. From Peru, a fine source is business guides, e.g. *Guía Lascano: Gran Guía del Comercio y de la Industria* (Lima: Lascano, 1926–1950s), Huánuco, Trujillo; or Cámara de Comercio de Lima/SNA, *Guía Comercial e Industrial del Perú* (Lima: La Unión, 1921), 28–30, 243, 458 (Vergil).

16 On Durand and Soberón, Dec.File 823.114, "Manufacture of derivatives of coca leaf," and "Shipment of cocaine," April–May 1932; *Guía Lascanos* ("Huánuco," 1928, 1932); and ongoing regional research in Archivo Sub-Regional del Huánuco (ARH), "Protocoles" (Roncillo) 1917–1930s (especially 21 May and 1 September 1917). Soberón's grandson – a drug reform activist in Peru – is completing a family history of this business.

17 For Japan, see Isabel Lausent-Herrera, "La presencia japonesa en el eje Huánuco-Pucallpa entre 1918 y 1982," *Revista Geográfica* (Mexico) 107 (1988), 93–118; RG 59, Dec.File 823.114 Peru/Narcotics, "Alleged traffic in cocaine and other alkaloids by Japanese agriculturalists," 15 January 1923 (with coverage of *Christian Science Monitor*); LN/OC 82–82A, "Manufacture and traffic of cocaine in Japan exclusive of her territories," 16 September 1922; and Karch, in Chapter 7 of this volume.

18 RG 59, Dec.File 823.114 Peru/Narcotics, Burdett, "Manufacture of derivatives of coca leaf in Peru," April 1932, 20–1; see early Decimal Files (1922–8) on drug administration, or Marcel Rubio C., *Legislación Peruana Sobre Drogas, 1920–1993* (Lima: CEDRO, 1994), 25–9, or bits in *Boletín de Ministerio de Salubridad del Perú* (1920s–40s).

19 These paragraphs are a brutal summary of prior section from intensive study of United States FBN reports, starting with 1919 United States Treasury, "Traffic in narcotic drugs" (Washington: GPO, 1920), 6–9, annualized by late 1920s in United States Treasury, FBN, "Traffic in opium and other dangerous drugs." On earlier United States view/protests on Peru, see 63rd Congress, Senate Doc. 157, "Second International Opium Conference," 1913, 10, or RG 43 (NA, International Conferences), box 41, H. Wright, 1 October 1912.

20 Similarly based on extensive use of United States documents, especially RG 170, FBN/DEA, 0660, 1920s, especially box 18 ("World narcotics factories," 1927–39)

and varied "Reports on coca"; or Dec.File 823.114, Peru/Narcotics, 1922–7, "Exportation of coca leaves from Peru." Generally, on FBN foreign policy, see Douglas C. Kinder and William Walker III, "Stable force in a storm: Harry J. Anslinger and United States narcotic foreign policy, 1930–1962," *The Journal of American History* 72(4) (1986), 908–27.

21 This section is based on survey of two decades of League of Nation's "OC" (Advisory Committee on Traffic in Opium) and Geneva Conference records (1920s–30s), plus new research in archives of Ministerio de Relaciones Exteriores del Perú (AREP). For very few examples, see LN/OC 153 (Peru, Agricultura, 12 July 1923); OC 158, "Letter from Bolivian government on the coca industry and preparation of cocaine," 28 August 1923; O.L. 198.1934XI, "Situation of certain countries of Latin America" (1934); Second Opium Conference, Geneva, O.172.M.47.1924.XI, Coca Leaf (1924, Committee C). For Bolivian resistance, Ana María Lema, "La coca de las Americas: Partido renido entre la Sociedad de Propietarios de Yungas y la Sociedad de Naciones," *I Coloquio Cocayapu* (La Paz: Cocayapu 1992), 1–12.

22 Geneva, Anti-Opium Information Bureau, "Strange omissions," 26 May 1931, 14; W.W. Willoughby, *Opium as an International Problem: The Geneva Conferences* (Baltimore: Johns Hopkins University Press, 1925), ch. 20. United States views in RG 170, box 7, Conferences on Production Limitation, 1931–8. For a distinct original interpretation, William B. McAllister "A limited enterprise: The history of international efforts to control addicting substances in the twentieth century" (Ph.D. thesis, History: University of Virginia, 1996).

23 On contexts, see Marcos Cueto, *Excelencia Científica en la Periferia: Actividades Científicas e Investigacion Biomédica en el Perú, 1890–1950* (Lima: Instituto de Estudios Peruanos, 1989), biography, 205, or "Andean biology in Peru – Scientific styles on the periphery," *ISIS* 80 (1989), 640–58. Nancy L. Stepan, *"The Hour of Eugenics": Race, Gender, and Nation in Latin America* (Ithaca: Cornell University Press, 1991), 180–1. C.A. Ricketts, *Ensayos de Legislación Pro-indígena* (Arequipa: Tip. Cuadros, 1936).

24 Carlos E. Paz Soldán, "El problema médico-social de la coca en el Perú," *Mercurio Peruano: Revista Mensual de Ciencias Sociales y Letras* 19 (1929), 135–6, 584–603; "La coca peruana y su futuro régimen político," *La Reforma Médica* (Lima) (January 1934) 69–77, (February 1934) 98–9. Cf. Washington view in William Reid, "Coca: A plant of the Andes," (PanAmerican Union, pam., 1918/1928/1937).

25 Paz Soldán, "Problema de la coca," parts 1–3 (1929).

26 Paz Soldán, "Problema de la coca," part 4 (1929), 597–603.

27 Paz Soldán, "La coca y su régimen político" (1934).

28 Joseph Gagliano, *Coca Prohibition in Peru: The Historical Debates* (Tucson: University-of Arizona Press, 1993), chs. 6–7 for indigenista politics, verging on Ricketts's view; JoAnn Kawell, "Going to the source," MS, Berkeley, 1997, ch.16, for splits on cocaine and coca; Dorothy Porter, "Social medicine and the new society: Medicine and scientific humanism in mid-twentieth-century Britain," *Journal of Historical Sociology* 9(2) (1996), 168–87.

29 On Pagador affair, RG 59, Dec.File 823.114 Peru/Narcotics, "Subject: Dr. Antonio Pagador," 12 December 1930 (Shreve corr., 3 November 1930); 511.4 A7/12 Hobson, 6 September 1930; RG 170 0660 Peru, Shreve to Fuller, November 1930.

30 RG 170 0660, "Fuller to Shreves," November 1930; Paz Soldán, "Problema de la coca," Epigraph; RG 170 0660, Peru, "Visit of Mr. E. Schaeffer" (Maywood), 10 March 1933; Paz Soldán, "La coca y su régimen político" (1934).

31 Gagliano, *Coca Prohibition*, ch. 6; RG 170 0660, Despatch 2799, 3 May 1933, "La Industria of Trujillo and the resolution of the League of Nations," (orig. *El Comercio*, 1 May 1933); C. Bües, "La coca en el Perú," *Boletín de la Dirección de Agricultura y Ganadería* V (July–September 1935), 3–75, rich in data.

32 Sociedad Nacional Agraria (Paz Soldán), *La Coca Peruana: Memorandum Sobre Su Situación Actual* (Lima: SNA, 1936), with detailed historical/statistical appendices.

33 *La Vida Agrícola: Revista de Agricultura y Ganadería* (Lima), "La coca en peligro," 1 March 1936 and SNA, "La cuestión de la coca"; Publicaciones Recibidas: "La coca Peruana," June 1936; "La cuestión de coca" (Dir. Gen. de Salubridad).

34 "Oficial: Producción Cocalera," (Benavides), *Vida Agrícola,* June 1936; "La situación de la industria cocalera," August 1936. They also carried technical info: Johannes Wille (La Molina), "Los insectos dañinos a la coca en el Perú," December 1937, 1003–9.

35 "La industria cocalera," *Comercio* (15 March, 9 May 1936), editorial; *La Prensa* (6 April 1936) (clippings, RG 59, Dec.File 823.114).

36 RG 59, Dec.File 823.114, Peru/Narcotics, clippings, 4 April; 13, 1 June 1936; RG 170 (FBN) 0660, Peru, "Subject: Approaching Narcotics Conference interests Peru," 13 April 1936; "Subject: Peru's Attitude at the Narcotics Conference," 1 June 1936; "Bureau of Narcotics," 14 August 1936.

37 Paz Soldán, "Como intentamos resolver en Washington el agudo problema de la crisis de la coca del Perú" (speech text), *Reforma Médica* (1 August 1936), 653–8, 662–3.

38 "La industria cocalera," *Comercio* (19 May 1936), and "Una Comisión estudiará la producción cocalera de la República," (15 March); RG 59, Dec.File 823.114 Peru/Narcotics, "Commission appointed to study the Peruvian coca industry," 23 March 1936. See Ricketts, *Ensayos pro-indígena,* "La oposición al proyecto de restringir el abuso de la coca" (on Huánuco), 33–52.

39 McAllister, "A limited enterprise," ch. 4; RG 59, Dec.File 823.114 20, April 1936 "Confidential biographic data" (Trujillo): Peru's delegate, an engineer, is dubbed "Personality: Pleasing" but "Influence: Not Important – eager for a diplomatic passport for his European vacation." Geneva, 13 October 1936, in LN/OC 1143(2), "List of firms authorized to manufacture drugs covered by the Convention," 17 March 1936. "Tráfico de estúpeficientes," *Boletín de Relaciones Exteriores*, (15 April, 31 January 1936).

40 LN, Com. on Traffic in Opium, OC 1760 "Latin American mission," 24 April 1939, esp. "Report of the Director." RG 59, Dec.File 823.114 Narcotics, 7 March 1938, with aims vis-à-vis Coca-Cola (Anslinger to Hayes).

41 LN OC 1760, Ekstrand, "Latin American mission," "Peru," 5–7, appendices. Paz Soldán, *Reforma Médica* (1 May 1938), editorial, 353.

42 "Visita de una misión de la Liga de las Naciones" *Boletín de Relaciones Exteriores* (6 January, 8 March 1938); "Memorandum del Director de la Sección del Trabajo de Opio y cuestiones sociales sobre el libro 'la Coca Peruana' ", April 1938, 248–59 (Ekstrand, Geneva, February 1938); "El control internacional de los estúpefacientes y la coca peruana," *Vida Agrícola* (July 1938), 595–7 (Spanish text).

43 Peru, Ministerio de Relaciones Exteriores, AREP, "7-0-D" Entrada, A. Jochmowitz al Ministro, Comité Central de Opio (Paris), 21 March 1938.

44 "Control de estúpeficientes," *Vida Agrícola* (July 1938); C.E. Paz Soldán, "Luchamos contra la esclavitud del cocaísmo indígena – sugestiones para una acción nacional," *Reforma Médica* (1 January 1939), 19–24 (speech to Congreso Nacional de Química); RG 170 FBN/DEA O660 Peru, "Coca," January 1938 (SNA, League); Ekstrand, "Mission," OC 1760, April 1939. Paz Soldán's coca writings (*Reforma Médica* through 1950) become militantly anti-coca.

45 Féderico Luzio, "Tecnología: La fabricación de cocaína en Huánuco," *Agronomía: Órgano del Centro de Estudiantes de la Molina* III (15) (1938) 44–55; Dante Binda A., "La cocaína: Problema industrial en el Perú," *Actas y Trabajos del Segundo Congreso Peruano de Química* I (23 October 1943), 375–9 (J. Kawell shared this find).

46 Besides US intelligence, ARH, Prefecturas (Huánuco), Leg. 44, 1938–40 overflows with shipment requests.

47 RG 170 FBN/DEA, "Maywood to Anslinger," February, May 1940, April–May 1942; "Narcotics in Peru," April 1942; RG 170, "Beverages," 1938–45; RG 59,

Dec.File 823.114 Peru/Narcotics, "Hartung," April 1940, Maywood politics; Pendergrast, *For God & Coca-Cola*, ch. 12.

48 RG 170 FBN/DEA 0660 Peru "Exports of coca, cocaine," 1943; Soberón deals (August 1941); "Raw cocaine in Peru," December 1941; "Materials for cocaine," January 1942 (etc.). RG 59, Dec.File 823.114 Peru/Narcotics, for many official orders/intelligence reports.

49 RG 170 0660 Peru, "Control of soda ash in Peru," March 1942; "Confidential," July 1943, 17 June, 1944; RG 59, Dec.File 823.114, April 1942, etc. This is obverse of wars as periods of enhanced drug production/collaboration: Jonathan Marshall, "Opium, tungsten, and the search for national security, 1940–1952," in William Walker III, *Drug Control Policy: Essays in Historical and Comparative Perspective* (University Park: Penn State Press, 1992), 89–116.

50 Peru, Ministerio de Agricultura, *La Acción Oficial en el Desarrollo Agrocopuario de la Colonización de Tingo María* (Lima: Min de Agricultura, 1947); Kawell, "Going to the source," ch. 17.

51 Gagliano, *Coca Prohibition*, 146–54; Luis Sainz, *La Coca: Estudio Médico-social de la Gran Toximanía Peruana* (Lima: Guardía Civil y Policíar 1938); Carlos Gutiérrez, Vicente Zapata Ortiz, "Estudios sobre la coca y la cocaína en el Perú," (Lima: Dir. de Educacion, 1947); Monge, "Réplica de la Delegación Peruana," *Perú Indígena* (September–December 1952). RG 170 FBN/DEA 0660 Peru, November 1942 (Ricketts).

52 RG 170 FBN/DEA, February 1940, Maywood–Anslinger; April 1940 and Hayes to Anslinger, March 1944; Min. de Relaciones Exteriores, September 1944; Dec.File 823.114, Peru/Narcotics, April 1940, March–April 1942, March 1944.

53 McAllister, "A limited enterprise," ch. 6; United Nations, EcoSoc Council, Commission on Narcotic Drugs, 1st–2nd Sessions, 1946–8; esp. "Illicit traffic in narcotic drugs," "World trends, 1939–45" (Lake Success, NY, 1947).

54 RG 170 FBN 0660, James C. Ryan, "Re: illicit cocaine traffic," NYC, 3 December 1949; a report copied throughout FBN; FBN, "Traffic in opium and other dangerous drugs," 1946–50. One gap: most FBN Peru records are missing from 1945–7 before UN era. See RG 59, Dec.File 823.114, 13 January 1947, first reports; RG 170 0660, Peru, Williams to Anslinger, "Re: illicit cocaine traffic," 17 May 1949. "Peru: The White Goddess," *Time* (11 April 1949).

55 Gagliano, *Coca Prohibition*, ch. 7, for respective coca politics.

56 UN, Annual Reports of Governments "Peru: Annual report for 1950," (E/NR 1950) "Laws and publications," 3–14; Spanish compendium is Rubio, *Legislación sobre drogas*, 82–93, plus fuller *El Peruano* (1947–50) and United States RG 59, Dec.File, 1947–50 (decree laws).

57 UN, Economic and Social Council, *Report of the Commission of Enquiry on the Coca Leaf* 5th Year, 12th Session, suppl. (Lake Success, July 1950) and related documents (E/1666, 8 June 1951), "Answer to statements of representatives of Peru and Bolivia in commission on narcotic drugs." Peru views in full issue of *Perú Indígena* III(7–8) (December 1952), esp. Monge "Réplica" (in English trans.), "Counter-reply of the Peruvian Commission for Study of the Coca Problem to the Commission of Enquiry of the UN on the Coca Leaf" (Lima: Min. de Salud Pública, 1951).

58 UN/ESC, *Annual Reports*, E/NR 1950, "Peru: Annual report for 1950" (17 January 1952), 25–7, "Mission of experts for the reorganization of the narcotics administration" (Logan Mission: full report lost). Com. on Narcotic Drugs (1947–50s), Session and Documents, for Peruvian role. UN E/NR 1951–4, Com. on Narcotic Drugs, "Annual report communicated by gov. of Peru" (13 March 1956).

59 United States files are intense here: RG 170 FBN/DEA, 0660 Peru, all 1949–50, as well as RG 59, Dec.File 823.114, Peru/Narcotics, G. Williams, "Memorandum for Com. Anslinger," "Re: illicit cocaine traffic," 17 May 1949; J. Edgar Hoover to Anslinger, "Subject: Peruvian narcotics traffic," 22 April 1949. "Afirman que la producción de cocaína peruana es una amenaza para el mundo," *La Prensa* (19 April

1949) (Anslinger pieces). Ethan Nadelmann, *Cops Across Borders: The Internationalization of U.S. Criminal Law Enforcement* (University Park: Penn State Press, 1993), chs. 2, 3, 5, for process at hand.

60 Harry J. Anslinger and W. Tompkins, *The Traffic in Narcotics* (New York: Funk and Wagnalls, 1953), 16–8, 281; Cf. FBN, "Traffic in opium and other dangerous drugs," (Washington, 1949–50) or RG 170 FBN/DEA 0660 "Peru," Dept. of State, "Memorandum of conversation," "Illicit traffic in cocaine from Peru," 2 May 1949.

61 Besides "oral history" evidence in Huánuco, one finds a few hot documents: ARH, Prefecturas, Leg. 73, 21 April 1949, shows a José Roncagliolo de la Torre (of the "Bolívar" factory) despatching approved cocaine (21 kilos) to Balarezo (a Durand relative) in Lima. Overall, "rumors" in Peru go both ways: Haya de la Torre was a "known" early aficionado of cocaine (though this 1949 scandal does not make history books), but many speak of "bored" 1940s military officers, too, among earliest users.

62 On APRA, drugs and United States: RG 59 LOTS files, "Subject files relating to Peru, 1950–58," a mine of documents, public and covert, esp. Morlock, "Proposed note to Peruvian Amb. on smuggling of cocaine," 24 March 1950; RG 170 FBN/DEA 0660 "Peru" all February–March 1950.

63 RG 59, Dec.File 823.114 Peru/Narcotics, Lobenstine, "Balarazo and the dope ring," 25 August 1949, a compendium of many press clips, police memos, intelligence reports.

64 UN, "Peru: Report for 1950," "Illicit traffic," 29–40, esp. 36–7 (Soberón, Ayllon); also RG 59, Dec.File 823.114, 1949–52, arrest profiles/reports, e.g. 25 August 1948, "Fabricación de cocaína clandestina," Otuzco (Ayllon); "Para reprimir el tráfico ilícito de estúpefacientes," *Comercio* (27 April 1949); RG 170 0660 Peru, "Statement made by Gustavo Prados ... in office of FBN," 15 May 1949. ARH, Prefecturas, Leg. 33/Exp. 463 "Inventario de la fábrica de cocaína de Don Andrés A. Soberón," May 1949. *Guía Lascano* (Huánuco, Trujillo), 1950–2, for businesses, and Huánuco "Sucesiones" (wills).

65 RG 170 FBN/DEA, box 54, "InterAmerican conferences, 1959–66," "Cocaine conferences," etc. FBNDD, "Traffic in opium and other dangerous drugs," (Washington, 1953–66).

66 UN Archives (New York) TE 322/Per (9), June 1957–19 September 1960; 26 February 1962, (15 December 1961) C. Caron, "Cocaína – Comercialización de la cocaína por el Perú." Peru, Caja de Depósitos y Consignaciones, *Memoria del Estanco de la Coca*, "Laboratorios fiscales de industrialización de la coca y sus derivados," annual reports, 1955–60s.

67 Primary sources for Peru: Joseph Gagliano, *Coca Prohibition in Peru: The Historical Debates* (Tucson: University of Arizona Press, 1994) and Fernando Cabieses, *La Coca: Dilema Trágico?* (Lima: ENACO, 1993?) are the two works on coca. JoAnn Kawell's "Going to the Source" (1997) makes good use of published historical sources on cocaine.

Part II

European axis, Asian circuits (Germany, Britain, the Netherlands and Java, Japan)

4 Germany and the transformations of cocaine, 1860–1920

H. Richard Friman

Standard histories of cocaine point to the drug's euphoric reception in the mid-1880s and its gradual de-legitimation in the medical and broader communities of the United States and Europe. But in some countries, scholars note, influential pharmaceutical industries obstructed such a shift, requiring pressures from international control efforts during the early 1900s to complete the transformation of cocaine from miracle drug to global menace. For example, classic texts by Arnold Taylor and S.D. Stein posit a powerful pharmaceutical industry behind the German government's resistance to controls on the cocaine trade. Drawing on United States and British archival materials, Taylor and Stein suggest further that the industry's influence was broken only with the Versailles Peace Treaty and its conditions requiring all signatories to adopt the drug control provisions of the Hague Convention.[1]

This traditional history, however, understates German control efforts on cocaine while overstating the impact of industry influence and international pressure. Many German control measures pre-dated international drug deliberations and subsequent dictates through Versailles for compliance with the emerging prohibition regime. Public and private German archives also reveal that rather than powerful pharmaceutical groups, policy-makers faced a fragmented cocaine industry with primary firms more interested in the regulatory environment facing other drugs such as morphine. The archival record further reveals that Germany's introduction of cocaine controls reflected the concerns of policy-makers with bureaucratic politics, broadly defined security interests, and problems of drug abuse, as well as international pressures.[2]

This chapter's first section offers a brief overview of the German cocaine industry and early steps towards government regulation. The second explores the international and domestic dynamics of control efforts during the Hague deliberations. The final section addresses German regulatory steps in the context of war and the Versailles Treaty.

The German cocaine industry

Traditional histories stress the political power of the German cocaine industry. Germany's "discovery" and early commercial production of cocaine, and the later prominence of German cocaine in European and American markets suggest this potential for political influence. However, such arguments fail to capture the organizational fragmentation and limited interest convergence that distinguished the cocaine industry and undermined its influence over German drug control policy.

Origins of the German cocaine industry

Despite interest among European explorers and chemists in the effects of Latin American coca leaves, little headway had been made by the mid-nineteenth century in extracting coca's active ingredients. In 1859, Albert Niemann, a graduate student working in the lab of Dr Friedrich Wöhler in Göttingen, Germany, made the first breakthrough. Experimenting with Peruvian coca leaves, Niemann extracted the primary alkaloid and named the ingredient "cocaine." Niemann published his findings in 1860 in a dissertation entitled "Über eine neue Base in der Kokablättern" ("On a new organic base in the coca leaves"). His work was continued by Wilhelm Lossen, a second chemist in the Wöhler lab, who in 1862 published his own dissertation that established the chemical formula for cocaine.

As noted by Hans W. Maier in his classic 1926 work on cocaine addiction "not much was done with the compound for the next two decades." This lag would end with published reports of experimentation by United States researchers with cocaine as a treatment for morphine addiction and, in turn, growing interest in the drug among European researchers. The latter include Karl Köller's influential discoveries of clinical uses of cocaine as a local anesthetic in eye surgery (1884), Theodor Aschenbrandt's experiments with cocaine as a stimulant for soldiers on field maneuvers (1883) and Sigmund Freud's therapeutic explorations with the drug (1884). Publications noting these experiments popularized the drug in Europe and abroad.[3]

The lag time posited by Maier, however, is partially misleading. Pharmaceutical companies had early taken note of the initial work of Niemann and Lossen. In 1862, the German pharmaceutical firm E. Merck, based in Darmstadt, began the first commercial production of cocaine hydrochloride (referred to as cocaine muriate) from Peruvian coca leaves. Initial production was limited, reflecting the low demand shaped by the scarcity of published research on cocaine's uses as well as the relatively high price of the drug. By the late 1870s, for example, Merck's annual production of cocaine remained less than 50 grams.[4]

Nonetheless, Merck's early foray into the market ideally placed the firm to dominate the production of the drug in Europe as popular interest grew. In the early 1880s, Merck officials had attempted to increase sales by sending informational pamphlets to European physicians. The brochures noted the American research on cocaine and stressed the similar use of Merck cocaine as a treatment for morphine addiction. By the mid-1880s, the path-breaking experiments of Köller, Freud, and Aschenbrandt had established Merck as the prime source for cocaine.

All three researchers had used Merck cocaine in their research and explicitly mentioned the company's product in publications of their results. Freud went even further, noting that "Merck's cocaine and its salts are, as has been proved, preparations which have the full or at least the essential effects of coca leaves."[5] Demand for and the price of Merck cocaine jumped dramatically. Merck sales records reveal that following the publication of Köller's discoveries in 1884, the price of cocaine more than doubled, increasing from 6 marks to 15 marks per gram. By February 1885, the price had almost quadrupled, peaking at 23 marks per gram. In the United States, the price of Merck cocaine also increased by over fivefold, from $2.50 per gram to a peak of $13 per gram in January 1885. Merck records (see Table 4.1) for this period also reveal a twentyfold increase in cocaine production, from 1.41 kilograms in 1883–4 to 30 kilograms in 1884–5.[6]

These references to Merck cocaine distinguished the company's product from lower quality solutions as new producers entered the market. In Germany alone, at least thirteen pharmaceutical companies diversified into cocaine production. Of these, Merck's primary competitors consisted of: Gehe & Co., located in Dresden and established in 1869; Knoll and Co., Ludwigshafen, 1866; I.D.

Table 4.1 Imports of Peruvian coca and crude cocaine by E. Merck and resulting production of cocaine hydrochloride, 1879–1900 (in kg)

Year	Merck production	Peruvian coca	Peruvian crude cocaine
1879–80	0.05	25	
1880–1	0.05	25	
1881–2	0.09	58	
1882–3	0.30	138	
1883–4	1.41	655	
1884–5	30	8,655	
1885–6	70	18,396	
1886–7	257	3,629	389
1887–8	300		375
1888–9	303		350
1889–90	511		595
1890–1	557		585
1891–2	436		434
1892–3	505		558
1893–4	626		656
1894–5	645		683
1895–6	791		1,801
1896–7	831		870
1897–8	1,509		1,819
1898–9	1,553		1,832
1899–1900	1,564		1,695

Source: 1908/1919 Manuscripts of Carl Scriba, Alkaloid Division, E. Merck, reprinted in Albrecht Hirschmüller, "E. Merck und das Kokain," *Gesnerus* 52 (1995), 119–20.

Note: Explanations for quantity variation in Merck's cocaine production figures relative to imports include uneven quality in coca and crude cocaine imports, and potential lag effects (e.g. not all imports being processed in a given year).

Riedel, Berlin, 1827; C.F. Böhringer und Söhne, Mannheim-Waldhof, 1859; and C.H. Böhringer Sohn, Nieder-Ingelheim, 1885. In the mid-1880s, Merck remained the leading producer, followed at a distance by Gehe.[7]

Merck's sharpest competition would come from the United States. Parke, Davis & Company emerged as the leading United States producer of cocaine in the 1880s. Established in 1866 as Duffield, Parke and Co., the company was renamed as Parke, Davis, & Company in 1871 and reincorporated and capitalized in Detroit in 1875. The company's expanded financial base facilitated expeditions to Latin America to collect new plant sources for drugs – such as H.H. Rusby's travels to the Andes in 1885 to procure coca leaves. By the 1890s, the company's offerings of cocaine products included "coca leaf cigarette, cheroots ... Coca Cordial, tablets, hypodermic injections, ointments and sprays."[8]

Parke, Davis and Merck's shift to crude cocaine

Beginning in mid-1885, the German cocaine industry ran into a series of market-related problems. Mounting interest in cocaine had sparked a booming trade in coca leaves. In turn, cocaine prices fell in Europe and the United States due to expanding supplies of the drug from established producers and new market entrants. Merck records reveal a sixfold drop in cocaine prices from February to October 1885, from 23 to 4 marks per gram. By 1887, cocaine prices had fallen further to less than 1 mark per gram.

Merck and Gehe temporarily suspended production of cocaine in mid-1885. Although possibly related to price shifts, the decision was blamed by both companies on problems with uneven quality in raw materials. Quality concerns stemmed from a production process that relied on extracting cocaine from dried coca leaves imported from the Andes and the East Indies. Dried leaves tended to lose their potency over time, increasing the difficulty of extracting higher-quality cocaine as well as the cost. The option of importing coca leaves with higher alkaloid content, such as those from Java, was initially inhibited by Dutch control over the East Indies trade route via Amsterdam. Thus, German producers tended to rely on imports of Peruvian and Bolivian leaf with shipments routed through Hamburg (for example, see the figures on Peruvian leaf imports by Merck in Table 4.1).[9]

In contrast, United States producers were able to take advantage of geo-graphical proximity and, in turn, a greater relative potency in nearby Latin American coca leaves. By 1885, with Merck's suspension of production, observers such as Freud were noting growing European interest in cocaine supplies from Parke, Davis, due to the product's higher quality (e.g. in terms of purity, color, solubility) and lower cost. Learning from the experience of Merck, representatives of Parke, Davis turned to Freud, supplying him with a sample of cocaine and an honorarium to test the drug. Merck's response was to publicly defend the quality of Merck cocaine, while shifting raw-material supplies from coca leaves to more durable imports of Peruvian crude cocaine.[10]

As sketched by Gootenberg's Chapter 3 in this volume, the Peruvian crude cocaine industry (producing a cocaine sulfate paste rather than refined pharmaceutical-grade cocaine) emerged in the late 1880s. Merck records reveal a shift from coca imports to heavy reliance on crude cocaine shipped through the Peruvian company, Kitz & Co., with offices in Lima and, by the late 1880s, with production facilities in (Amazonian) Pozuzo. Starting with initial imports of 389 kilos of crude cocaine in 1886–7, Merck by the late 1890s counted on Kitz & Co. for roughly 1,800 kilos per year. In addition to this change of inputs in the production process, Merck established offices "to bolster sales" in the United States in 1887. By 1899, Merck had established production facilities in the United States as well. By the turn of the century then, the Parke, Davis challenge to Merck cocaine had ended.[11]

Cocaine's first transformations

While weathering this competitive business challenge from the United States, the German cocaine industry was less successful in avoiding a growing backlash against the drug. In the opening stage of this backlash, however, the German cocaine industry faced few restrictions.

During the mid-1880s, medical publications across Europe and the United States began to report on the risks of cocaine addiction and the drug's toxic side effects, especially in attempts to use cocaine as a "cure" for morphine addiction. A similar wave of criticism emerged in Germany. Leading German medical journals such as the *Deutsche Medizinal-Zeitung* and the *Centralblatt für Nervenheilkunde* published the concerns of Albrecht Friedrich Erlenmeyer, Louis Lewin, and others in the medical community. As cocaine's medicinal uses were being called into question, researchers were also discovering new drugs that offered less toxic alternatives to cocaine's role as an anesthetic.[12]

Despite the proliferation of criticisms and emerging research on alternatives, in the mid-1890s German scientific publications were still noting potential therapeutic uses for cocaine. With the medical community split, there appeared to be little impetus towards a stricter control regime targeted at cocaine. German drug regulations remained broadly focused. In general, health and safety issues fell primarily into the purview of the individual German states. Nonetheless, selected imperial ordinances resulted in national-level pharmacy laws that were "careful to restrict powerful drugs to pharmacies and physicians."[13] National regulations from 1872, for example, granted pharmacies the exclusive authority to sell drugs and chemical preparations to the public. Drug regulations began to tighten gradually during the 1890s and early 1900s, affecting cocaine as well as morphine and its derivatives. A Prussian Public Notice from 22 June 1896 introduced the requirement of prescriptions for repeat sales of powerful medicines. New national quality standards were gradually introduced through revised editions of the *Imperial Pharmacopoeia*. In addition, national provisions for commerce in medicines were introduced in 1901.[14]

In 1910, however, the regulatory focus of the German government narrowed. On 4 March, the Reichstag (the lower house of the German national legislature) passed a broad resolution calling for stronger measures to deal with the unauthorized distribution and misuse of morphine and cocaine. The origins of the Reichstag measure are not entirely clear. The leading German medical journals of the era reveal no surge in opposition to cocaine in the medical community. But inter-agency memos by the Imperial Health Office (*Kaiserliche Gesundheitsamt*) do suggest that drug problems were increasing in Germany. A report issued in May by the Imperial Health Office noted loose prescription practices by doctors, the availability of morphine candies (bon bons and pralines), and the spread of morphine shops in Berlin and Hamburg that offered discount injections (5–10 marks for the first, the second for half price) to ease "delicate nerves." The Imperial Health Office also noted the more recent emergence of cocaine usage, "especially among those who feel that morphine is not enough."[15]

In contrast, Erika Hickel's work on State policy towards the chemical industry in Imperial Germany suggests the centrality of bureaucratic politics behind regulatory steps more than changing drug-use conditions. Hickel notes that the limited statutory authority of the Imperial Health Office to shape policy within the executive agencies of the German government often led office representatives to approach the legislature with draft resolutions. The Reichstag measure of March 1910 initially stressed the latitude granted to doctors in their prescription practices for morphine and cocaine. The Imperial Health Office also called attention to the paucity of regulations on the wholesale trade as the primary source of uncontrolled supply. The solution posed by the Imperial Health Office was to revise the 1901 pharmacy code to grant greater power to pharmacists, and in turn provide the Imperial Health Office more authority over the wholesale trade.[16]

By 1911, little progress had registered at the ministerial level but a version of the Imperial Health Office's recommendations had made its way into the Reichstag. On 6 January, Dr Louis Merck, writing to the Foreign Office on behalf of Merck, C.F. Böhringer, Gehe, Knoll, and Riedel, noted his objections to a proposal under consideration in the Reichstag. The proposal would have specifically limited the handling of morphine and cocaine to pharmacists. Noting that most drug producers sold to large wholesalers rather than pharmacists, Merck argued that the Reichstag proposal posed a threat to an annual wholesale trade estimated at 60–80 million marks. Through the Spring of 1911, the Imperial Health Office continued its efforts to clarify its position on regulating the wholesale trade in communications with other ministries. In May, the Interior Ministry, noting the concerns over control measures, suggested to the Foreign Office that a meeting be held that June to debate the question and further the "direction that Germany should take ... especially in light of the upcoming international opium conference [Hague]."[17] As argued below, the issue of control efforts would become caught up and delayed in deliberations over the Hague Opium Conference.

Fragmentation in the German cocaine industry

The preceding discussion of industry opposition to regulatory steps against the wholesale trade risks overstating the political force of the German cocaine industry. By the early 1900s, the industry was distinguished more by organizational fragmentation and limited convergence of interest.

As part of broader trends towards cartelization in the German chemical industry (stemming from rising raw materials costs and economic dislocation in the late 1870s), pharmaceutical producers established price-fixing cartels for a range of products in the late 1800s. These cartels sought to maintain high domestic price levels while driving down export prices to facilitate external competitiveness. By 1896, thirty-five cartels were in place on pharmaceutical products including arrangements in cocaine and morphine. Although offering a unifying benefit of price stability, the cartels also became a source of tension among producers. Pricing cartels helped to protect the market share of established cocaine producers like Merck at the expense of relatively new market entrants such as C.H. Böhringer. These tensions would express themselves in 1911 as C.H. Böhringer representatives emerged as the primary opponents to regulatory steps against cocaine. Later, during the 1920s, C.H. Böhringer officials would also become the leading German suspects in the illicit international cocaine trade (including the massive and infamous Naarden trans-shipment case of 1927–8).[18]

In addition to price cartels, German cocaine producers organized themselves into several pharmaceutical industry associations. But their institutions were often not very consistent or influential. For example, Merck and Gehe were the only cocaine producers among the founding members of the Association for Safeguarding the Interests of the Chemical Industry (*Verein zur Wahrung der Interessen der chemischen Industrie*) established in 1877.[19] The cocaine industry was better represented by a greater participation of firms in the Central Information Bureau for Trademark Protection (*Zentralauskunftsstelle für Markenschutz*, ZEMA) and the Interest Association of the Chemical-Pharmaceutical Factories (*Interessenverband der chemische-pharmazeutischen Fabriken*, CEPHA), both established in 1905.[20]

However, these chemical industry associations failed to offer the cocaine industry a viable framework for mobilizing against prejudicial regulation. Industry efforts would face potential resistance from a broader and in some cases more powerful membership – including firms such as Bayer, Höchst, and Schering – who had little stake in the cocaine trade. As a result, in 1906, Merck and four other major cocaine producers (Gehe, C.F. Böhringer, Riedel, and Knoll) established their own interest association. Merck, Böhringer, and Knoll also turned to sharing selective production information, purchases of crude cocaine and marketing. The newly formed Association to Protect the Interests of the German Chemical Industry (*Verein zur Wahrung der Interessen der chemischen Industrie Deutschland*) sported a name strikingly similar to that of the broader chemical industry association of 1877. Whether this was by design, for example to suggest the need for protection of one portion of the industry from another, or to suggest affiliation with the larger organization, is unclear. For purposes of distinction, I will refer to the 1906 group as VCI.

Despite this small step towards organizational solidarity, it is important to note that interest convergence within the cocaine industry remained limited. Cocaine was never the primary product for any of the firms that dominated the industry, including Merck. When founded in 1827, Merck began with morphine as its key product and the company became the first commercial distributor of the drug. Cocaine production became increasingly central to the firm only in the 1880s. However, by 1893, cocaine products added up to but a small portion of the 1,156 different pharmaceutical preparations exhibited by Merck at the Chicago World Fair. By the early 1900s, Merck's product list had diversified even further. Morphine had fallen from Merck's first tier to second tier of product categories. Despite a surge in production (see Table 4.2), cocaine still ranked fourth out of a total of twenty-two categories in the second tier.[21]

In contrast to Merck, Gehe's leading products were quinine derivatives. Knoll originated from former Gehe personnel who left Gehe to patent a process they had obtained in England for making codeine from morphine. More similar to Merck, C.F. Böhringer und Söhne, C.H. Böhringer Sohn, and Riedel were producers of morphine and morphine derivatives (such as codeine). C.F. Böhringer's product list contained sixty-six items including codeine and cocaine, while morphine, codeine, cocaine, and quinine became vital products for rival

Table 4.2 Imports of coca and crude cocaine by E. Merck and resulting production of cocaine hydrochloride, 1900–18 (in kg)

Year	Merck production	Peruvian crude	Java coca	Java crude
1900–1	1,418	1,991		
1901–2	1,886	2,116		
1902–3	2,454	2,745		
1903–4	2,157	2,821		
1904–5	2,426	2,885		
1905–6	2,146	2,487	58,967	919
1907	1,881	953	94,018	1,647
1908	3,642	1,634	220,429	3,721
1909	4,183	1,239	238,066	3,972
1910	5,241	3,151	186,127	3,183
1911	4,681	2,072	261,254	4,080
1912	6,049	1,384	422,776	6,552
1913	8,683	1,226	724,189	10,683
1914	6,212	791	487,245	7,295
1915	265		203,972	2,966
1916	44		68,380	829
1917	1,246			
1918	1,738		6,744	72

Source: 1919 Manuscript of Carl Scriba, Alkaloid Division, E. Merck, reprinted in Albrecht Hirschmüller, "E. Merck und das Kokain," *Gesnerus* 52 (1995), 120–1.

Note: See Table 4.1.[22]

C.H. Böhringer only after 1905. During the early 1900s, access to cheaper imports of coca leaves and crude cocaine from Java as well as growing imports of Peruvian crude cocaine (as Peruvian exporters began to face trade restrictions on crude cocaine in the United States) facilitated new market entrants in cocaine production such as C.H. Böhringer. Throughout these years, however, Merck continued to dominate the trade (Table 4.2).[23]

In sum, though weathering a limited domestic backlash against cocaine among the medical community and initial government moves towards drug control, the German cocaine industry was anything but a cohesive force. Dominated by Merck, the industry still varied in terms of the quality of its output, the size of its producers, and the interests of its members in other pharmaceutical products. From an organizational standpoint, the industry's firms belonged to an array of price cartels and interest associations. The latter were dominated by larger chemical producers who were more likely to overshadow – rather than mobilize for – the interests of cocaine producers. Moreover, the cocaine industry's own business association only involved the five major firms and excluded at least eight others involved in the production of cocaine.

Germany and the Hague Convention

By 1911, the German debate over regulating the wholesale distribution of morphine and cocaine became caught up in broader American efforts to establish an international prohibition regime. German responses to these efforts reflected an initial sense among policy-makers that domestic drug problems did not warrant additional restrictions, and that such restrictions would also place Germany at a competitive disadvantage relative to non-signatory states.

Origins of international pressures

In 1905–6, United States officials turned to curtailing the international opium trade, especially the British trade from India to China. By 1909, these efforts had led to the convening of the Shanghai Opium Commission. Several considerations underlay the United States campaign, including political pressure from missionaries and "moral entrepreneurs," and desires of American policy-makers to challenge British influence in China. The decision of British officials to participate in drug control negotiations was no less complex, shaped by the need to appease the growing political strength of anti-opium forces in Britain while protecting broader strategic interests of opium revenues in colonial India. British diplomatic skills at Shanghai deflected the United States plan, resulting in vague final agreement of non-binding resolutions.[24]

Following Shanghai, United States officials pressed for a second round of negotiations that would lead to binding agreements. In the rush to gain British participation, however, American policy-makers again were outmaneuvered. In the preliminary negotiations leading up to the 1911 Hague Opium Conference,

British diplomats conditioned their participation on demands that the negotiations over opium be broadened to encompass morphine and cocaine. Having broached such a step at Shanghai with little success, United States officials responded positively to the suggestion without exploring the ramifications of the additional British amendments. These conditions included the demand that Britain receive "satisfactory assurances" that the Hague participants were ready to discuss "restricting of manufacturing, sale and distribution" of cocaine, morphine and opium, and that the participants would collect and share data on domestic production and trade in these industries before conference proceedings. With the definition of "satisfactory" left to the British, the United States unwittingly gave the primary target of its control efforts the deciding voice in the agenda of the conference.

Underlying such conditions was British concern with growing problems with addiction in the Crown colonies as well as for protecting its own pharmaceutical industry against foreign competitors. Unilateral restrictions on cocaine and morphine by Great Britain would merely open the international market further to powerful competitors abroad, especially German firms. The British preconditions for the Hague Conference, by contrast, would place pressure on Germany to either divulge information about the extent of its industry and steps to curtail it, or risk becoming a pariah state in international control efforts. With the United States acceding to the British demands in October 1910, this trade-off became the Germans' dilemma.

Germany and the British conditions

In early 1910, the German Foreign Office received the United States proposal for the Hague Conference. Inter-ministerial correspondence through mid-year shows how the proposal circulated to agencies including the Interior Ministry, Justice Ministry, the Imperial Health Office, and Chancellor's Office. In general, agency reactions supported the Conference's stated goal of action against drug problems but expressed reservations over proposals to curtail the international trade in opium and manufactured opium products (e.g. codeine and morphine). In November, the Interior Ministry notified Merck of the Government's intent to participate in the Hague negotiations.

The following week, Merck officials communicated on behalf of VCI the association's willingness to meet with Interior Ministry officials to discuss the Hague proposals. German archival records reveal that the Interior Ministry waited seven months before arranging such a meeting, and an additional four months before forwarding a formal request for industry information and for detailed discussions. During this eleven-month period, three deadlines for the onset of the Hague Conference came and went. Meanwhile, the German Foreign Office continued to inform its American counterparts that Germany was taking steps to comply with the British conditions.

The fact that such steps were not taking place appeared unrelated to any government apprehension over industry opposition to the Hague Conference.

The VCI stance on the Conference was similar to that of German policy-makers. In November, for example, Merck had acknowledged the need for action to address drug problems but noted that the Hague proposals appeared more likely to "hurt legitimate trade and commerce."[25] Rather than direct industry pressure, domestic drug dilemmas and considerations of relative industrial competitiveness appeared to be driving the actions of German officials.

Drug control was already under active deliberation in Germany by 1911, focused on the Reichstag and Imperial Health Office proposals for increased regulation on drug wholesalers. In this context, becoming one of the first major drug-producing countries to meet the British conditions would do little for German drug control and would risk placing the pharmaceutical industry at a competitive disadvantage. Thus, the Germans delayed. Such a strategy held out ,the chance that other producing countries would comply first, or that the Hague Conference would be derailed by either other hold-outs (such as Portugal and Japan) or by growing American frustration with the British position.

By mid-1911, however, the German position became untenable. State Department records reveal that the United States Embassy directly approached the German Foreign Minister on 10 May 1911 to see if Germany would be ready to participate by October. On 24 May, the Embassy reported the Foreign Minister's reply that the October date was "being considered by the departments concerned."[26] Although this claim was not precisely accurate, movement had begun among German policy-makers. On 18 May, the State Secretary of the Interior had contacted the Foreign Office suggesting that an inter-agency meeting be set for 8 June to discuss the question of "stronger measures to deal with the unauthorized distribution and misuse of narcotic drugs."[27]

The 18 May memo along with confidential minutes from the resulting meeting noted the 1910 Reichstag's resolution, the Imperial Health Office proposals, and the upcoming Hague Conference – in that order. For the first time, the meeting brought together senior officials from the Interior Ministry, Foreign Office, Ministry of Commerce and Industry, and the Imperial Health Office as well as representatives from Merck, Gehe, Riedel, and the Pharmacists' Association to explore the issue of expanded control measures.[28]

The plan for excluding wholesalers in favor of pharmacists in the morphine trade dominated the agenda of the June meeting. Industry representatives remained opposed to such a step, repeating their earlier concerns; pharmacists backed the Imperial Health Office. Other government participants raised a third option of allowing large producers to, in effect, serve as wholesalers. The final agreement on this issue revealed a slight shift in the status quo towards a compromise position – by limiting the right to engage in morphine distribution to manufacturers, specially *licensed* wholesalers and pharmacists.

If the German cocaine industry was organizationally fragmented and lacked "interest convergence," as just argued, how were three of its leading firms able to influence the policy-making process? Issues about morphine production and abuse rather than cocaine determined the government's inclusion of these firms in deliberations, partially offsetting the industry's organizational fragmentation.

More important, these three producers shared a strong, common interest in continuing the lucrative practice of bulk morphine sales to wholesalers. In fact, cocaine received little attention here. The word itself appeared only twice in the minutes, once in the introduction, and again in item six of the agenda to determine if the proposed compromise regulations for morphine should extend to cocaine. Rather than detailed debate or discussion of the cocaine question, the extension was simply approved.[29]

By October 1911, the Hague Conference agenda overshadowed further German debates over drug control. On 24 October, the Interior Ministry hosted a second meeting of government officials and industry representatives explicitly focused on the upcoming Hague Conference and once again dominated by issues of morphine controls. Notes from the meeting again reveal little discord between government and industry positions. On the question of adding new domestic controls on morphine and cocaine as suggested by the British, the meeting concluded that their new wholesale provisions made sufficient regulation. Domestic drug conditions did not merit additional steps. Moreover, new restrictions made no sense in the absence of similar steps by drug-producing countries not attending the Hague Conference. The Hague proposals for regulating the international trade in narcotics met with either little objection or doubts as to their effectiveness.[30]

However, consensus between industry and government officials, and the shared interest within the industry, should not be overstated. On 25 October, the Interior Ministry wrote to Merck requesting data on the morphine and cocaine industry as demanded by the British conditions. The request included a list of firms the government believed engaged in cocaine and morphine production. On 1 November, Louis Merck relayed the request to companies specified by the ministry but added the following recommendations: that the information be provided only to the German government, that the data not be updated and that references to production and trade figures remain vague. As the memo noted, "we all know our position relative to foreign countries but it is not in our interest to let them know."[31]

The responses of the companies as received over the next two days were less cooperative; most advocated simply rejecting the government's request. Merck chose to avoid a direct confrontation with the German government that the industry had little chance of winning. His reply to the Interior Ministry on 3 November assumed a more conciliatory tone. Merck noted the industry's support for the international fight against drug abuse and for control measures but expressed doubts on providing sensitive data to potential competitors. Merck requested that the government refrain from revealing statistical information provided by the sector. To protect industry interests, Merck had adopted a strategy of select passive resistance, relying on the provision of vague, dated, and incomplete information rather than open confrontation.

The Hague Convention of 1911–12 fell short of American as well as British expectations. First, the manufacture, distribution, and sale of cocaine and morphine remained under national auspices, with signatories "required only to 'use their best efforts' to control" drug industries. Similar requirements applied to the licensing of drug exporters and to linking exports to authorization from importing nations. Citing potential problems of jurisdictional disputes between national and state authorities, the German delegation had blocked more restrictive language. Second, German and French concerns over the threat posed by non-signatories deadlocked the conference on the issue of ratification. Efforts by the United States to break this deadlock would lead to additional Hague Conferences in 1913 and 1914, and partial ratification and implementation of the convention by sixteen countries in 1915. Although signing in 1913, German officials continued to dwell on the problem of non-signatories and refused to ratify the accord.[32]

In sum, by 1913, cocaine continued to face only limited regulation. New restrictions on the wholesale trade in morphine and cocaine introduced in 1911 were focused mainly on morphine. German policy-makers clearly resisted more extensive control measures, such as those envisioned by the United States and British delegations to the Hague Convention. Rather than massive industry pressure, however, this stance appeared to reflect government concerns over risks posed by non-signatories and their sense that further regulatory steps remained unwarranted.

The war, aftermaths, and cocaine's transformation

By 1917, faced with the growing impact of World War I, the concerns of German policy-makers with drug abuse and security began to shift towards tighter regulation. The social dislocation of the war's immediate aftermath prompted additional control provisions. Contrary to arguments of traditional histories, the transformation of cocaine was already underway by the time German officials faced the dictates of Versailles. Implementing these new control provisions, however, would prove to be a difficult task as cocaine also transformed into Germany's illicit drug of choice in the 1920s.

Wartime controls

By the onset of World War I, the import of the Hague Convention and the threat of non-signatories had faded. German policy-makers faced far more pressing security concerns. The disruption of raw-material imports and heightened demand for medical supplies led to new regulations around the German pharmaceutical industry.

As seen in Table 4.2, Peruvian exports of crude cocaine to Merck halted after 1914 (Gootenberg's Chapter 3 suggests a corresponding increase in Peruvian exports to France, Britain, and the United States). German producers were forced into reliance on the dwindling supplies of coca and crude cocaine from Java. Merck production figures for the war years reveal the result. In 1913, Merck alone was producing almost 9,000 kilograms of cocaine; by 1915–16, annual production had fallen to under 500 kilograms (Table 4.2).

In 1917, the War Ministry's Health Department turned to centralizing stockpiles and drug disbursement. The reasons for the shift were not limited to the need to safeguard stockpiles. Interior Ministry officials pointed to the threats posed by the diversion of drug supplies from legitimate channels, including a noticeable domestic problem of drug abuse. Health Department officials drew on authority granted under a March 1917 regulation concerning commerce in opium and other narcotics (including cocaine). Ironically, the war had empowered the former Imperial Health Office, enabling health officials to obtain regulations similar to those sought in 1910. The financial reservations of the pharmaceutical industry that had blocked the Imperial Health Office seven years earlier became irrelevant.

The 1917 order designated pharmacists as the primary drug wholesalers and retailers. The Health Department specifically delegated control over the disbursement of drug stockpiles to the German Pharmacists' Trading Corporation (*Handellsgesellschaft Deutscher Apotheker*) rather than the broader gamut of wholesalers seen in 1914. The order also limited drug disbursement to "medical uses" and imposed maximum penalties of a year in prison and/or a fine of 10,000 marks for violations of these provisions. These new penalties reflected the seriousness of the change. The maximum prison time and fines for drug offenses in 1911 had been only six weeks and 150 marks.[33]

Control in the aftermath of war

The extensive political and socio-economic dislocation in Germany immediately after the war upped drug demand and led to further regulation. Initially, the German Demobilization Office turned to a December 1918 order authorizing steps to control traffic in opium and manufactured opium products. The Demobilization Office began by requiring all parties in possession of a certain quantity of drugs, such as more than one kilogram of morphine, to provide notification of their holdings. The decree clarified further the 1917 regulations on those allowed in drug distribution. All parties engaged in drug distribution were now required to maintain detailed ledgers of their transactions – noting the name, position and address of the supplier/receiver, and the date and quantity of each transaction. Maximum penalties for violation of the new regulations consisted of up to six months in jail and/or a fine of 10,000 marks. But the new regulations did not apply to cocaine, which remained under the provisions of 1917. The absence of detailed notification requirements for cocaine thus created a loophole for diversion of drug supplies away from legitimate distribution channels.

By 1920, problems with diversions of cocaine supplies from military stockpiles and the spread of cocaine abuse resulted in steps by the Weimar Government to block this gap. Cocaine availability was growing with "the chaos that prevailed in the distribution of army stocks" and a surge in street-level trafficking. Street sales were often adulterated cocaine mixed with boric acid, novocaine, and other fillers, and sold in quantities of one to six grams at seven to eight times the legal price of one mark. The combination of postwar trauma and increasing cocaine availability also resulted in an epidemic of hospital admissions for cocaine-related problems. In Berlin alone, cocaine-related admissions to university clinics rose from an average of 1.75 percent of admissions in 1913 to 3 percent in 1918, 7.5 percent in 1920, to fully 10 percent in 1921.[34]

The government's new regulations of 20 July 1920 retained core elements of earlier control provisions. Commerce in opium, morphine and other opium alkaloids, and now cocaine, was restricted to individuals with a permit granted by government authorities. For sellers with permits, sales were limited to those legally allowed to acquire drugs (such as wholesalers, large producers, pharmacists, and scientific institutes). Only pharmacists with permits would licitly receive or sell such products, and only in medicinal form. The new regulations retained the ledger and criminal provisions of 1918 and extended them to transactions in cocaine. In addition, the regulations authorized the National Health Office to require information from all parties in the production, storage (such as in bond), or import of cocaine and narcotics (concerning the nature, quantity, location, and scale of commerce).

Domestic difficulties and the Hague Convention revisited

Extant narratives argue that the Versailles Peace Treaty forced Germany to override long-standing pressure from the pharmaceutical industry on the issue of drug controls. Article 295 of the Versailles Peace Treaty of 1919 required signatories, including a defeated Germany, to implement the Hague Convention's provisions within twelve months. Other scholars such as Sebastian Scheerer suggest that German officials turned to reconsidering the Hague Convention in 1920 with their own control provisions on domestic commerce already in place. Scheerer notes that Germany only needed to adopt measures on export trade to comply with Article 295, doing so in December 1920. The archival record, however, supports a slightly different story. German officials were worried about domestic drug conditions and the Versailles dictates as early as 1919, and the pharmaceutical industry exerted little pressure over these deliberations.

In May 1919, the Interior Ministry called for a meeting of government officials to discuss control provisions (concerning import, export, and home distribution) for opium, morphine, and cocaine. The Interior Ministry noted that such discussions were necessary from the standpoint of public health, and that discussions should be held "before the final decision of the peace negotiations [at Versailles]."[35] At the 17 May meeting, representatives from the Economics and Interior Ministries, and the Health Office and Opium Commissioner argued for retaining the existing system of domestic distribution based on the provisions of 1917 and 1918. Given domestic drug needs in postwar Germany, however, representatives did not expect exports to be "an issue in the foreseeable future."[36]

Discussions focused explicitly on cocaine emerged during July of 1919. In correspondence with the Interior Ministry, Health Office representatives noted the growing problems with cocaine in the later years of the war and the views of "some doctors" that cocaine was "more dangerous than morphine." The Health Office also passed on the recommendation, "albeit radical," of Professor W. Strass, Director of the Institute of Pharmacology at Freiburg, that Germany should embrace a full policy of cocaine prohibition. The Health Office noted the potential problem with outside smuggling of cocaine if prohibition were tried, but also suggested that "since cocaine production is concentrated in a few areas in Germany greater oversight is possible." The report made no mention of the interests of the pharmaceutical industry or its supposed reaction to such steps.[37]

Though noting the concerns of some doctors, the Health Office's report did not picture the German medical community as a strong political force pushing against cocaine. Bruno Glaserfeld, a Berlin doctor writing in the medical journal, the *Deutsche Medizinische Wochenschrift*, in 1920, worried about the absence of discussions in the German medical journals of the "cocaine epidemic" and threats posed by "morphine and cocaine addiction."[38] The classic works in the German medical literature on the dangers of cocaine – by writers such as Louis Lewin, Ernst Jöel, and F. Fränkel – would not come until the mid-1920s, well after the Government's regulatory moves against cocaine.[39]

Throughout 1919, inter-ministerial deliberations continued on the question of extending the 1918 provisions on opiates to cocaine. Interior Ministry officials noted the general concerns of the cocaine industry with proposals for new restrictions. The industry's argument, as summarized by the Interior Ministry in mid-1920, was that the regulations of December 1918 made any additional provisions superfluous. Since the 1918 regulations did not address cocaine, however, the argument was not very convincing.[40]

Throughout 1920, discussions of cocaine became caught up in debates over implementing the provisions of the Hague Convention. On 30 April, the Foreign Office notified the Interior Ministry of receipt of the Versailles dictates (i.e. Article 295) and the need for action within twelve months. To avoid a potential domestic backlash over Germany's forced introduction of implementing legislation, the Foreign Office argued against publicizing details of the Hague agreement and called on the Interior Ministry to recommend the appropriate regulatory steps. Ministry officials followed this advice by largely closing the pharmaceutical industry out of the deliberations that followed.

In May 1920, the firm C.H. Böhringer wrote to both the Health Office and the Interior Ministry requesting a meeting, noting that it had heard from Merck officials about preliminary discussions around the impact of Article 295. The Health Office replied to the company that "it was too early to tell who would participate."[41] In reality, there would be little industry participation. Over the protests of firms such as C.H. Böhringer, for example, German officials simply extended domestic regulations to cocaine in July 1920.

From October through late November, Interior Ministry officials turned to the international trade provisions required by the Hague Convention. Officials circulated draft proposals of implementing legislation to allied ministries and to the Chancellor's Office for approval. However, the Interior Ministry did not schedule a meeting with industry representatives until 6 December, well after approval of the draft proposal. Three days following the industry meeting the Interior Ministry sent the draft legislation on to the Reichstag which passed the legislation on 17 December "without objection." The new provisions were implemented in February 1921.[42]

In sum, domestic drug problems and the need to secure drug stockpiles during the war prompted the German Government to create new regulations on pharmaceuticals in 1917. Postwar dislocations added to regulatory provisions for opium and morphine in 1918, ahead of international pressures for compliance with the Hague Convention. German steps against cocaine emerged in the mid-1920s as policy-makers faced mounting public problems with cocaine abuse. By the late 1920s, these steps became part of broader legislation passed to comply with the dictates of Article 295. In contrast to 1911 and the pharmaceutical industry's efforts to limit regulation of the wholesale trade, the industry played a minor role in postwar deliberations over drug control. The war and its dictates had shifted the bargaining process towards controls and the rulings of 1917 and 1918 changed the baseline against which regulatory issues would be judged. By 1919, the Weimar Government allowed scant industry input into the policy-making process. Firms adamantly opposed to regulation, such as C.H. Böhringer, were simply ignored. Others were consulted, but only after regulatory proposals had the approval of government offices.

Conclusion

Cocaine underwent a transformation from miracle drug to social menace in Germany, home to the world's leading cocaine producer, E. Merck. Most histories attribute this change mainly to the impact of international pressures. The Hague deliberations and the mandatory incorporation of the Hague Convention into the 1919 Versailles Peace Treaty, according to this argument, were able to override the political influence of a powerful German cocaine industry.

This chapter suggests an alternative interpretation that is based on an ongoing process of transformation from the late-nineteenth century through the early 1920s. In this long-term shift, the voice of the German pharmaceutical industry was weakened by problems of organizational fragmentation and limited collective interest on the issue of cocaine. Leading firms in this dispersed cocaine industry were more often interested in the regulatory environment around other drugs such as morphine. Unlike the United States and British cases discussed in this volume, the medical community, moral entrepreneurs, and media were largely silent during the German transformation. This would start to change with broader reactions to dramatic social changes of the mid- to late 1920s.[43]

More than international or business pressures, policy-makers in Imperial and Weimar Germany appeared to act from "bureaucratic politics," broadly defined

security interests (in protecting competitiveness and, later, in securing supplies), and perceptions of domestic drug abuse. These considerations resulted in regulations in 1911, and more extended controls in 1917, 1918, and 1920. Prewar issues of morphine distribution and addiction in the early twentieth century expanded into inter-ministerial deliberations over questions of access to medical supplies and curtailing drug abuse during and after the war. In the shift towards the domestic regulation of cocaine in 1920, neither the industry nor international pressure alone played a determining role.

Finally, although this chapter explores a time frame of roughly sixty years, its contribution to the history of cocaine's transformation remains incomplete. In the aftermath of the new regulations, German cocaine production fell off through the 1920s but problems with addiction and illicit trafficking, both domestic and now international, were on the rise. An estimated 10–20,000 cocaine users were found in Berlin by the late 1920s, getting cocaine on the street or in establishments linked to organized crime. German pharmaceutical corporations attracted international outcry for willing or unknowing participation in episodes of cocaine trans-shipment into Europe, the United States, and East Asia.[44] Cocaine, already deemed a social menace in Germany by 1920, would prove hard to expunge.[45]

Acknowledgments

The author wishes to thank the staffs of the German Central State Archive (Potsdam), Merck Archive (Darmstadt), United States National Archives (Washington, DC), the German Foreign Office Political Archive (Bonn), and the Interlibrary Loan Department at Marquette University; Paul Gootenberg, Lisa Kahraman, and volume contributors for comments during the revision process; and Paul Bovee, Xin Qing, and Haiyan Qu for their research assistance. Financial assistance for the larger project behind this chapter was provided by the American Council of Learned Societies, American Political Science Association, Bradley Institute for Democracy and Public Values, and Marquette University.

Primary sources: Germany

This chapter draws on United States, British, and German archival sources. For the United States, the chapter relies on State Department Diplomatic Records (Record Group 59), decimal file "International conferences, narcotics, 1910–29" (cited as 511.4A1/document /correspondents/date), from the United States National Archives, now in College Park, MD. British archival materials from the Foreign Office on early international control efforts have been complied and published in a useful multi-volume set, *The Opium Trade, 1910–1941* (Scholarly Resources, 1974). These materials are identified by document number, correspondents, and date.

For Germany, the chapter draws on public and private archives that have received scant attention in existing historiography on drug control. This gap partly reflects the scattered location, incomplete holdings, and misfiling of German archival records for the period. During my research in Germany in 1990–1, archive records of the Foreign Ministry were located in collections in Potsdam and Bonn. These include materials from the German Central Archive (Potsdam), Foreign Office Records, Division IIm, file "Drug and medical conferences" (cited as IIm volume/document/correspondents/date). This file covers the period 1910–11 and contains correspondence between the Foreign Office and Interior Ministry, and the Interior Ministry and Health Office (at times coded as III B document). The main repository of Foreign Office files is Bonn's Political Archive. Relevant files in this archive include German Foreign Office, Division II, file "The Hague embassy: opium 1907–11" (cited as II U/document/correspondents/date).

Records on drug control from 1912 through the 1920s are not in the Political Archive, nor were archivists with whom I spoke aware of their possible location or existence. The extensive photocopying of German archival records and publications of such records by United States occupation authorities also failed to reveal files on drug control subjects. Ironically, perhaps the most complete record of this period – including Foreign Office, Interior, Health, and company correspondence – is misfiled in the archives of the Interior Ministry located (in 1991) at the German Central State Archive in Potsdam. The relevant files were found in the Interior Ministry Records, Division II 5A, file "Distribution of opium and morphine" (cited as II 5A, volume/document if available [or page, 1919–]/correspondents/date).

The chapter also relies on the company archives of E. Merck, located in Darmstadt, Germany. Scholars have used the Merck collection for early links between Merck and Freud, but less attention has focused on Merck's interactions with other pharmaceutical companies and the German Government. Merck records include reports from the import and production divisions (*Jahresberichten der Einkaufs-Abteilung* and *Jahresbericht, Fabrik Abteilung* Ia) as well as files on international conferences. The latter include correspondence between firms, and firms and ministries. The primary file used here is coded as Merck Archive, file "Opium, Opium Konferenz," (by document title and/or correspondents/date). Other primary materials, such as *Guide Through the Exhibition of the German Chemical Industry, Colombian Exposition in Chicago 1893* (Berlin: Juliee Sittenfeld, n.d. [prob. 1893]) were obtained by request to the Merck archives in the United States.

Notes

1 Arnold H. Taylor, *American Diplomacy and the Narcotics Traffic, 1900–1939: A Study in Humanitarian Reform* (Durham: Duke University Press, 1969); S H Stern, *International Diplomacy, State Administration, and Narcotics Control: The Origins of a Social Problem* (Aldershot, UK: Gower Publishers, 1985).

2 This chapter expands on arguments developed in H. Richard Friman, *NarcoDiplomacy: Exporting the US War on Drugs* (Ithaca: Cornell University Press, 1996).

3 See Oriana J. Kalant, *Maier's Cocaine Addiction* (Toronto: Addiction Research Foundation, 1987), x, 19–21, 23, 278; Lester Grinspoon and James B. Bakalar, *Cocaine: A Drug and its Social Evolution* (New York: Basic Books, 1976), 17–20, 21, 23; Theodor Aschenbrandt, "Die psysiologische Wirkung und Bedeutung des Cocain. muriat. auf den menschlichen Organismus," *Deutsche Medicinische Wochenschrift* 50 (12 December 1883), 730–2; Karl Köller, "On the use of cocaine for producing an anesthesia in the eye," *The Lancet* (6 December 1884), 990–2; and Sigmund Freud, "Über Coca," in Robert Byck, MD, ed., *The Cocaine Papers: Sigmund Freud* (New York: Stonehill Publishing, 1974), 53–4.

4 Berndt Georg Thamm, *Drogen Report: Und nun auch noch Crack?* (Bergisch Gladbach: Gustav Lübbe, 1988), 85; Albrecht Hirschmüller, "E. Merck und das Kokain: Zu Sigmund Freuds Kokainstudien und ihren Beziehungen zu der Darmstädter Firma," *Gesnerus* 52 (1995), 116–32; Steven B. Karch, *The Pathology of Drug Abuse*, second edition, (New York: CRC Press, 1996), 1–10.

5 Freud, "Über Coca" (1974), 63.

6 Hirschmüller, "E. Merck und das Kokain" (1995), 119, 124–5, 130. To solidify its position in the British market, Merck also offered a limited price reduction (to 18 pence per grain) and made supplies of the drug available to "one or two well-known observers in order that its properties may be thoroughly investigated." Anon., "The price of cocaine," *The Lancet* (12 January 1885), 30.

7 Wilhelm Vershofen, *Wirtschaftsgeschichte der Chemisch-Pharmazeutischen Industrie, Dritter Band, 1870–1914* (Aulendorf: Editio Cantor KG, 1958), 38–9; and State Department Diplomatic Records, file International Conferences Narcotics, 1910–29, 511.4A1/no. 962 (Consul General, Berlin to Secretary of State, 7 January 1911).

8 Harry Loynd, "Parke Davis: The never ending search for better medicines," in *Addresses: The Newcomen Society in North America* No. 4 (New York: Princeton University Press, 1957), 12–15; Hermann Schultze, *Die Entwicklung der chemischen Industrie in Deutschland seit dem Jahre 1875* (Halle an der Saale: Tausch & Grosse, 1908), 106; and David F. Musto, *The American Disease: Origins of Narcotic Control* (New York: Oxford University Press, 1973), 7 (quote).

9 Hans Maier, *Der Kokainismus: Geschichte/Pathologie Medizinische und behördliche Bekämpfung* (Leipzig: Georg Thieme Verlag, 1926), 20; and Louis Lewin, *Phantastica: Die Betäubenden und Erregenden Genussmittel* (Berlin: Georg Stilke, 1924), 69.

10 Hirschmüller, "E. Merck und das Kokain" (1995), 131; and Karl-Ludwig Täschner und Werner Richtberg, *Koka und Kokain: Konsum und Wirkung* (Köln: Deutscher Ärte-Verlag, 1988), 27.

11 The shift also reflects the transformation of cocaine in United States markets. In addition to Chapter 2 by Spillane in this volume, see H. Wayne Morgan, *Drugs in America: A Social History, 1800–1980* (Syracuse: Syracuse University Press, 1981), 91; and David T. Courtwright, *Dark Paradise: Opiate Addiction in America before 1940* (Cambridge: Harvard University Press, 1982), 97–8.

12 Grinspoon and Bakalar, *Cocaine* (1976), 23; and Courtwright, *Dark Paradise* (1982), 97.

13 Musto, *The American Disease* (1973), 9–10. Musto contrasts the German situation with the United States where state and local regulations only began to emerge in the early 1900s.

14 See Erika Hickel, "Das Kaiserliche Gesundheitsamt (Imperial Health Office) and the chemical industry in Germany during the Second Empire: Partners or adversaries?," in Roy Porter and M. Teich, eds, *Drugs and Narcotics in History* (Cambridge: Cambridge University Press, 1995), 99–102. Hickel discusses in considerable detail how firms sought to influence the setting of purity standards.

15 IIm 20558/n.a. [coded as III B 3074] (Health Office to Interior Ministry, 25 May 1910, in III B 3074, Interior Ministry to Foreign Office, 15 June 1910). Maier (Kalant, *Maier's Cocaine Addiction* [1987], 40) argues that by 1910 "cocaine use in Central Europe was still limited to certain segments of the population of the large cities, particularly the decadent artistic circles in Paris, Berlin, London, and Munich."

16 Hickel, "Das Kaiserliche Gesundheitsamt," 99; IIm 20558/n.a. [III B 3074] (Interior Ministry tò Foreign Office, 15 June 1910; and Imperial Health Office to Interior Ministry, 25 May 1910 [in III B 3074]).

17 IIm 20558/5251 (Interior Ministry to Foreign Office, 26 June 1911); IIm 20558/n.a. (Louis Merck to Foreign Office, 6 January 1911); IIm 20558/n.a. (Imperial Health Office to Foreign Office, 1 April, 27 April 1911 [as III B 3029]); and IIm 20558/4090 (Interior Ministry to Foreign Office, 18 May 1911 [also as III B 3029]).

18 Schultze, *Die Entwicklung der chenischen Industrie* (1908), 289–90, 304; and see Friman, *NarcoDiplomacy* (1996), 20–32.

19 Vershofen, *Wirtschaftsgeschichte* (1958), 128–9; and Hickel, "Das Kaiserliche Gesundheitsamt," 97.
20 Vershofen, *Wirtschaftsgeschichte* (1958), 131–5.
21 Schultze, *Die Entwicklung der chemischen Industrie* (1908), 87; Vershofen, *Wirtschaftsgeschichte* (1958), 38–40; and *Guide Through the Exhibition of the German Chemical Industry, Columbian Exposition in Chicago 1893* (Berlin: Juliee Sittenfeld, n.d. [prob. 1893]).
22 The Merck figures in this table partially understate total crude cocaine purchases and resulting refined cocaine production by the company. For example, the inability of Kitz & Co. to meet Merck demand for crude cocaine as early as 1900 had led to Merck purchases of crude cocaine on the Hamburg market (as well as Java coca leaf purchases in 1904–5 of 5,000 kilos). Merck Archives, *Jahresbericht, Einkaufs-Abteilung*, 1904–5; and *Jahresbericht, Fabrik Abteilung Ia*, 1904–5.
23 Hirschmüller ("E. Merck und das Kokain" (1995), 121) notes that Merck's access to Java coca was facilitated by its share in a Java coca plantation. On Java trade see the chapters by Marcel de Kort and Steven Karch in this volume.
24 The literature here is extensive: see, for example, Taylor, *American Diplomacy and the Narcotics Traffic* (1969); Stein, *International Diplomacy* (1985); Friman, *NarcoDiplomacy* (1996); Bruce Johnson, "Righteousness before revenue: The forgotten moral crusade against the Indo-Chinese opium trade," *Journal of Drug Issues* 5 (1975), 307–16; and William O. Walker III, *Opium and Foreign Policy: The Anglo-American Search for Order in Asia, 1912–1954* (Chapel Hill: University of North Carolina Press, 1991).
25 Merck Archive, file Opium, Opium Konferenz (Merck to Interior Ministry, 21 November 1910; and Gehe to Merck, 18 November 1910).
26 511.4A1/1114 (United States Embassy, Berlin, to Department of State, 19 May 1911), 1133 (United States Embassy, Berlin, to Department of State, 24 May 1911).
27 IIm 20558/4090 (State Secretary of Interior to Foreign Office, 18 May 1911).
28 IIm 20558/5251 (Interior Ministry to Foreign Office, 26 June 1911).
29 IIm 20558/5251 (Interior Ministry to Foreign Office, 26 June 1911).
30 For example, the United States proposal that countries export only to those with proper import controls was viewed by participants as effective as a "punch in the water," useless given the dynamics of transit trade. Merck Archive, file Opium, Opium Konferenz ("Notes concerning a meeting on 24 October 1911 on the Hague Convention," 27 October 1911).
31 Merck Archive, file Opium, Opium Konferenz (Merck to Böhringer und Söhne, usw., 1 November 1911). As noted in 1911 by United States consular officials, "no statistics or reliable estimates of production and consumption of morphine and cocaine in Germany can be given, as no data are available for that purpose." 511.4A1/962 (Consul General, Berlin, to Secretary of State, 7 January 1911).
32 Friman, *NarcoDiplomacy* (1996), 21–2. For a more detailed discussion of the Hague deliberations, see Taylor, *American Diplomacy and Narcotics Traffic* (1969); and Stein, *International Diplomacy* (1985).
33 II 5A 10394/n.a. (Health Office to Interior Ministry, 23 July 1918; Interior Ministry to Chancellor, 8 August 1918); and Sebastian Scheerer, *Die Genese der Betäubungsmittelgesetze in der Bundesrepublik Deutschland und in den Niederlanden* (Göttingen: Otto Schwartz 1982), 41–2. On the 1911 provisions, see IIm 20558/5251 (Interior Ministry to Foreign Office, 26 June 1911).
34 Scheerer, *Die Genese der Betäubungsmittelgesetze* (1982), 43–7; and Maier (Kalant, *Maier's Cocaine Addiction* (1987), 49, 67) citing statistics from K. Bonhöffer and G. Ilberg, "Über Verbreitung und Bekämpfung des Morphinismus and Kokainismus," *Allg. Z. Psychiatrie* 83 (1925–6), 228.
35 II 5A 10395/pp. 26 (Economic Ministry to Interior Ministry, 8 May 1919), 28 (Brief by Dr Bourwieg, Interior Ministry, 19 May 1919).

36 II 5A 10395/pp. 30–2 ("Protocol over the meeting concerning the management of opium, opium alkaloids, and cocaine, 17 May 1919", 20 May 1919).
37 II 5A 10395/pp. 39–41 (Health Office to Interior Ministry, 19 July 1919).
38 Bruno Glaserfeld, "Über das gehäufte Auftreten des Kokainismus in Berlin," *Deutsche Medizinische Wochenschrift* (1920), 185–6.
39 For a literature review and discussion of cocaine research during the mid-1920s, see Berndt Georg Thamm, *Andenschnee: Die lange Linie des Kokain* (Basel: Sphinx Verlag, 1986).
40 II 5A 10395/p. 148. (Interior Ministry brief, regarding 17 May 1920 meeting on cocaine, 19 May 1920).
41 II 5A 10395/p. 194 (Foreign Office to Interior Ministry, 30 April 1920); II 5A 10395/pp. 217 (C.H. Böhringer Sohn to Interior Ministry, 27 May 1920); 219, (Health Office to Interior Ministry, 15 May 1920).
42 II 5A 10395/p. 377 (Interior Ministry to Economics Ministry, Finance Ministry, Statistical Office, Commissar for Export and Import, and the Prussian Ministries for Commerce and Industry and Public Welfare, 30 November 1920); 406 (Interior Ministry to Reichstag, 9 December 1920), 444 (Reichstag, 49th Session, 17 December 1920), 447 (President, Reichstag to Interior Ministry, 17 December 1920).
43 See for example: Walter Laqueur, *Weimar: A Cultural History* (New York: Putnam, 1974); Eberhard Kolb, *The Weimar Republic*, trans. P.S. Falla (London: Unwin Hyman, 1988); and Paul W. Chase, "The politics of morality in Weimar Germany: Public controversy and parliamentary debate over changes in moral behavior in the twenties." Unpublished Ph.D. dissertation (History), SUNY-Stony Brook, 1992.
44 Albert Wissler, *Die Opiumfrage: Eine Studie zur weltwirt schaftlichen und weltpolitischen Lage der Gegenwart* (Jena: Gustav Fischer 1931), 137; Thamm, *Andenschnee* (1986), 34; *New York Times* 16 August 1925; and Friman, *NarcoDiplomacy* (1996), 23–34.
45 Ibid. One difficulty was the disruption caused to German law enforcement by the war and the political problems of Weimar. For example, see Hsi-Huey Liang, *The Berlin Police Force in the Weimar Republic* (Berkeley: University of California Press, 1970); Raymond B. Fosdick, *European Police Systems* (New York: The Century Co., 1915); Johannes Buder, *Die Reorganisation des preussischen Polizei 1918–1923* (Frankfurt: Peter Lang, 1986); Richard Bessel, "Policing, professionalism and politics in Weimar Germany," in Clive Emsley and Barbara Weinberger, eds, *Policing in Western Europe: Politics, Professionalism and Public Order, 1850–1940* (Westport: Greenwood Press, 1991), 187–218; and Elaine Glovka Spencer, *Police and the Social Order in the German Cities* (DeKalb: Northern Illinois University Press, 1992).

5 Cocaine girls

Sex, drugs, and modernity in London during and after the First World War

Marek Kohn

Cocaine, drug panics, and "modernity"

At the turn of the century, cocaine was regarded in Britain as a useful element of the pharmacopoeia, rather than a miraculous one. Risks associated with its use were recognized, but were perceived to be largely confined to a particular category of person. In this perspective, the typical cocaine victim was highly strung, vulnerable to mental or intellectual pressure, and of relatively high social standing. Cocaine was seen as a menace to such individuals, but not to society.

That perception changed within the space of a few months during the First World War, when the drug was identified as a threat to soldiers. It was banned under emergency regulations, which were transferred to permanent legislation after the war. Cocaine dominated the first British underground drug scene, from around the middle of the war to the mid-1920s.

Strongly associated with women – prostitutes, actresses, nightclub dancers, "flappers" – it was at the center of a discourse that used anxiety about delinquent drug use as a means of articulating deeper fears about the transformations Britain was undergoing; particularly those involving female emancipation, pleasure, morality, and perceived threats from the outside world, symbolized by drug-dealing "men of color." The drug panic was a spasm of reaction, as Britain struggled to come to terms with modernity.

Cocaine in London, 1901–14

The first underground drug scene in Britain was largely contained within a single square mile of a single city, and lasted less than a decade. It might seem hardly worth bothering with, but in the context of this project it is particularly attractive. In the British historical record, it is possible to specify the moment when cocaine turned from miracle to menace: a phase about six months long, starting at the end of 1915, and culminating in a few weeks during which concern turned to moral panic. At that point, the possession of cocaine was made a criminal offense.

This chapter looks at the events of this phase in some detail, and then sketches out the subsequent development of the first British drug underground. There are three main episodes: the appearance of drug use as a subject of public and official concern in 1916; the first major drug scandal, following the death of an actress just after the Armistice in 1918; and the agitation about drugs that formed part of a wider reaction against postwar nightlife in the early 1920s. Throughout this period, cocaine was the most popular drug, and the most fervently condemned.

The action of this story takes place at the beginning of the twentieth century, in the sense nicely expressed by Eric Hobsbawm in the subtitle of his book, *Age of Extremes: The Short Twentieth Century, 1914–1991*.[1] Edwardian Britain was a perseveration of the Victorian era. Britons began to realize what the twentieth century meant when they found that the war against Germany would not be over by Christmas 1914. The drug underground was a product of wartime conditions, and the reaction against it was part of a wider reaction against modernity.

This early drug scene entailed several distinctive aspects of modernity that reached their full dimensions towards the end of the century. After the war, it was associated with an entertainment sector that was energetically transforming itself from an exclusive service for the élite into a consumer industry, expanding from nightclubs to dance halls. In these venues, drugs were associated with music of African-American derivation. They were associated with people of color as well, being perceived as agents of race-mixing. And above all, they were part of a moral sea change, which embraced the pursuit of pleasure for its own sake.

Both the transformation of mores that the drug underground implied, and the transformation of cocaine into a social menace, can be better appreciated in the light of a tragic incident at the beginning of the calendar twentieth century. On 16 July 1901, in the Bloomsbury district of London, Ida and Edith Yeoland committed suicide by swallowing cocaine. Having struggled to make careers for themselves on the stage, the sisters had decided, still both in their twenties, that they did not want to struggle any more.

In a note addressed to her mother, Edith Yeoland wrote that "It is not the fault of circumstance that has led to this – not a bit; for we should be the same under any condition. It is in ourselves, our temperaments in which our unhappiness dwells." She thus identified their unhappiness as constitutional, a view affirmed at the inquest in testimony to her sensitive, excitable temperament, her poor health, and proneness to depression.[2]

When Edith wrote that "we haven't the nerve to push," she meant not that they lacked boldness, but that they lacked nervous energy. The individuals believed to be peculiarly at risk from the pressures of modern life were those with the most refined and sensitive nervous systems, those who worked by brain rather than hand; professional men, businessmen, and "new" women, attempting to defy the inherent weakness of their sex by making their own way in the world. These "neurasthenic" – that is, "weak-nerved" – types were also those considered vulnerable to the "drug habit," as they might be tempted to use stimulants to provide the energy their systems naturally lacked.

Although Edith predicted in her note that people would call her and Ida "cowards, brutal and mad," their double suicide was reported with respectful sympathy. Commentators treated them as respectable women who were temperamentally unsuited to the precarious occupation they had chosen. There was no suggestion that their use of cocaine implied depravity, although the habitual taking of cocaine was depicted as a terrible vice:

> The habit grows rapidly; a mild 10 per cent solution obtained at a chemist's to cure a toothache has given many people a first taste of the joys and horrors of cocaine. The first effect of a dose is extreme exhilaration and mental brilliancy. The imagination becomes aflame. The after-effects – reaction, utter loss of moral responsibility, a blotched complexion, and the lunatic asylum or death.
>
> Yet any chemist will tell you that it has been increasingly in demand by women of late years.[3]

This account, by a columnist known as Guinevere, indicates some of the predominant perceptions of cocaine at the turn of the century. The habit was recognized to derive from routine medical use and ready availability; it was not associated with any subculture or other social grouping, beyond the general association with the professional and allied classes. (Although a tiny set of *fin de siècle* aesthetes experimented with drugs such as hashish and opium, cocaine held little interest for them.)[4]

These features are apparent in the case of the Yeolands. They were daughters of a silk merchant; they obtained the three bottles of cocaine with which they poisoned themselves by sending their landlady's servant to pick it up from a nearby chemist. A number of empty bottles were found in their room, suggesting that they had acquired the "habit." This is also suggested by the fact that they chose cocaine, presumably because they were familiar with it, rather than another poison. Opiates were also readily available, while carbolic acid had been the most commonly used poison in suicides over the preceding decade.

Guinevere's account also shows that cocaine was, significantly, already beginning to be identified as a women's drug. The association was not yet dominant, however, as another article prompted by the tragedy shows. The *Daily Mail* stressed the dangers of cocaine, including allegedly inevitable death, but did not allege that it stimulated violent or orgiastic excesses. The "fiend" was actually said to become more refined, but also more dishonest; which perhaps has a grain of truth in it.[5]

The paper informed its readers that any West End chemist could tell of cocaine victims, among whom were the "cleverest" people – doctors, writers, politicians, artists. Cocaine had not, however, reached the common people. There is no evidence to suggest otherwise. While stories of the so-called opium dens of Limehouse had long been a perennial of popular journalism, establishing thè genre of voyeuristic drug reportage and confirming that the public had an appetite for it, no equivalent reports of a working-class cocaine scene were to emerge until the First World War. As for so much of the century, Britain was about fifteen years behind the United States. In 1903, the inventory of cocaine-using types drawn up by the Committee on the Acquirement of Drug Habits already included "bohemians, gamblers, high- and low-class prostitutes, night porters, bellboys, burglars, racketeers, pimps, and casual laborers."[6]

It should perhaps be borne in mind that such claims were shaped by precon-ceived ideas about what class of person would be likely to take cocaine. The person who bought the cocaine for the Yeolands was a servant; perhaps other working-class individuals also purchased cocaine for their own use, or that of their peers. They could have done so without constituting a subculture, and they would not have been committing criminal offenses, so they might well have escaped the attention of officials or charity workers.

Alternatively, the principal enthusiasm for cocaine in the 1870s and 1880s had been among doctors. In the absence of modern mass media, familiarity with the drug may not have diffused far beyond the medical profession, penetrating only adjacent layers of society. The sequence, "doctors, writers, politicians, artists," suggests how first-hand knowledge of the drug's use might have moved across overlapping social circles.

It seems likely that a second source of diffusion was introduced to Britain – or more specifically the West End of London – in the years just before the outbreak of the Great War. Looking back from the perspective of 1922, the crime writer, Edgar Wallace, said that cocaine had been introduced to London nightlife by a visiting American theatrical troupe, performing a show called *Come Over Here*, and a second group of American chorus girls who appeared in another production. He recalled that he had first come across the drug in 1911, when one such performer had shown him a silver box of it.[7]

Whether or not Wallace was justified in making such a precise claim, the first London drug underground was so localized that it could well have been seeded by two small parties of visitors. The West End was a fertile habitat for an underground drug scene because it was small and crowded. Those in search of pleasure made their way there, as did those seeking to make a living out of selling pleasure, in various forms. The result was that theater, song, dance, spectacle, drinking, nightclubbing, and sex were all concentrated in a small zone right in the center of the metropolis. In other words, in the West End, pleasure was polymorphous. Hedonists would tend to encounter more than one variety, and many would be on the lookout for new forms.

For those selling such services, a stimulant drug had a particular appeal. Wallace remarked that the chorus girl who showed him the box of cocaine had been listless before the show, then suddenly appeared very lively when on stage. Cocaine enabled tired, poorly paid women to perform energetically and vivaciously. For very similar reasons, the drug also held an attraction for prostitutes. Nowadays, prostitutes who use opiates or cocaine are generally assumed to sell sex in order to support their habits. Before prohibition, the cost of cocaine was relatively modest, suggesting that when prostitutes took the drug, it was to support them in their work.

The nature of the economy in which such women made their living was fundamental to the development of the underground drug scene. The West End was a zone of casual employment, with no clear boundaries between the legitimate and the criminal sectors. For many women, prostitution might have been one option among a range of uncertain occupations from which they could derive a usually meager income. A woman could have performed sweated labor as a dressmaker, secured a temporary engagement in a chorus line, or sold sexual services, doing a bit of this and a bit of that as the opportunities arose.

A sense of this occupational milieu emerges from a small survey, conducted in 1921, of women who appeared on prostitution charges in two West End courts. Ten described themselves as domestic servants, and seventeen as dressmakers, the twin pillars of the low-wage female economy. Eight said they were chorus girls, three were clerical workers, and two were waitresses. (Just one woman actually identified herself as a prostitute.) A similar picture emerges from surveys conducted in Continental Europe in the 1890s and 1900s.[8]

The prominence of chorus girls in the court registers is an important clue to how the London underground drug scene may have arisen. Women who worked both as prostitutes and in the chorus would have mixed with street criminals on one hand, and women who had progressed beyond the chorus on the other, while the more successful of these actresses would be admitted to élite society circles. In the nightclubs (the vogue for which began in 1911) people of all ranks and stripes would rub shoulders – indeed, this was one of the main objections to such establishments. West End nightlife, based on theaters and clubs, was an island of social promiscuity in an era of rigid class barriers. It was a vertical section through a horizontal society.

Evolutionary theorists sometimes call this kind of structure a pre-adaptation. It takes shape in an organism under one set of evolutionary influences; conditions change, and it turns out to be suitable for a new purpose, as when fins turned into limbs. The West End of London was pre-adapted for a locally intense cocaine scene. There was an elective community committed to hedonistic pursuits. There was sufficient income, some of it derived from very wealthy individuals, to support the establishments where this community gathered. The drug itself could be readily obtained if pharmacists were prepared to disregard the regulations supposed to govern its sale. These were hardly stringent: pharmacists were supposed to know their customers, or to have been introduced to them, and to keep records of the transactions. But they shifted cocaine towards the black market – though probably not so far as to create a price barrier to its initial spread. A formidable population of local criminals would have the street wisdom to know which pharmacists to approach, and how; while the criminal charges that could be brought against them were flimsy at best.

The West End's war

With the outbreak of war, the central location of the West End became another element in the ecology of the embryonic drug underground, possibly a decisive one. Central London became the logistical focus of the war. Troops were funneled in from the regions, or from overseas, and dispatched to the Front from the southern railway termini, the resonantly named Victoria and Waterloo. London was also a magnet for servicemen on leave, whether from France or from camps in southern England.

Various concerns were expressed about the moral life of the wartime capital. For much of the war, YMCA officials pestered the police with reports that soldiers were being drugged by prostitutes and robbed in the vicinity of the rail termini, on the basis of claims made by servicemen who woke up to find their wallets missing, but insisted they had drunk no more than a single glass of beer.[9] This was essentially an expression of concern about the men's moral welfare, using the allegations of robbery in a vain attempt to get the police to crack down on prostitutes. The police certainly had their work cut out dealing with expressions of the camp-follower outlook, to which the bushes of Hyde Park and the register of the Marlborough Street Police Court bore witness.

A strident moralism soon became a feature of war policy. Concern over the effect of drinking on industrial production prompted David Lloyd George's famous declaration in 1915 that "We are fighting Germans, Austrians and Drink, and so far as I can see, the greatest of these deadly foes is Drink." Though the class the then Minister of Munitions was worried about was the proletariat, whom the war had brought full employment and raised wages, it was especially important that all levels of society should be seen to be in it together. To this end, the King announced in April 1915 that he and his family would abstain from alcohol for the duration.

Neither the State nor the influential temperance lobby placed all their faith in voluntary measures. Hitherto, London pubs had been allowed to open between five in the morning and half past twelve at night. In November 1915, they were restricted to two hours at lunchtime and three in the evening. (They remained subject to a similar regime until the late 1980s, closing at half past ten in much of the country.) Beer was made weaker but trebled in price; the effect of these and other measures was to halve alcohol consumption during the war, and to cut drunkenness convictions by three-quarters. Against this background, any other form of intoxication would stand out all the more starkly.

So too would any class of recreational venue that failed to show appropriate restraint. The principal instrument of wartime emergency regulation was the "Defence of the Realm Act" (DORA). Introduced as a counter to espionage or sabotage, it gradually expanded into a compendium of state interference: freezing rents, controlling the price of milk, preventing people from loitering near bridges, and requiring the registration of racing pigeons. Under its "Beauty Sleep Order," restaurants were obliged to turn their lights off at ten, and theaters to finish their performances by ten-thirty.

Nightclubs, however, were not covered by the order, and to the indignation of a lobby led by *The Times* newspaper, London clubs continued to defy the spirit of patriotic sobriety by staging events such as an "Apache night" and a "Bacchanalia revel."[10] In November 1915, the Home Secretary responded with the Clubs (Temporary Provisions) Act, though this measure still permitted nightclubs to stay open till midnight at weekends. Shortly afterwards, however, a uniform closing time of nine-thirty was set for restaurants, pubs, and nightclubs alike. In response, the clubs went underground; by the end of the year, there were 150 illegal clubs in Soho alone.

It was just at that point that hints of a vogue for drug-taking began to surface in the press. Quex, the gossip columnist of the *Evening News*, reported a conversation with a celebrated French actress, who spoke of her regret that many of her fellow actresses in Paris had "succumbed to the opium craze – one of the results of the war." The police in London were keeping an eye on the matter, Quex informed his readers. "It is an evil which has grown insidiously since the war."[11]

The following week, Quex brought the topic closer to home:

> I see that other people are turning their attention to the growing craze for opium smoking, to which I referred last week. West End Bohemia is hearing some dark stories of what is going on. But still more prevalent is the use of that exciting drug cocaine. It is so easy to take – just snuffed up the nose; and no one seems to know why the girls who suffer from this body and soul racking habit find the drug so easy to obtain.
>
> In the ladies' cloakroom of a certain establishment two bucketfuls of thrown-away small circular cardboard boxes were discovered by the cleaners the other day – discarded cocaine boxes.[12]

"That exciting drug" might have thrived in the West End even without the constraints placed upon legitimate recreation. But if people were breaking the rules simply by staying out late at night, they might feel less attached to other norms. And by going underground for their entertainment, they would probably have come into closer contact with the delinquent and criminal elements at large in the West End. By analogy with the idea of pre-adaptation, we might say that the social group that took up cocaine was pre-criminalized by the regime imposed on nightlife.

It is also possible that the impediments placed in the way of alcohol consumption encouraged some people to turn to other intoxicants. One contemporary argument to this effect noted specifically that bottled stout, the chorus girls' favorite tipple, had become unavailable.[13] The eccentricity of the suggestion highlights the limited persuasiveness of such explanations in general. More important, surely, were the milieu and mores that encouraged young women to seek intoxication at all.

All considerations of drug use must take availability into account, however, and the alcohol drought must be noted as a factor in the ecology of the drug scene. By the same token, so must the availability of cocaine. According to Quex, it was there in bucketfuls. Whatever the true quantities, however, it seems reasonable to presume that demand could be met from retail outlets. Import by smuggling would have been difficult, since the world's major manufacturer of cocaine was Germany. However, stocks of German cocaine held in Britain were large enough to service a contraband export traffic to India.[14]

Early attempts by the police to suppress cocaine dealing were ineffective, but documents accumulated during their investigations afford us a glimpse of the nascent cocaine economy in extreme close-up. One night in the spring of 1916, two detectives arrested a man called William Johnson in a street off Charing Cross Road, after they saw him accost two women passing by. "I am only trying to sell cocaine," he is said to have protested. Johnson had eleven boxes of the drug in his possession. He told the officers that he sold these for 2 shillings and sixpence ("half a crown") each, making ninepence profit. The boxes contained two and a half grains of the drug, for which the wholesale price was a penny a grain.

Press reports around this time said that half-crown boxes generally contained one and a half grains. This suggests that cocaine was sold in units of between a tenth and a sixth of a gram. By comparison, a survey of New York cocaine sniffers in 1983 recorded an average weekly consumption of four and a half grams, while heavy users might consume such a quantity in a day. The West End trade appears to have been geared to casual or light users only, which supports the idea that local pharmacists could have met the demand.

Johnson had been a porter at a nearby café, said by the police to be "patronised chiefly by prostitutes and Continental undesirables." Aged twenty-six, he had a string of convictions for larceny, and lived with a prostitute. He got his supplies from a thief called Alfy Benjamin, named as a member of a drug-dealing gang in a letter received by the police, purporting to come from exiled Belgian detectives. The informants made a point of identifying several members of the gang as Jewish. Despite the passionate xenophobia and racism that was to inflame the public hue and cry over drugs, however, it never included a significant anti-Semitic strain. This was perhaps a curious omission, given the rich potential of anti-Semitic conspiracy lore on which it might have drawn.

Benjamin obtained the cocaine from a pharmacist's at the back of Leicester Square, the heart of the theatrical and entertainment district. Two years later, this shop was named as a source of drugs, both cocaine and heroin, in a scandal following the death of an actress. Cross-examined in court, the pharmacist, Thomas Wooldridge, was forced to claim that he had "forgotten" about 6 ounces of cocaine he was found to have supplied. Strategically located, and cultivating actresses as customers, Wooldridge was certainly a principal supplier to the West End drug underground.

Police operations during the first few months of 1916 confirmed the existence of an underground drug trade based on cocaine. The reason for their attentions, and the factor that turned dark rumors in gossip columns into Britain's first full-blown drug panic, was the identification of cocaine as a threat to the soldiery. It was accompanied by the labeling of cocaine use as a transatlantic import. The cultural microclimate was suitable, the supply networks were activated, and now the key symbolic elements of the drug panic came together. Cocaine turned into a social menace once it signified foreign threat as well as sex, hedonism, young women, and moral peril. That was an explosive combination.

By January 1916, a Canadian major stationed near Folkestone had been trying for some time to find out who was supplying cocaine to men under his command, forty of whom, by his reckoning, were addicted to the drug. That month, a corporal finally trapped the dealers by buying packets of "snow" from a man called Horace Kingsley and a woman called Rose Edwards. According to Edwards, a London prostitute, she in turn obtained the drug from a man in a West End pub – "He sells it to all of us girls." The price she charged the corporal, two and sixpence, suggest that norms had already emerged in the clandestine drug market.[15]

The pair's use of the slang term was significant. It was a sign that a subculture was emerging. So was the fact that it was an imported term. Whether they picked it up from their Canadian customers, or whether it was already current in their native West End haunts, the cocaine underground was acquiring an American accent.

The involvement of servicemen gave the law a purchase over the dealers. Kingsley was charged with "selling a powder to members of HM Forces, with intent to make them less capable of performing their duties." Existing laws were framed to counter doping in the transitive sense, where one party administers drugs to another for nefarious purposes. They did not recognize the phenomenon of voluntary intoxication by agents other than alcohol. In this instance, however, the dubious premises of the charges were overlooked. Kingsley and Edwards got six months' hard labor.

The same week, more respectable defendants were also convicted on charges involving the supply of cocaine, and morphine, to soldiers. The long-established pharmacists, Savory & Moore, were fined over packages of drugs advertised in *The Times* as a "useful present for friends at the front." They were charged with selling morphine and cocaine to one particular individual without an introduction and without recording his name and address. Harrods, the famous department store, was also fined for selling these preparations. *The Times* described cocaine as a threat to soldiers "more deadly than bullets."[16]

The week before that, a young Canadian officer called Georges Codere had been convicted of bludgeoning a canteen sergeant to death in order to rob him. Witnesses testified to Codere's violent and bizarre behavior; one said that it was as if he had been doping himself.[17] This seems to have been the basis of subsequent remarks in the press that Codere was a cocaine addict. In turn, Codere and the Folkestone case seem to have formed the basis of the public belief that Canadians had brought the cocaine craze to Britain.

A more likely scenario is that Canadian soldiers, who had a reputation for ferocity in battle and unruliness off duty, encouraged the growth of the cocaine underground by increasing demand in the emerging local market. Canadians would have participated in the classical delinquent subcultures that had become established in the United States by this time. Delinquents in North America have traditionally been peripatetic, seeking out new haunts and keeping a step ahead of the consequences of their actions. They would therefore have been likely to encounter and transmit subcultural drug-taking practices.

The way of life is described in Francis Chester's *Shot Full: The Autobiography of a Drug Addict.*[18] Chester tells of leaving the ailing family farm in Canada and getting a job as a messenger boy in New York, where he finds he is delivering packages of cocaine, known as "joy dust." He starts to use drugs, and sells "decks" – paper packets – of heroin for a dollar a time. After falling into an itinerant life of jail, hopping freight trains, and working petty scams, he heads back to Canada, taking a morphine habit with him. Eventually, finding it difficult to afford drugs on what he makes from casual work, he joins the army.

In October 1915, his unit arrives in England, and is posted to Folkestone. He spends much of his time malingering or absent without leave, heading first for Leicester Square to look for drugs. He draws a blank in two favorite haunts of overseas soldiers, the Leicester Lounge and the Province Lounge (though the latter – correctly, the Hotel Provence – was named in the Belgians' letter to the police as the place where William Johnson's "woman" sold cocaine). He hears, however, that "junk" is sold around Shaftesbury Avenue:

> secreted in the packets of postcards of 'Views from London' which were so popular with Dominion visitors. One packet cost only 5s. A woman pedlar told me that she sold ten times more 'snow' than she did morphine, and it was only the Colonials who used it, except some of the ladies of pleasure.

Perhaps, at 5 shillings rather than two and six, he was being quoted the tourist price. But although Chester obviously embroiders, exaggerates, and invents, his account appears to be based on real experience in the drug underworld. The participation of Canadians like him in the British drug scene would have introduced a new delinquent cohort, increasing the proportion of such characters involved. Chester's account of the background to his enlistment also suggests that the Canadian forces may have been something of a haven for delinquents, like the French Foreign Legion. These would be at the extreme of a selective tendency that would tend to stock overseas contingents, less well-placed than domestic regiments to benefit from the patriotic spirit, with men who were readier than the average to take risks and depart from norms.

Canadian soldiers were also alleged to be victims rather than perpetrators. "We have received several complaints in this district respecting cocaine," a police inspector noted in the file raised in response to the Belgians' accusations, "and in many cases it was alleged that it was given to Canadian soldiers by prostitutes in order that they could be robbed." This seems to have been an elaboration on the soldier-doping claims that had arisen in late 1915; these tended to specify cocaine, in evident ignorance of its stimulant properties, as the drug's notoriety grew.

A doctor interviewed by the police said in May 1916 that cocaine use had "greatly increased during the last year or so." Though most of the users he encountered were prostitutes, he had occasionally seen Canadian soldiers under its influence.

In the opinion of one of the sergeants who arrested William Johnson, there was no point in taking further action against the cocaine traffic without greater legal sanctions. After the Folkestone case, the authorities gave themselves firmer powers regarding military personnel. An Army Council order issued on 11 May 1916 banned the unauthorized supply to soldiers of drugs including cocaine, morphine, opium, heroin, barbiturates, and cannabis. A few convictions were secured under this measure. But as far as the police were aware, soldiers were at most an incidental element in the street trade. William Johnson had been trying to sell cocaine to fellow civilians. As he was not seen to actually make a sale, he was acquitted. Even if he had been convicted, he would have been liable to a maximum penalty of £5. The law was designed for the pharmacist's shop, not for the street.

The Assistant Commissioner of Police, who favored making the unauthorized sale of drugs illegal (he made no comment on whether to criminalize their possession), recognized that the police had lost the battle but might thereby win the war:

> The prominence given in the Press to the failure of the prosecution in this case would probably make it easy to pass a Bill to amend the law: it will – unless there is legislation – embolden traffickers in this dangerous drug. There is evidently more money to be made out of it than most people wld [*sic*] have supposed.

His assessment was shrewd. Although the police failed to secure a conviction, the hearing had given them a platform from which to set out a case for strengthening the law, a measure endorsed by the magistrate. The police counsel suggested this could be achieved by an addition to the Defence of the Realm Act; and that was the course eventually taken.

Primed by the Johnson case and the earlier incidents, the press made up for a lack of further news developments with increasingly lurid stories, backed up by a clutch of sensationalist drug films imported from the United States, with titles like *The Curse Of A Nation*, *The Curse Of The Poppy*, and *Black Fear*. The style and the themes of the stories also betray the influence of American drug rhetoric; sometimes explicitly, as in a reference to cocaine having "demoralised the negroes of Alabama, and caused outrages of the most terrible description." The headlines to that particular article give a vivid impression of what the public was now being told about cocaine: "Vicious Drug Powder – Cocaine Driving Hundreds Mad – Women And Aliens Prey On Soldiers ... LONDON IN THE GRIP OF THE DRUG CRAZE ... SECRET 'COKE' PARTIES OF 'SNOW SNIFTERS'."[19]

Quite suddenly, the drug panic had arrived. "From a habit much more vicious but fortunately much more rare even than that of veronal [a barbiturate], the use of cocaine has become in six months a veritable mania, an obsession only too terribly common among the women who haunt the West End at night," the *Daily Chronicle* announced. It described the sight of soldiers, desperate for the drug, crawling on their hands and knees into chemist's shops. In the editorial column, the paper called for possession of cocaine to be criminalized.[20]

"Practically unknown a few years ago, cocaine-taking has spread like wildfire in all classes of the community until, next to alcoholism, it is far and away the commonest form of drug-taking," stated the *Evening News*.[21] Another article in the same paper claimed that "Social workers, mental experts and police officials all bear testimony to the ravages of the drug habit among young women, especially of the leisured class that regards itself as Bohemian." The piece identified nightclubs as foci for the drug's spread, claiming that cocaine had become popular in these venues to dispel fatigue; this was also its appeal to weary soldiers. It suggested that the traffickers were individuals who had been run out of Paris and Belgium by police action and the war.[22]

We should of course be aware of the danger of projecting the immense power of today's media back upon an earlier age. But it seems reasonable to believe that Britain's first media drug panic would have had some influence upon policy-makers. They would not have seen what the sensationalist *Umpire* had to say about the "negroes" of Alabama, but they would have read in *The Times* that cocaine was calculated to kill the natives of India in three months.

The broad tendencies in mores and social policy were also conducive to stricter regulation. Above all, the Great War years saw a massive extension of the powers of the State, while, at the same time, prevailing standards of moral orthodoxy were not seriously challenged until after the war had ended. One of the most significant characteristics of the new powers established during the emergency was their tendency to become entrenched afterwards. Pub opening hours were one example; drug criminalization was another.

It is difficult to discern any clear direction in the specific area of drug control. Britain had been lukewarm about the 1909 Shanghai Opium Commission, the first of the prewar series of international drug conferences promoted by the United States: the British considered that they had already taken the necessary action to curtail the opium traffic from India to China. They were concerned during this period that any international control regime should not compromise the interests of British drug companies, who led world morphine production. Britain did, however, accept the decision of the 1912 Hague Conference that the use of cocaine, morphine, and opium be confined to "legitimate medical purposes."

Historian Virginia Berridge argues that, by 1914, it looked likely that when Britain eventually did implement the Hague Convention, it would do so by "little more than the extension of existing pharmacy laws governed by professional self-regulation." She observes that no government department wanted the responsibility of controlling drugs. The Foreign Office, the Board of Trade, and the Home Office all managed to pass the buck, leaving it with an equally reluctant Privy Council Office, which would presumably have been inclined to leave the professions to look after themselves.[23]

With the onset of war and the expansion of the State, ministries became more involved in the control of drugs. As well as the West End cocaine scene, they faced the issue of drug smuggling from British ports; cocaine to India, opium and morphine to the Far East. Alfred Holt & Co., who owned a shipping line implicated in the traffic, circulated a memorandum on the subject to Government departments. At an interdepartmental meeting to discuss the memorandum, held on 19 June 1916, Sir Malcolm Delevingne of the Home Office argued that the "most convenient" way of dealing with the problem would be by a Regulation under the Defence of the Realm Act. He acknowledged the difficulty that "its bearing on the 'Defence of the Realm' is neither very direct nor important," but argued that "the only alternative method would be legislation which may be difficult to get and would possibly not be regarded as uncontroversial."

Delevingne's concern was mainly with the international traffic – an interest that sustained over an energetic twenty-year career, and culminated in his involvement in forming the League of Nations drug policy. The police and army were more concerned with local issues. "At present there is believed to be an extensive sale to all and sundry by retailers of Malthusian appliances, quack medicines and that class of offensive literature which we have long and vainly sought powers to deal with," the Commissioner of the Metropolitan Police, Sir Edward Henry, complained to the Home Office.

He reported that among the known dealers caught in possession of cocaine were a pair of thieves and a man charged with soliciting males for immoral purposes. Henry favored criminalization, and the imprisonment of some of those convicted of possessing cocaine.

> It might then be possible to deal severely with the unauthorized persons who, using as their tools burglars, thieves, prostitutes, sodomites, men living upon the earnings of women and other nefarious persons, are at present with impunity doing such infinite harm

In other words, he was concerned with suppressing the activities of the petty criminal underworld. From such a perspective, all such activities ought to be unequivocally criminal. The fact that cocaine users were only committing trivial infractions was an anomaly that ought to be rectified.

Despite Henry's vehemence, the controls he favored fell far short of comprehensive drug prohibition. His animus was specifically directed against cocaine, "the most baneful drug in the whole Pharmacopoeia"; on the other hand, he opposed sanctions against opium, "which in most of its forms is a more or less beneficent drug." British establishment figures quite often took a benign view of opium; partly, perhaps, as collective self-justification for Britain's involvement in the opium trade, partly because their observation of opium use by colonial subjects suggested that its effects were not catastrophic. But for Henry, as for drug prohibitionists in general, cocaine was damned by the company it kept.

The edict that resulted from the discussions, Defence of the Realm Regulation 40B, concentrated on cocaine. Issued on 28 July 1916, it outlawed possession of the drug for everybody except doctors, pharmacists, veterinary surgeons, and holders of prescriptions for it, which were non-repeatable. Possession of opium was also banned.

After "DORA," 1916–22

In the short term, the effects of DORA 40B were scarcely dramatic. A trickle of defendants was convicted for breaking its stipulations on cocaine – a Canadian soldier here, a young woman there. DORA 40B probably subdued the West End cocaine scene, and certainly drove it firmly underground. But the regulation failed to extirpate clandestine drug use, as was revealed by investigations following the death of a well-known actress after a Victory Ball in November 1918.

The ensuing scandal was the pivot upon which the entire drug panic turned. It bridged the first phase, of 1916, and the second, which reached its peak in 1922. Whereas the narratives of the 1916 hysteria had lacked major characters – and none of the minor ones were at all sympathetic – Billie Carleton personified the dope drama. She allowed the public to understand drug-taking in terms of a single, personal tragedy, and stood as the type-specimen for cocaine victims for many years afterwards. The trial of her friend, Reggie de Veulle, who was charged with her manslaughter, was the first major criminal case related to cocaine and the underground drug scene. Its centerpiece was the description of an occasion on which a "circle of degenerates" including Carleton and de Veulle spent the night reclining on cushions in pajamas and nightdresses, smoking opium brought from Limehouse. De Veulle's wife admitted trying the pipe, but insisted she did not inhale.[24]

A number of points about the judicial aspects of the case are worth noting. First, though the inquest concluded that Carleton had died of a cocaine overdose, this appears unlikely. She certainly used cocaine, and had done so on the night of her death; she undoubtedly died as a result of taking drugs, but on the available evidence the agent responsible appears to have been a depressant rather than a stimulant; possibly the barbiturate veronal. Both coroner and judge emphasized the toxicity of cocaine, suggesting that even a very small dose might well prove fatal.

Second, this was the first major episode in which an attempt was made to impose the categories of victim and culprit upon a relationship of drug-taking equals, each of whom supplied drugs to the other. But the evidence scarcely supported the idea of de Veulle as a lecherous seducer and corrupter of young womanhood, in the mold of Victorian melodrama. Moreover, the illegality of drug taking had not yet been consolidated. At the inquest, the coroner acknowledged that the jury might "not feel inclined to press hardly" in a case where the illegality arose solely from emergency war regulations, or might feel that such regulations ought not to be the basis of a constructive manslaughter charge. Nevertheless, the case occurred after a decisive shift in both the public perception and the control of drugs such as cocaine. Before jailing de Veulle on a secondary charge of conspiracy to supply cocaine, the judge observed that it was "a strange thing to reflect that until quite lately these drugs could be bought by all and sundry like so much grocery."[25]

The case consolidated the symbolic structures of the drug panic. The Lime-house connection had involved a Chinese man and his Scottish wife, dealing in cocaine as well as opium. Drugs were understood to dissolve barriers of race and sex as well as of class. The clandestine nature of the practice spoke to the kind of paranoid mentality that had been firmly convinced that Zeppelin airships were launched not from Germany, but the backyards of German bakers in London.[26] Just as rumors of conspiracy had flourished during the war, conspiracies involving the drug traffic thrived in popular fiction. Sax Rohmer linked drugs and the Yellow Peril in the figure of Fu Manchu, an oriental genius at the center of a secret network bent on world domination. Rohmer also produced an exuberant fantasy, "Dope," based on the Carleton episode.

In 1920, DORA 40B was transferred to permanent legislation as the Danger-ous Drugs Act. By then, the jazz craze was under way, touching off a boom in nightclubs and dance halls. This, the British apprehensively realized, was the sound of the new world; chaotic, Dionysian, American, African, and altogether Other.

Young women were seen to be at the forefront of the dance craze, which was one manifestation of a general reaction against the trauma of war. It had overtones of mania and undertones of desperation, personified in the figure of Freda Kempton. She was a "dance instructress," or paid dancing partner, in a West End club. Her way of life kept her up all night, dancing and making the rounds of the West End club circuit. It is easy to see why she found cocaine useful, though she had to chew gum to mask the grinding of her teeth. Her income as well as her social life would have depended on being able to remain energetic and vivacious.

In April 1922, however, she committed suicide by swallowing cocaine. The reason is uncertain, but she appears to have been depressed for some time before. Her death triggered a new hue and cry about "dope," this time aimed at nightclubs - "dance-dope dens" - many of which were operating illegally. It also introduced a new figure to the dope narrative, a Chinese restaurateur named Brilliant Chang. Though he never faced charges arising from the allegation that he had supplied Kempton with the fatal dose, he became the object of keen police attention. Several of his employees were arrested on drug charges, after being seen offering cocaine to women in the restaurant or in the streets of Soho nearby. They joined a stream of working-class street dealers, male and female, apprehended by police action during this period. By the mid-1920s, the drug underground had faded out. The efforts of the police no doubt played a part, but it had probably run its course anyway.

What the dope narrative gained with Chang, who was eventually jailed for cocaine possession in 1924, was a counterpart to the figure of the female victim. The genre remained that of the Victorian melodrama, but since Reggie de Veulle had so signally failed to live up to the stereotype required of the male lead, the part had remained vacant. Chang was alleged to have supplied cocaine to Billie Carleton, and imagined connections between the two have been a feature of tales from the first British drug underground ever since.[27]

He was portrayed – with some justice – as an ardent seducer of young white women, for whom he was said to hold a mysterious appeal. Yet he was not only short in stature, but a member of a race perceived as effeminate in character. The explanation for the mysterious attraction must therefore be that oriental men were using drugs as aids to seduction. Hence the paradigmatic expression of the dope menace: that drug taking encouraged miscegenation between young White women and men of color.

The women themselves were depicted in terms of traditional notions of female frailty, with emphasis on the morbid variety classically associated with tuberculosis. In the words of one reporter, the "predominating type" was "young, thin, underdressed, perpetually seized with hysterical laughter, ogling, foolish."[28] Another described the sight of "three girl-addicts to cocaine" in a club.

> One was a frail-looking creature of about twenty in a flimsy frock that left three-quarters of her back bare. During the intervals of her vivacious danc-ing in an underground room, she gave herself over to almost hysterical attacks of inane, purposeless laughter, and now and then stroked the man sitting with her.[29]

Billie Carleton was said to have had "a certain frail beauty of that perishable, moth-like substance that does not last long in the wear and tear of this rough-and-ready world."[30] Three years later, a columnist wrote of Freda Kempton that "She was young, she was beautiful, and she danced ... it is evident that she was a foolish little moth whose wings were scorched by the flame of vicious luxury."[31]

Their tragedies, and the images of the "cocaine girls" haunting the West End, were to be read as awful warnings against female emancipation. Women had worked in factories during the war, driven ambulances under fire, and now many of them had been granted the vote. This was understood as a formal recognition of their capability to serve the nation in capacities outside the home. But their rights remained conditional. Women under twenty-seven were still denied the franchise, and conservative opinion derided the idea of "votes for flappers."

The young women of the West End, associated with the sale or the pursuit of pleasure, rather than with patriotic responsibility, were used as examples of the true nature of womanhood. Like the Yeoland sisters, they lacked nervous strength, and were ill-equipped to survive unprotected in the real world. The moral of the dope story was that the Victorians had been right about womanhood after all. It was not simply that cocaine accentuated the neurotic symptoms and self-destructive tendencies of those drawn to it, but that these symptoms were the female psyche writ large. Cocaine thus served to weave together several themes: young women's behavior, miscegenation, criminal delinquency, and hedonism in general. To varying degrees and in different ways, each of these was perceived as a menace.

Primary sources: Great Britain

Historians have neglected the milieu discussed in this chapter, making the sources rather more primary than one might wish. Virginia Berridge has published three articles about drugs during this period and Terry M. Parssinen has considered it in his book, *Secret Passions, Secret Remedies: Narcotic Drugs in British Society, 1820–1930* (Manchester/Philadelphia: Manchester University Press, 1983). These works served as the primer and point of departure for my book, *Dope Girls: The Birth of the British Drug Underground* (London: Lawrence & Wishart, 1992), on which this chapter is based. The great bulk of my research material came from the British Library's newspaper archive at Colindale, in North London. I concentrated on the popular press, for the vividness of their accounts, the vehemence of their pronouncements on moral and social issues, and their attention to detail. Among the many are the *Daily Chronicle*, the *Daily Mail*, the *Daily Sketch*, the *Empire News*, the *Evening News*, the *Folkestone Herald*, *John Bull*, the *News of the World*, *The Stage*, the *Sunday Pictorial*, and the *Umpire* – as well as *The Times* (of London). Memoirs of the age were also quite valuable.

The general history of British cocaine remains to be written: the British (especially in botany and medicine) played a notable if secondary role in the development of the drug. On coca promotion and botany, archives of the Royal Botanical Gardens (at Kew) hold interesting papers, as well as key published studies in their *Bulletin of Miscellaneous Information*. British drug-industry, pharmacy, and medical journals (*Chemist and Druggist*, *Pharmaceutical Journal and Transactions*, *The Lancet*, *British Medical Journal*, etc.) carry a good deal about cocaine in the late nineteenth century: one of the finer collections is found at London's Wellcome Institute for the History of Medicine. And the British *Pharmacopoeia* is a vital source, given keen interest in coca and cocaine among leading pharmacists like William Martindale. The Public Records Office in London (in Kew again) no doubt holds scattered untapped data on cocaine history, under jurisdiction of both the Foreign and Home Offices. Here, I consulted DPP4 50 and MEPO2 1698, prosecutor and police reports on London during the war. An accessible series of diplomatic papers on British roles in early drug-control conferences (in ten volumes) is *The Opium Trade, 1910–1941* (Wilmington, DE, Scholarly Resources, 1974). Finally, several British pharmaceutical firms were initially engaged in the making and marketing of cocaine (and coca wines), notably May & Baker and Burroughs-Wellcome, and who, someday perhaps, will allow researchers a peak at their pertinent papers.

Notes

1 Eric Hobsbawm, *Age of Extremes: The Short Twentieth Century, 1914–1991* (London: Michael Joseph, 1994). [Editor's note: the United States edition sports a different subtitle.] This chapter uses British spelling in original quotes and for British institutions; Paul Gootenberg assisted in composing "Primary sources."
2 *The Stage*, 18 July 1901, 25 July 1901; *Daily Mail*, 20 July 1901; *Reynolds's Newspaper*, 21 July 1901.
3 Quoted in *Daily Mail*, 22 July 1901.
4 Virginia Berridge, "The origins of the English drug 'scene' 1890–1930," *Medical History* 32 (1988), 51–64.
5 *Daily Mail*, 10 August 1901.
6 Lester Grinspoon and James B. Bakalar, *Cocaine: A Drug and its Social Evolution* (New York: Basic Books, 1985).
7 *John Bull*, 6 May 1922.
8 Hermann Mannheim, *Social Aspects of Crime in England between the Wars* (London: Allen & Unwin, 1940); Abraham Flexner, *Prostitution In Europe* (New York: Century Publishers, 1914).
9 Public Record Office (London), Metropolitan Police, MEPO2 1698 (1915).
10 *The Times*, 13 and 15 October 1915; 8, 19, and 20 November 1915.
11 *Evening News*, 29 December 1915.
12 *Evening News*, 3 January 1916.
13 *Empire News*, 8 December 1918.
14 Terry M. Parssinen, *Secret Passions, Secret Remedies: Narcotic Drugs in British Society, 1820–1930* (Manchester/Philadelphia: Manchester University Press, 1983).
15 *Folkestone & Hythe Advertiser*, 12 February 1916; *Folkestone Herald*, 12 February 1916.
16 *The Times*, 11–12 February 1916; Virginia Berridge, "War conditions and narcotics control: The passing of Defence of the Realm Act Regulation 40B," *Journal of Social Policy* 7 (1978), 285–304; "Drugs and social policy: The establishment of drug control in Britain 1900–30," *British Journal of Addiction* 79 (1984), 17–29.
17 *The Times*, 5 February 1916; Public Record Office (PRO), Director for Public Prosecutions, DPP4 50 (1916).
18 Francis Chester, *Shot Full: The Autobiography of a Drug Addict* (London: Methuen, 1938).
19 *Umpire*, 23 July 1916.
20 *Daily Chronicle*, 19 July 1916.
21 *Evening News*, 13 June 1916.
22 *Evening News*, 14 June 1916.
23 Berridge, "Drugs and social policy" (1984); "War conditions and narcotics" (1978).
24 *Daily Sketch*, 21 December 1918; *News of the World*, 26 January 1919.
25 *The Times*, 8 April 1919.
26 Michael MacDonagh, *In London During the Great War* (London: Eyre & Spottiswoode, 1935).
27 Including the recollections of Annie Lai, who by the time of her death was probably the last person to remember Chang from personal acquaintance, and a 1992 television production entitled *White Girls on Dope*, written by Tariq Ali (Bandung Productions for Channel 4, UK).
28 *Daily Express*, 14 March 1922.
29 *Evening News*, 14 March 1922.
30 *Sunday Pictorial*, 1 December 1918.
31 *Daily Express*, 10 March 1922.

6 Doctors, diplomats, and businessmen

Conflicting interests in the Netherlands and Dutch East Indies, 1860–1950

Marcel de Kort

This is a history of doctors, diplomats, and businessmen.[1] These three groups played a determining role in the transformation of cocaine from miracle to menace between 1860 and 1950. In the nineteenth century, doctors were among the first to hail cocaine as a great discovery but they also contributed to the definition of addiction as a disease. Moreover, it was they who rejected the use of the white powder outside the medical realm. This change in attitudes towards cocaine in the medical world must be seen as the underlying implicit cause for the national and international restriction of production, trade, and use during the first decades of the twentieth century.

The increasing popularity of coca and cocaine gave Dutch businessmen the idea of planting coca in the colony of the Dutch East Indies and of exporting its leaf to the West. This was a brilliant success by the beginning of the twentieth century as the Netherlands became the largest producer of coca and cocaine in the world. This situation ended in the 1920s as a result of the implementation of international treaties and national laws. Dutch diplomats tried to protect their economic interests by arguing that limits on the legal trade and production of cocaine would spur illegal trade that would be almost impossible to control. This was to prove a prophetic insight. By the beginning of the 1930s, the illegal drug trade in Europe took off and the battle against drugs was declared.

From medicine to mood-altering drug, 1884–1919

Early popular medicine

As was the case in most European countries in the nineteenth century, self-medication and popular medicine played a major role in health care in the Netherlands. A significant segment of the population, primarily the lower classes, was deprived of medical help from legally recognized physicians and depended to a large extent on self-medication. In the last decades of the century, products known as "secret medicines," "patent medicines," or "specialties" became especially widespread. Druggists, pharmacists, and grocers sold these packaged remedies, the ingredients of which were frequently unknown. Advertisements for innumerable specialties filled newspapers and magazines with claims of effectiveness for many types of ailments. Coca and opiates were vital ingredients in these specialties. In the 1870s many specialties with coca were introduced as new wonder drugs, some in pill form, like "Dr Alvarez's Coca Pills," but primarily in liquid form, such as an "Anti-nausea" for nervousness, "Quina-coca," and "Vin de Coca du Pérou de Chevrier." Dr Sampson's Coca Preparations, according to its advertisements, could cure almost any illness. Remedy Number One helped against throat, breast, and lung complaints; Number Two against digestive problems and hemorrhoids; Number Three against "general nervous weakness, hypochondria, hysteria, etc. and particularly against certain weak conditions (sperm loss, impotence, etc.)." "Dr Sampson's Coca Spirits" relieved "cranial gout and blinding headaches."[2]

Cocaine in medical practice

Initially, recognized physicians also prescribed such specialties for their patients. This changed, however, towards the end of the nineteenth century when medicine began to turn towards scientific methods. Academically trained doctors rejected natural philosophy medicine and believed that their new clinical methods, based on scientific knowledge, provided better results. The tendency towards a more scientific approach to medicine went hand in hand with the professionalization of medical practice. One of the characteristics of this professionalization was the support and dependency of patients, which was enhanced by physician power to write prescriptions, in a more closely regulated drug trade.[3] Competition arose between academically trained doctors and the proponents of popular medical practices. As part of this struggle, doctors began to campaign strongly against the unregulated trade in remedies. At first no reference was made to possible addictive effects of these patent medicines. Only around 1900, when addiction became defined by scientific medicine as an illness, did doctors begin to point out the dependency that such remedies could cause.

The Dutch Opium Act of 1919 outlawed the production and trade in specialties containing opium and cocaine. It was only permissible to prescribe, administer, or deal in opiates and cocaine for medical or scientific purposes. Possession of these substances, however, was not outlawed until the revision of this Act in 1928. As a result of the Opium Act, modern medicine and pharmacists acquired a monopoly on the prescription and supply of these substances. Nonetheless, even after 1919, specialties containing opiates, coca, or cocaine frequently showed up in drugstores. But, all in all, the matter had already been decided; scientific medicine had seriously reduced the role of self-medication and popular medicine, and cocaine and opiates were labeled perilous substances that only trained doctors had the right to administer. In forging this monopoly, a clear line was drawn between cocaine as a useful medicine and as a forbidden mood-altering drug.

Views on cocaine cannot be considered apart from the changing role of opiates in medicine during the second half of the nineteenth century. Morphine, which was isolated by Sertürner in 1803, only became widespread in the second half of the nineteenth century with the invention of the hypodermic needle. Morphine turned out to be a superb painkiller which could be effectively administered with a needle subcutaneously and later intravenously. About ten years after first use of the hypodermic needles, physicians concluded that morphine was addictive. They described a "hunger" or "craving" for morphine, which was named "morphinomania" or "morphinism." By the turn of the century morphinism was considered a serious medical problem. Until then it was known how difficult it was sometimes to quit opiates, but this was not seen as an illness or a moral problem. It was at most a vice or case of missing willpower.

Attitudes changed once morphine addiction was defined as an disease. The concept of opiate addiction as an illness is closely related to the progress of scientific medicine during the last decades of the nineteenth century. Great strides were taken in the localization of tuberculosis, cholera, and diphtheria through bacteriology, for example, but this was not the only change in the field: illnesses were now conceptualized more generally as deviations from the norm. On this basis, social phenomena such as homosexuality, masturbation, criminality, and addiction were described as diseases and therefore could be medically studied, treated, and contained.

At first morphine addicts received most attention from doctors, but near the end of the century "cocainism" also became a matter of interest to the medical world. Friederich Gaedeke, Albert Niemann, and Wilhelm Lossen succeeded in producing cocaine from the leaves of the coca plant in 1855, 1860, and 1862, respectively. The introduction of cocaine into medicine in 1884 is generally attributed to Karl Köller. In the Netherlands of this period extensive research was devoted to the application of cocaine to medical practice. Cocaine was initially welcomed, just as morphine had been, as a miracle drug. In 1884 the *Nederlandsch Tijdschrift voor Geneeskunde (Dutch Medical Journal)* spoke very highly of this substance; its only drawback was its pricey-ness.[4] In the Netherlands, Van der Sijp was the first to conduct research on the use of the drug in ophthalmology. In his dissertation there is no mention of the possible side effects of cocaine, nor does he reveal if the substance was used outside of medical practice.[5] Similarly, in 1885, Römer published a thesis on the results of research on acute cocaine poisoning in medical treatment.[6] Acute poisoning must have been a popular subject because three years later Bitter wrote a dissertation about blocking cocaine poisoning by breathing amyl nitrate. Bitter concentrated on what was called "acute cocaine poisoning" and left aside "chronic poisoning," or cocainism. He proposes in his dissertation that chronic cocainism manifests itself in "numerous disorders in the psychic life" as well as in poor digestion, weight loss, and insomnia.[7] The first objections to the use of cocaine only appeared in the *Nederlandsch Tijdschrift voor Geneeskunde*, in 1899; here it was claimed that Murias Cocaini had a harmful effect on the system and was sometimes addictive, for which reasons doctors should beware in prescribing.[8] •

Initially, it mattered little to which drug one was addicted. Both opiates and cocaine had destructive effects. However, starting in the beginning of the twentieth century, doctors became more and more convinced that there were more risks associated with cocaine than with morphine.[9] In 1904, the neurologist, Bolten, noted that a cocaine addict quickly found himself in a situation in which he could no longer carry on his work because of visions, hallucinations, and overwhelming apathy. A morphinist, on the other hand, was still able to work to some extent after years of addiction.[10] A morphine addict could be cured with a certain amount of work, but no successful therapy was known for the cocaine addict:

> the almost completely destroyed interest in work, the heart neurosis, the total apathy and physical destruction as well as the psychic defects can no longer be turned around through any type of treatment method, however scrupulous it may be.[11]

As opposed to the soporific effect of opiates, cocaine's stimulating effects no doubt contributed to the more negative opinions about this substance. More important, however, was the changed status of cocaine in medicine. Morphine remained one of the most commonly used painkillers in medical practice and was still considered to be an essential medicine. In contrast, cocaine became progressively replaced in the 1920s and 1930s by such drugs as novocaine, a cocaine replacement that has anesthetizing but no addictive characteristics. Doctors then viewed cocaine injections as superfluous and strongly advised against them. Cocaine was slowly coming to be seen as a recreational substance rather than a true medicine.

The many press reports about cocaine abuse in the "decadent world capitals" like Paris, Berlin, London, and New York only strengthened this view. Sniffing, it was reported, had taken on epidemic proportions among the prostitutes of Montmartre, as well as among artists, writers, and others who indulged in nightlife.[12] Reports from the United States related that the Black population in the southern states suffered serious psychic disorders and that criminal inclinations surfaced under the influence of cocaine.[13] Worse still, many doctors saw a connection between the use of cocaine and homosexuality. The drug was believed to cause impotence in men with the result that "latent bisexual inclinations" came to the fore. After detoxification, they maintained, such homosexual feelings would disappear again completely.[14] Although seen as a problem drug, cocaine could still be used as a medicine. In 1929, for example, a written questionnaire revealed that cocaine was still being used by ear–nose–throat specialists in particular. In their field they "would not want to do without" cocaine as a surface anesthetic.[15]

Dutch drug policy from 1919 to 1940

After passage of the Opium Act in 1919, doctors could still prescribe maintenance doses of opiates and cocaine for their patients. This was regularly done but the scale of this practice is not known. Not only the medical world but the Dutch Government also opposed restricting these rights of medical science.

Addicts were seen explicitly as patients, and not as criminals. Only a doctor, in a professional capacity, could determine what sort of treatment was appropriate. The State Public Health Inspectorate did not wish to limit a doctor's right to prescribe. This institution wrote in 1938:

> The fight against drug addiction must be handled in a totally different way and be looked upon from the human side. Do not pursue these addicts, as it will finally drive them to the dealers, but offer these people help. Addicts are not criminals but wretches, the morally weak, most of whom did not become addicted through any fault of their own, and lack the power to suppress the inclination. ... Along with measures taken to trace these people, a way must be found to give them a withdrawal program and by means of follow up, send them back to society, as has already been done with so many others. ... State money will surely be spent more efficiently that way than on an expensive and elaborate control machinery used to chase doctors, druggists and patients, while not solving the problem itself.[16]

The right of doctors to prescribe substances covered by the Opium Act did lead in a few cases to excesses in medical usage. An example was an ear–nose–throat doctor in Rotterdam: "Dr X" and his wife were frequent users of cocaine. The white powder was also the medicine Dr X preferred to prescribe for his patients: "cases are on record of patients using 12–18 grams a month for many months at a stretch. ... One of Dr X's patients was so addicted to the drug that he would carry his spray equipment containing a cocaine solution out in the open and would go into public conveniences to have a spray."[17] Yet, most of Dr X's patients experienced few problems from their regular use of cocaine and in general were quite positive about this treatment. Nonetheless, the Rotterdam police who brought this matter to light reported Dr X's habits to the medical disciplinary board.

However, such excesses did not lead to a revision of the drug policy. If the goal was keeping addicts from having to get drugs from the illegal market, it turned out to be extremely effective. Up until the 1960s, the Netherlands did not have a drug problem that provoked mass social outcry. Drug addiction remained an isolated medical problem.

Not much is known about the recreational or non-medical consumption of drugs and in all probability it remained limited to a small scale. The "Chinatowns" in Rotterdam and Amsterdam were the centers of opium smoking in the Netherlands. Opium smoking enjoyed great popularity in the Chinese community, as an estimated 50 to 75 percent of Chinese were smokers. In general, possession of opium for personal use was allowed, but those caught with more than 2 grams were prosecuted and fined between 25 and 50 guilders.

Source material on the recreational use of cocaine is scarce. An underground cocaine scene and resulting "moral panic" as described by Kohn for London (Chapter 5) was never to occur in the Netherlands, for whatever reasons. It was known that sniffing the white powder was fairly common among prostitutes and sailors. Along the waterfront amid a collection of bordellos, cafés, and cabarets, it was relatively easy to buy coke, according to police. This cocaine came both from illegal sources and from pharmacies that did not strictly adhere to the provisions of the Opium Act. The police did not pursue users and only occasionally arrested small dealers. In general, the police tolerated use and petty dealing, concentrating, as seen below, on large-scale trades.

Comparisons: the United States, Britain, and the Netherlands

The nineteenth-century story of drugs in the Netherlands hardly differs from that of other countries. In the United States, Great Britain, France, and Germany cocaine and‘ opiates were also important ingredients for self-medication and in official medicine. In the United States and Europe, written reports on addiction display mounting concern during the second half of the century. The Netherlands was an exception in that there was hardly any research into the size and nature of addiction, and the Dutch based their opinions mainly on foreign research. However, at the beginning of the twentieth century when national drug policies were formulated, different approaches were "chosen."

The American Harrison Act (1914), the British Dangerous Drugs Act (1920), and the Dutch Opium Act (1919) show many similarities. All three acts were a result of the treaty of the International Opium Conference of the Hague in 1912. However, the Americans moved quickly towards a criminalization of drug use whereas the British and the Dutch advocated their medical approach. Several reasons for these differences can be pointed out. First, in England and Holland the number of recreational or deviant drug users was limited. Most addicts were "victims" of careless medical practice and were treated as patients. In the United States the user populations had changed a great deal at the beginning of the twentieth century. Cocaine and opiates were defined as hedonism rather than as medical drugs, with users typecast as deviant and criminal (and often of a different ethnicity).

According to Stein, the lack of influence of the American medical profession on the federal level was another reason for their prohibitionist approach. The Harrison Act was federal law. Medical practice, however, was loosely regulated by state authorities rather than by the central Government. And the American medical profession was no match for the later Federal Bureau of Narcotics, which strongly advocated the crime-control approach.[18] The British and Dutch medical professions carried more clout in public-health policy than their American counterparts. As a result, the Dutch Opium Act was not seen as penal law to be enforced by cops, but as a regulation to control the production and distribution of certain pharmaceutical products.

Coca leaf from the Dutch East Indies

Due to the increasing popularity of coca in the specialties industry and cocaine in medicine, the Dutch investigated at an early stage the possibility of growing the coca plant in the Dutch East Indies (mainly Java, but also the islands of Madura and Sumatra). In 1878, a Belgian firm sent the first coca bushes from South America to the botanical garden of Buitenzorg on Java, the most important island in the colony. In 1883, cultivation began. Three years later planting started on a commercial scale on the islands of Java, Madura, and to a lesser extent on Sumatra.

The coca plant grown on Java, the *Erythroxylon novogranatense*, was a distinct variety from Peruvian coca, *Erythroxylon coca Lamark*. In general, Java coca was of better quality; it was less susceptible to diseases and contained 1.5 percent and sometimes even 2 percent alkaloid, whereas Peruvian coca rarely surpassed 1.2 percent.[19] Java coca yielded twice as much cocaine as the coca from the Peruvian leaf. One disadvantage, however, was that it took longer and involved more intermediate steps to extract pure cocaine from Java coca.[20] Consequently, Peru could provide raw *cocaine* (as Gootenberg shows in Chapter 3), primarily to German firms, whereas Java coca had to be inefficiently transported in leaf form. Thus, initially, Java coca could not compete with coca from Peru. But the quality of the crop on Java continued to improve and close attention was paid to packing and transportation. At the beginning of the century, prospects for Dutch coca planters looked very encouraging.

Between 1890 and 1900 only a small amount of coca was planted, some 500 acres. According to Reens, the first small batch of coca leaves from Java, which was of poor quality, was offered for sale in London in 1890.[21] Until 1900, the sole customer for the leaves was the German company Farbwerke, which alone had the patent for processing of Java coca into cocaine (via the ecgogine method), and as a result could influence prices considerably. The outlook improved in 1900 when the *Nederlandsche Cocainefabriek* (Dutch Cocaine Factory) was established. At the time the Netherlands had no patent law and consequently the extraction method of Farbwerke could be copied without objections. After the German patent expired in 1903, other German companies could also extract cocaine from Java coca and demand for the leaf quickly skyrocketed.

At the start of the twentieth century, 100 kilograms of leaves containing an average alkaloid percentage sold for NLG 50. The cocaine that could be produced yielded no less than NLG 726.[22] With such profit margins it proved lucrative to set up a factory in the Dutch East Indies as well. In 1914 attempts were made, but because of World War I it was impossible to obtain the materials necessary to begin production. The financier of the project, the Geo Wehry company, was no longer willing to invest after the war and this N.V. Preanger company liquidated in 1921.[23] The prospects of profitable cocaine production seemed too cloudy after the war to start another factory.

Figure 6.1 shows that export of coca leaves from Java rose quickly. The bulk of the shipments were traded in Amsterdam in the Koka auction house, but there was also direct shipment from Java to other countries. In 1909 the Dutch

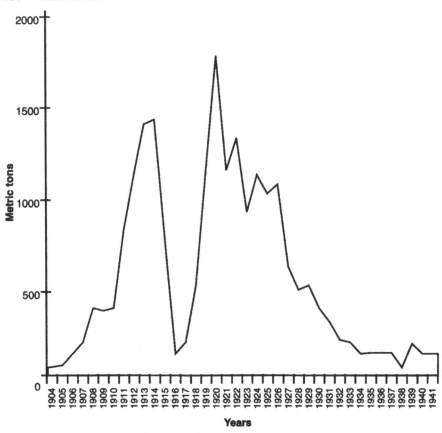

Figure 6.1 Coca leaf exports, Dutch East Indies, 1904–41
Source: Association of Coca Producers Annual Report.

East Indies' share of world production was 17 percent; in 1911, 22 percent. South American countries were pushed from the top of the list of coca exporters by the Dutch East Indies in 1911.[24] Around 1910, after a period of glut on the world market, Amsterdam took over from Hamburg the position of global coca trade center. In 1905, almost 1,600 metric tons of coca leaves and more than 5 tons of raw cocaine entered the harbor of Hamburg from Peru, but by 1913 this had sunk to 35 metric tons of leaves and approximately 2.5 tons of raw cocaine.

World War I hurt the international coca and cocaine trades. Not only did the war hinder deliveries, but prices also dropped. Before 1914 there was a co-operative arrangement between the largest European cocaine manufacturers, which maintained high prices through price-setting agreements. After the war broke out, each manufacturer tried to boost its own sales, with the result that prices fell despite growing overall demand. Coca leaf prices also plunged. By exporting their product directly to other countries, such as the United States, Britain, and Japan, planters tried to cushion their losses. After the war, such third-country exports played an ever larger role. In 1930, about 60–70 percent of colonial coca went to Amsterdam, 25 percent to Japan, and the remainder to the United States, Germany, Switzerland, and France.

After the war the Netherlands slowly but surely lost its leading position in the trade and production of cocaine. Although the number of firms producing coca increased from 72 in 1922, to 88 in 1923, and 96 in 1924, this only caused overproduction. To counteract this uncertain situation, the major Dutch importers decided to join forces. They did away with the Koka auction house and set minimum prices. Cocaine prices slackened with shrinking demand in the postwar years, while at the same time the supply of leaves increased because of this price setting. The outcome was enormous stocks in the Amsterdam warehouses. Added to that was the adverse impact of competition from South American coca.

To stabilize the market, the co-operative group of coca producers, renamed the Coca Producers Society in 1925, decided to conclude an agreement with the convention of German cocaine manufacturers, with whom Dutch manufacturers also had forged contracts. The Association of Coca Producers, essentially a cartel, was made up of importers and producers of coca leaves, such as the Colonial Bank and the Dutch Trade Company. Day-to-day management was in the hands of the Coca Bureau. In 1926 it was agreed to lower minimum prices because of low sales. In time, international regulation and competition from Peruvian leaf forced the Coca Bureau to advise members to stop harvests and replace coca bushes with other crops.[25]

There was also dissatisfaction over the agreement with the convention of cocaine manufacturers. The manufacturers did lower their price of a kilo of cocaine to NLG 500, but this did not boost sales.[26] A new contract improved the situation in 1927. It mandated that manufacturers would buy only Java leaves and only from plantations that were members of the Association; in addition a minimum purchase quota was set. The price of leaves was coupled to the price of cocaine.[27]

The definitive end to the dominant Dutch position in coca trading came in 1928. In that year, the Netherlands implemented its certificate system for drug import/export, as it had agreed to in ratifying the 1925 Geneva Convention. This system was designed to regulate international traffic in anesthetic drugs by restricting trade to drugs for "medical and scientific purposes." Just before implementation of this system, however, a million kilograms of leaves were rapidly sent out from Amsterdam warehouses.[28]

Despite this modest revival in 1928, the annual reports of the Association of Coca Producers became gloomier and gloomier. Stocks increased, sales fell, and the competition continued from Peru leaf. In 1931, stocks in the Amsterdam warehouses were sufficient to provide all of Europe with cocaine for five years.[29] In the following years the amount of leaf delivered dropped sharply and the number of members declined with each successive year. Many planters turned to more promising crops. The last annual report of the Association, in 1949, reported only eleven members and a total of 1,500 kilograms delivered.[30] In that year the Dutch Government recognized the independence of Indonesia, which spelt the end of the association.

Cocaine production in the Netherlands

Although it was claimed in the Netherlands that cocaine was manufactured exclusively for medicinal purposes, the truth is harder to determine. This can be deduced from the decline of coca and cocaine production after 1928, when new international regulations banned casual use of the drug. The percentage of cocaine produced solely for medical purposes is difficult to estimate. Gavit notes that in 1922 the amount of cocaine required for world medical use was estimated at 12,000 kilograms. The production of coca leaves in the Dutch East Indies alone, 1,283,503 kilos, would have been sufficient to meet these needs. The combined export from Peru and Bolivia, however, would also have met them.[31] Such estimates lack reliability, unfortunately. We will never know, for example, how much cocaine supposedly intended for medicine ended up as mood-altering drugs. It may be assumed that as the white powder lost legitimacy in medical practice, more and more cocaine produced in the 1920s and 1930s was being used recreationally.

The largest manufacturer of cocaine in the Netherlands was the Nederlandsche Cocainefabriek (NCF), established in March of 1900. To avoid complete dependence on the German Farbwerke for coca sales, the Colonial Bank took the initiative to promote processing in the Netherlands. The first location in Amsterdam was a trial operation and limited in size. It soon became apparent that the cocaine produced was of excellent quality and could compete with that of Germany. Production capacity increased and the factory had to be quickly expanded. Despite competition in the Netherlands from the Cheiron factory in Bussum, and the Brocades and Steehman company in Meppel, as well as from foreign (primarily German) factories, the NCF was able to expand its market share substantially. In 1910 it could claim to be the largest single cocaine manufacturer in the world.[32] However, as Friman's Chapter 4 shows, in aggregate German factories produced more cocaine than the Dutch. As a result of NCF successes, the factory outgrew its old premises by 1910 and moved to a new building elsewhere in Amsterdam.

The company experienced enormous expansion during World War I in particular. Acts of war raised demand to unknown levels while cutting off supply lines and foreign-market competitors. The Netherlands, which remained neutral during the war, imposed embargoes on the export of medicine. However, when the NCF requested an exemption to this regulation because of its vast supplies and large foreign markets, this was granted as early as the first year of the war.[33] The period of 1914–18 was a troubling time for the coca producers in the Dutch East Indies and for foreign cocaine makers; in contrast, the NCF was booming.

Although the NCF experienced sharp competition from other manufacturers after the war, it continued to play an important role in the production of various sorts of anesthetics. The European Convention of Cocaine Producers, founded in 1924, had eight members. In addition to the Nederlandsche Cocainefabriek, the largest participants were: C.F. Boehringer Söhne, F. Hoffmann-La Roche, and E. Merck. Three companies – one French, one German, and one British – did not join the convention.[34] The Dutch NCF produced approximately 20 percent of world production in the beginning of the 1920s. This share later slipped to 18 percent of total production of the Convention and by 1930 to 13 percent. In 1931 it was agreed in the International Limitation Treaty that the NCF would receive a quota of 10.28 percent. This came down to the production of 250 to 300 kilograms a year, whereas originally the company had regularly topped 1,500 annually.[35] In 1926 the company produced 1,025 kilos; in 1927, 692; and in 1928, 668.

Despite this shrinkage of the 1920s, the company continued to perform well. The *Pharmaceutisch Weekblad (Pharmaceutical Weekly)* wrote at the time of the twenty-fifth anniversary of the firm:

> Despite great foreign competition, it has succeeded in gaining a premier position in the world market with its products. Its main product, cocaine for medicinal purposes, has achieved recognized superiority throughout the world. Without a doubt, this company belongs to the modern industries that will carry the fame of our nation abroad with resounding success.[36]

Due to the decreasing legitimacy of cocaine in medicine and to increased competition, the company was forced to diversify its line with other products. In 1921 it began production of novocaine, which had been discovered much earlier but whose production only became relevant after imposition of legal restrictions on commercial cocaine. About ten years later, they started to process raw opium into morphine and heroin, and in 1941 they began production of ephedrine, a medical stimulant.[37] This diversified line served the company well; before World War II, they controlled two-thirds of the Dutch market for opiates.

During the war, the NCF factory escaped direct damage and in 1945 it appeared to be a "perfectly healthy company."[38] Cocaine, however, was no longer important here, though small amounts of coca continued to be imported to Amsterdam from the Dutch East Indies (and later Indonesia) for processing. Even after World War II, the cocaine factory was allowed to produce drugs for licit medical purposes.

International treaties and Dutch opposition

The Dutch Opium Act of 1919 was born from external pressure rather than internal pressures by broad segments of the population. It was basically a reflection of the ratification of the International Opium Convention of the Hague in 1912.

Until World War II, the Netherlands participated in all international drug conferences. Starting with the Opium Commission in Shanghai in 1909, to the conference for the Trafficking Treaty of 1936, the position of Dutch delegations was determined to a considerable degree by economic interests. International measures seriously threatened coca cultivation in the Dutch East Indies and the production of cocaine at home. From a fiscal perspective, the opium trade in the Dutch East Indies was even more vital. The Dutch had a weighty interest in the opium trade for centuries.[39] Their ships ferried opium from Turkey and Bengal to the Malay Archipelago, where distribution was generally turned over to Chinese concessionaires known as "opium farmers." Relatively speaking, use of opium prevailed among the ethnic Chinese, but in absolute terms opium smoking was most popular among East Indian populations. According to Vanvugt, the Dutch position with regard to the sale and use of opium was determined largely by the financial weight of the trade in government coffers. Colonial revenues were dependent on opium profits. Between 1876 and 1915, these amounted to 703.3 million guilders, an income that reduced the national balance of payments deficit in this period by 70 percent.[40]

At the end of the nineteenth century, when it became apparent that profits from opium farmers were on the decline, the government decided to introduce a State-controlled monopoly system, known as the "*opiumregie*" in Dutch. Under the farm system, sale of opium was left to the farmers. The highest bidder was allowed to hold a monopoly on sales in a specific district for a set period of time. Early in the twentieth century the farm system was phased out and the Dutch State itself took direct charge of the trade, production, and sale of the drug.

The debate touched off by the switch from farming-out to State monopoly was accompanied by a vast number of books, brochures, and pamphlets on opium. Contentiously written, these publications focused on three topics: opium smuggling in the Dutch East Indies; the potentially adverse effects of opium smoking; and the transition from farming to monopoly. Financial issues were pivotal and every policy change was preceded by figuring its consequences for the treasury. Thus, measures against smuggling were deemed essential, for smuggling was an assault on revenues. The advantages of a monopoly system were strongly advocated in these documents. A monopoly would decrease contraband traffic, it was predicted, because official opium in uniform packaging could be easily distinguished from the illegal kind. Second, a monopoly meant higher revenues, as State income from opium farms fell considerably towards the end of the nineteenth century. Finally, a reduction in the number of smokers could be achieved most effectively by a monopoly.

In practice, Dutch policy on opium was defined, as we said above, by the financial interests of the State. During the course of the 1920s and 1930s the contribution of opium to the national treasury slowly declined. The monopoly continued to provide 4–5 percent of the State income from the Dutch East Indies, however. The actual end to the monopoly system came with the Japanese occupation in 1942. The Dutch intended to restore the monopoly after the Japanese surrender. But in March 1943, the Americans threatened through their spokesman, FBN chief Harry J. Anslinger, that as soon as American troops reached the Dutch East Indies they would confiscate all opium stocks, close opium dens, and impose a general ban on opium smoking. If the Netherlands planned to make opium available, no American troops would be sent. Reacting to this threat, the Netherlands decided to impose an absolute and permanent prohibition on opium after the Japanese surrender.[41]

The Netherlands was by no means the sole country in the world with material interests in the production and trade of drugs. Germany made codeine and cocaine and England morphine. Iran had poppy cultivation and Portugal allowed opium in Macao; France worked opium in Indo-China. Yet, the Netherlands was viewed by the Americans as one of the worst "evil-doers," especially because of Dutch coca production. Java and the Netherlands were mentioned in the same breath as Peru and Bolivia. From 1931–40, the League of Nations referred to the Netherlands as one of the largest producing and exporting countries for cocaine.[42]

During international conferences, European countries – and certainly the Netherlands – found themselves confronted with not only humanitarian and moral considerations, but also with fiscal, trade, and colonial concerns. Understandably, the Europeans had great difficulty with absolute restrictions on the production and trade in drugs, helping to stall implementation of the international regulation system. The position of American delegations was simpler and single-minded. The economic interest of the United States was limited here, as was domestic opposition to international regulation of drugs. The United States initiated the Opium Commission in Shanghai (1909) and wielded their influence on the agendas of other conferences. The Americans argued ceaselessly for far-reaching controls and accused the Europeans of apathy about the drug problem. It was the United States, however, that was not particularly co-operative when it came to international negotiations. Co-operation depended primarily on their participation in the League of Nations, though they refused to ratify the Peace Treaty of Versailles and never joined the League. On one hand, the isolationist Americans acted independently, while, on the other hand, they demanded collaboration from others. These contradictions were hard ones for Europeans to grasp.

As seen above, the Dutch were concerned mainly with protecting their economic interests. At each conference the opium monopoly was put forward as the optimal system to combat both use and smuggling. The Americans resolutely opposed such a system and proposed total prohibitions of trade and use of opium. Nonetheless, the Dutch succeeded in convincing others of the virtues of their opium monopoly. A 1930 report by a committee of the League of Nations endorsed the Dutch national monopoly, and dismissed general prohibitions, such as those imposed by the Americans on the Philippines. According to the Dutch, their system emerged after extensive study and experience, and therefore worked rather well. The problem was not a State monopoly, but the challenges of contraband.

Circumvention of the State monopoly in the East Indies by means of smuggling was a constant concern to the Dutch. They strove to combat opium smuggling in various ways. In the nineteenth century a special opium police force was formed whose task was to track down illegal opium. Under a State monopoly, it was possible to prevent smuggling through pricing policy. If the price was low, the amount of illegal opium fell, though usage increased; if the price was high, the black market grew and less legal opium was consumed. On the basis of this experience, the Dutch came to the conclusion that if there was a demand for drugs, supply would inevitably follow. Only if demand fell to negligible levels would it be possible to impose prohibitions. From the Dutch perspective, restriction of drug demand was a national matter that could not be resolved via international treaties. Reduced demand was a question of "national education" to which it was frequently added that the United States had the most flagrant drug problem: "Only by raising the moral level of the population can the American people rid itself of this deep-seated evil."[43]

The Dutch rejected American attempts for a comprehensive ban on opium smoking and global restriction of raw materials for opiates and cocaine. The Dutch adviser on international opium affairs and head of Dutch delegations to the conferences of the League of Nations, W.G. van Wettum, labeled the American standpoint "destructive idealism."[44] A drug-free world was a wonderful ideal, but in Dutch eyes unrealistic or even harmful. Experience in the East Indies had taught them, after all, that a total prohibition would inevitably mean insuperable illegal trade. Illegal trade, they believed, could never be completely stemmed and would lead to "uncontrollable difficulties."[45] After seventeen years of international experience, van Wettum wrote in 1926 that the Americans had no notion of drug dilemmas and formed opinions "without thorough study." Inexperienced peoples made "frequently fanatical opponents."[46]

Despite much criticism of the American mindset, the Dutch could not stop the slow movement towards restriction of the production and trade in opiates and cocaine after 1920. The Dutch knew how to successfully defend their opium monopoly, but the negative impact of international measures on the production of coca and cocaine could not be halted. For financial and economic purposes the opium monopoly was far more important for the Dutch than interests in coca and cocaine. Even compared to coffee and quinine, coca was a minor commercial crop. The fact that international codes did not affect the opium monopoly was a victory for Dutch diplomacy, making the decline of coca and cocaine seem less consequential.

In 1924 and 1925, the second Geneva Conference was held under the auspices of the League of Nations to discuss restrictions on production of raw materials for manufacturing and trade in morphine, cocaine, and heroin. According to the Americans, reduction in the production of raw opium and coca leaf was the sole means for solving the drug problem. The Netherlands staunchly opposed this and proposed an alternative plan, based on State monopolies, covering even the cultivation of coca leaves. As the largest producer and exporter of coca leaf, and with weighty cocaine factories, the Netherlands would end up with a practical monopoly. The plan was dismissed by the other countries but so were the American proposals.

At the second Geneva Conference it was decided to implement a certificate system. All imported and exported drugs had to be sealed with country certificates. In this way it would be possible to ascertain the ultimate destination of the drugs; moreover it would reveal the scale of the drug trades. One result of the implementation of this system was that the export of coca leaves dropped sharply at the end of the 1920s, and it became difficult for producers to trade cocaine not intended for medical or scientific use. A second blow to cocaine production came a few years later.

The tenth meeting of the League of Nations in 1929 decided to restrict the production of drugs and the 1931 Limitation Treaty placed new production restrictions on the manufacturers. In the Netherlands there were serious objections to this treaty, which was perceived as a protectionist measure to defend the industry of other nations. It was believed that production restrictions might result in price hikes and in turn stimulate illegal trade. Despite these grave objections, the Netherlands participated in the Limitation Conference, rather than lose face, and then ratified the treaty.

The Netherlands held limited influence on the international stage at the beginning of the twentieth century. It overestimated its pull, based on large colonial territories and a past history as a world power. Although initially successful in protecting its economic interests, by the eve of World War II an elaborate international control system was in place that allowed no room for State monopolies or free trading in coca or cocaine.

Chatterjee has labeled the Dutch position as "pseudo-obligation ... neither self-induced nor genuine."[47] With each treaty, the Netherlands reserved the right to withdraw in case of contradictory interests. Yet despite numerous objections, the Netherlands ratified every drug treaty. The Dutch position was shaped by conflicting and ambiguous interests on varied aspects of the drug problem. Above all were economic interests, though constrained by other views. The use of drugs was legal only for medical or research ends, but the Dutch saw recreation consumption of opiates and cocaine as a social and medical danger. Nonetheless, drastic restrictions of legal production and trade would lead to a larger and uncontainable black market, following the experience of the Dutch East Indies. In Dutch eyes, growing illegal trade in the interwar period was a *result* of international regulation.

Drug trades and drug control, 1920–40

Drug control, 1920–40

Narcotics laws involve what Schur and Bedau call "victimless crimes."[48] Though sale of drugs does leave victims, the vast majority of drug buyers do not react like the victims of such crimes as assault, robbery, or burglary. This means that in enforcing drug laws, police cannot base their actions on reports or complaints filed by victims but must rely on their own investigations and on informers. The extent to which illegal drugs are seen as a problem therefore depends upon the priorities of the police and the courts.

Initially, the Opium Act of 1919 was not so much a criminal or repressive code for the police and the courts, but rather a preventive or administrative measure to regulate the flow of trade in specific pharmaceutical products. In 1920, for example, it seems that Rotterdam's police were still unaware of the existence of the Opium Act. A short time later, however, the police and the justice system placed mounting emphasis on combating illegal traffic in narcotics.

Between 1920 and 1940, it was primarily police in the port city of Rotterdam who threw themselves into the fight against drug trafficking, for several reasons. First, because of the harbor and its geographical location, Rotterdam became an important drug-trading center, as recognized at the time. Second, the largest Chinatown in Western Europe was located there, and the opium smoking in its boarding houses for sailors represented the most visible form of recreational drug use. Last, the Rotterdam police commissioners had a keen interest in drug control. Under the leadership of Police Commissioner A.H. Sirks, the Rotterdam police developed into the country's specialized force in the field of drug control. Although a specialized Opium Investigation Bureau was only set up in 1928, by the mid-1920s policemen were being assigned more and more frequently to investigate the smuggling of Opium Act substances. There was also growing co-operation on the international level. In 1931 Sirks met in Geneva with Harry J. Anslinger and the Egyptian narcotics fighter, Russel Pascha, about the possibilities for information sharing. The Americans became exceptionally active in Europe in those years. United States narcotics agents from the Treasury Department stationed in Paris traveled to the Netherlands several times a year to confer with Rotterdam police. Despite their criticism of the position of Dutch delegations at international conferences, the Americans were full of praise about the co-operation of the Rotterdam police:

> The benefit of the splendid narcotics law enforcement facilities of the Netherlands Government, intelligently and efficiently administered by the unusually well qualified officials in charge, has generously been accorded to the United States Bureau of Narcotics.[49]

The League of Nations advised member states in 1930 to set up centralized and uniform police surveillance. The Rotterdam force made the obvious choice for this role in the Netherlands, and by 1932 the entire Dutch Office for the Control of Narcotics Smuggling was placed under authority of the Rotterdam police.

Drug control took on a professional profile in the period of 1920–40. While in 1920 there was little knowledge about the existence of the Opium Act, twenty years later in Rotterdam a full-time central agency meticulously followed developments in the Netherlands and co-operated on a regular basis with its foreign counterparts.

Drug trades, 1920–40

The drug trade between 1920 and 1940 was extremely diverse. The police and customs officers encountered all kinds of illegal substances, varying in amounts from a few grams to dozens of kilos. However, a distinction can be made between high-level trade and intermediate-level trade. High-level trade was usually semi-legal. In theory, all companies or individuals with valid permits could obtain large quantities of drugs from pharmaceutical companies. For illegal dealers at the intermediate level, obtaining legal drugs from companies was not a possibility. Here, dealers were primarily concerned with the smuggling of opium and cocaine, though the smuggling routes for opium and cocaine varied.

Opium was generally transported from Turkey through Marseille, France, and then on through Belgium to the Netherlands by boat or train. Cocaine was supplied by the Western European pharmaceutical industry. It is striking that cocaine of the Nederlandsche Cocainefabriek was almost never found in the smuggled lots. The majority of illegal cocaine was produced in Germany, with the result that the eastern and southern sections of the Netherlands were those confronted with contraband. Cocaine was carried into the Netherlands not only for local use but also for trans-shipment to other countries such as Britain, Belgium, or France.

The first reports of Dutch citizens involved in smuggling occurred in 1925 in England. Henricus Augustus Boon, a 29-year-old Dutch national residing in London was found guilty of illegal possession of the white powder. According to the British, he was a smuggler who traveled regularly to the Netherlands and France to obtain cocaine. He was also suspected of arranging marriages of convenience during these trips.[50]

A year later, Rotterdam police discovered a Dutch group in attempts to smuggle cocaine to America by boat. An undercover agent declared that this ring was able to deliver 5 kilos of cocaine a week at a price of NLG 750 to NLG 800 per kilo. The drugs were transported from the German cities of Hamburg or Bremen to Amsterdam and from there smuggled to the United States.[51]

In 1927, Sirks reported that cocaine smuggling was becoming more common. According to Sirks, coke was transported to Rotterdam from Germany by train, with a second route via Paris and Antwerp.[52] A few years later came disturbing reports about cocaine trades in the eastern, and more frequently in the southern, parts of the country. Information on suspected perpetrators was regularly exchanged at international police meetings. Nonetheless, only occasionally did arrests follow, yielding truly modest amounts of cocaine, from a few grams to a couple of hundredgrams. Likely, no large-scale dealing (involving dozens of kilos) was developing.

During the course of the 1930s, these reports of cocaine smuggling became less and less frequent. Every once in a while an arrest or confiscation would register, but compared with the situation around 1930 smuggling of "narcotic substances" had declined significantly by the end of the decade.[53]

Faced with the more stringent national and international regulations, producers and traders of opiates and cocaine faced difficult choices. Would they accept the lower turnover from the loss of markets for non-medical uses, and turn to the production and trade of other products? Or would they opt for a semi-legal and later fully illegal status and continue to sell substances used as recreational drugs? Both paths were taken. The Nederlandsche Cocainefabriek turned to production of other pharmaceutical products and followed the new codes, as far as is known. There were other companies, however, that tried to evade the rules.

As mentioned, the Opium conferences in Geneva had resolved to introduce a certificate system which required drug-exporting companies to show a certificate from the receiving country. To import drugs, a similar document was needed. This regulatory system was intended to impede trade in opiates and cocaine outside legally recognized channels. Many European countries adopted this system by the mid-1920s, but the Netherlands followed only in 1928. In the meantime, pharmaceutical firms, some still well known today, such as Boehringer (Germany) and Hoffman-La Roche (Switzerland), were able to deal legally in large quantities of drugs using indirect connections in the Netherlands. Seizure in 1928 of a box concealing 60 kilos of heroin in Rotterdam harbor led to the discovery of the most extensive circumvention of international codes up to World War II. Originating at the Chemische Fabriek Naarden (Netherlands), the box was placed in the Belgian seaport of Antwerp on a boat bound for China, sailing, however, via Rotterdam. The Naarden factory was found to have imported and exported huge quantities of drugs between early 1927 and mid-1928. According to the League's Opium Commission (the OAC), it succeeded in marketing an estimated 950 kilos of morphine, 3,000 of heroin, and 90 of cocaine in that eighteen-month period.

Calling the small town of Naarden the center of underground narcotics trafficking, the Opium Commission further alleged that the factory controlled at least half of world production of heroin. The company was not prosecuted, however. Authorities in the Netherlands concluded that, while acting contrary to its spirit, it had not actually violated a single Dutch law. The discovery of the practices of the Naarden factory made it clear to the League of Nations, however, that the international regulation system was rather leaky. The case gave a strong impetus to moves to limit drug manufacturing, leading to the Limitation Treaty of 1931.

After introduction of the certificate system in the Netherlands in 1928, a former employee of the Chemische Fabriek Naarden continued the search for legal loopholes. In collaboration with Swiss and French firms, he sought substances that could be converted into heroin and cocaine but that did not fall under laws. The resulting drugs were Dionyl (an opiate) and Atoin (a derivative of cocaine), which today might be called "designer drugs." The companies first hoped to manufacture the drugs at the French firm, Comptoir Central des Alcaloïdes, as it was seemingly not covered under French narcotics law. When

Dionyl turned out to be covered by French law after all, production was switched to another substance, Peronine, also convertible to heroin.

Eventually, however, tightening of European legislation forced manufacturers to relocate in Turkey. Not a signatory to the Geneva Convention, Turkey became a center of opiate production in the early 1930s. Three factories existed, set up with the aid of Europeans and the Japanese, each capable of producing 500–2,000 kilograms of heroin per month, precursors of the famous "French connection" of the 1950s. Morphine was moved from Turkey to Marseille, France, where it was converted into heroin for the American market. Clearly, as drug regulations in Europe became stricter, larger dealers found other means and locations for their activities.

Conclusions

The transformation of cocaine from miracle to menace in the Netherlands between 1860 and 1950 resulted from a multiplicity of factors at various levels. Initially, coca and cocaine were considered important medicines both for self-medication and in scientific medicine. This changed around the turn of the century when "addiction" became defined as an illness and a clear line was drawn between medicines and mood-altering drugs. Cocaine was a useful anesthetic in the hands of a doctor, but a dangerous mind-altering substance outside of medical practice.

The Opium Act of 1919 prohibited production and trade of cocaine for non-medical or non-scientific purposes. In 1928, possession came under prohibitions. Doctors and pharmacists embraced the Opium Act as it provided them a monopoly on these drugs. This Act, however, was not a direct result of the medical profession's changing perspectives on cocaine and opiates. It was more a repercussion of ratification of the treaty drawn up at the Hague International Opium Conference of 1912. Subsequent international restrictions on production and trade stemming from the League of Nations between 1920 and 1940 were viewed with great skepticism in the Netherlands, for two reasons. First of all, the experience with opium licensing and the State monopoly in the Dutch East Indies had shown that overly strict constraints on legal supplies of drugs inevitably lead to illicit dealing, and it was the illegal trade in the Dutch East Indies that proved extremely difficult to stem. The second more important reason was that international regulation damaged financial interests in the production of coca and cocaine, and in the opium trades.

The Dutch insisted that cutting demand would prove more effective than limiting supply. However, the limitation of demand was a national question, not one that could be regulated at the level of the League. Despite these serious objections, the Netherlands ratified all the treaties formulated before World War II. Dutch power in the international sphere was too slight to impede development of the international regulatory system, while United States influence proved decisive. Despite American absence from the League, almost all of the

American proposals dating from the beginning of the century became inscribed in international drug treaties.

Although it was clear by the 1930s that the international regime heavily influenced Dutch interests in coca and cocaine and that the State monopoly would eventually be abandoned, World War II was the true turning point. The loss of colonial possessions in Asia brought an abrupt end to the State monopoly and to Dutch cultivation of coca leaves.

After the war, cocaine slowly but surely was forgotten and was only rarely encountered among dealers and addicts. It was only around 1980 that this white powder again appeared on the illegal drug scene, while the prewar experience had been lost to collective memory. Cocaine was a "new" substance, *the* drug of the 1980s.

Continuity in Dutch drug policy?

Nowadays, Dutch drug policy stands outside the mainstream of international drug control. The official objective of Dutch drug policy is to reduce the risks of drug use for the individual, their immediate environs, and to society at large. This objective has made harm reduction a core concept and led to liberal policies on cannabis (though not cocaine). Cannabis was decriminalized more than twenty years ago; though still a scheduled substance, small-scale sale and use in so-called "coffee shops" is tolerated. The Dutch also hold a stronger faith in prevention and other public-health strategies, such as low-threshold methadone maintenance, needle-exchange programs, and social and medical assistance for drug users. A "war on drugs" leading to a "drug-free society" is deemed unrealistic.

It is a misleading conclusion, however, to interpret today's "liberal" policy as originating in the pre-1945 period, when global prohibitions were similarly dubbed as "destructive idealism." Current Dutch drug policy was formulated at the beginning of the 1970s. During the wide-ranging drug policy debates of the 1970s those past experiences were never brought up. The period preceding World War II had all but disappeared from collective memory.

However, both Dutch skepticism towards the American standpoint before World War II and our current liberal drug policy are indeed rooted in Dutch attitudes towards the role of the State in moral questions. The Netherlands has always been a heterogeneous nation where agreement on economic and social issues is vital to national politics. But when it comes to moral issues, dogmatic attitudes rarely breed a consensus. Today, this "pragmatic" Dutch approach is practiced towards issues like abortion, prostitution, and euthanasia – as well as drugs.

Primary sources: the Netherlands and Java

Information on nineteenth-century medical use of coca and cocaine in the Netherlands can be found in medical and pharmaceutical journals like the *Nederlandsch Tijdschrift voor Geneeskunde* and the *Pharmaceutisch Weekblad*. Dutch researchers were most interested in the use of cocaine in medical practice (and not in other roles): for example, J.W.C.M. van der Sijp, *Cocaïne* (Utrecht, 1885); J.A. Römer, *Hydrochloras Cocaini* (Leiden, 1885); Hendrik Bitter Jz., *Experimenteele Onderzoekingen over Bestrijding van Cocaïnevergiftiging door Inademing van Amylnitriet* (Helder, 1888).

Strong sources on coca cultivation in the Dutch Indies are handbooks on agriculture in the Dutch colonies and journals on colonial affairs: especially A.W.K. de Jong's contributions in *Dr. K.W. van Gorkum's Oost-Indische Cultures*, vol. III (Amsterdam, 1919, second edition); C.J.J. van Hall and C. van de Koppel, eds, *De Landbouw in de Indische Archipel, Volume IIA, Voedingsgewassen en Geneesmiddelen* ('s-Gravenhage, 1948).

The National Archives in the Hague have much material on coca cultivation, international conferences, and Dutch involvement in legal and illegal drug trades, especially in files of the Ministry of Foreign Affairs and Justice Department (these are given English titles in the notes). Material on health policy is scarcer: most were lost during World War II, due to a single well-placed bombshell. There are ample sources on the opium monopoly in the Dutch Indies, even secondary studies in English (see Bibliography). Despite serious tries, I was unable to locate the archive of the Dutch Office for the Control of Narcotics Smuggling. Archives of the NCF are likely rich sources on the production of cocaine in the Netherlands, but access is difficult as the NCF was taken over by Akzo Nobel, a multinational corporation, in the 1970s.

Notes

1 This chapter is based on my Ph.D. thesis: *Tussen patiënt en delinquent. De geschiedenis van het Nederlandse drugsbeleid* (Hilversum: Verloren Publishers, 1995). ("Between patient and delinquent: The history of drug policy in the Netherlands"). I thank Lisa Kahraman and Paul Gootenberg in editorial revisions.
2 *Dagblad van Zuid-Holland en 's-Gravenhage* (12/13 October 1877).
3 See Eliot Freidson, *Profession of Medicine: A Study of the Sociology of Applied Knowledge* (New York: Dodd & Mead, 1970) 11–22, 44.
4 *Nederlandsch Tijdschrift voor Geneeskunde* (1884), 1141.
5 J.W.C.M. van der Sijp, "Cocaïne" (Ph.D. thesis, University of Utrecht, 1885).
6 J.A. Römer, *Hydrochloras Cocaini* (Leiden: Van Doesburgh Pub., 1885).
7 Hendrik Bitter Jz., *Experimenteele Onderzoekingen over Bestrijding van Cocaïnevergiftiging door Inademing van Amylnitriet* (Helder: de Boer pub., 1888), 5–6.
8 *Nederlandsch Tijdschrift voor Geneeskunde* (1899), 621.
9 See G.C. Bolten, "Geschiedkundige bijzonderheden aangaande morphinisme en cocaïnisme," *Nederlandsch Tijdschrift voor Geneeskunde* II (1923), 1670–3; P.H.G. van Gilse, E. Laqueur, and A.J. Steenhauer, *De Cocaine en Hare Vervangmiddelen als Oppervlakte Anaesthetica* (Leiden: A.W. Sijthoff pub., 1929), 20.
10 G.C. Bolten, "Over cocaïne-intoxicatie," *Nederlandsch Tijdschrift voor Geneeskunde* (1904), 673–87.
11 Bolten, "Over cocaïne-intoxicatie" (1904), 687.
12 See for example: *Nederlandsch Tijdschrift voor Geneeskunde* (1913), 133–5; *De Telegraaf* (14 January 1913), 2; *Pharmaceutisch Weekblad* (1921), 684. On cocaine use in France see Cyril V. Berger, *La "Coco", poison moderne* (Paris: n.p., 1924).
13 Bolten, "Geschiedkundige bijzonderheden," (1923) 1672–3. See also David F. Musto, *The American Disease: Origins of Narcotic Control*, (New York: Oxford University Press, 1987, second edition), 6–8.
14 *Nederlandsch Tijdschrift voor Geneeskunde* (1932), 4882–3; Hans W. Maier, *Der Kokainismus, Geschichte, Pathologie, Medizinische und Behördliche Bekämpfung* (Leipzig: Tieme pub., 1926) 65–73; P.H.G. van Gilse, E. Laqueur, and A.J. Steenhauer, *De Cocaine en Hare Vervangmiddelen als Oppervlakte Anaesthetica* (Leiden: A.W. Sijthoff pub., 1929), 21.
15 Van Gilse, Laqueur, and Steenhauer, *De cocaïne* (1929), 44.

16 Letter by Chief of State Supervision of Public Health to the Ministry of Justice, 2-11, 1938, p. 9. Record office, Ministry of VWS, Sub-department of Public Health 1918–56, 1.772.833.07.76 M.B. Concerning selling, delivering, and administering of narcotics for medical purposes, 1939–63.

17 Report by Chief Commissioner of the Rotterdam Police to the Ministry of Justice and Social Services, 17 July 1938, p. 8. Record office, Ministry of VWS, Sub-department of Public Health 1918–56, 1.772.833.07.76 M.B. Concerning selling, delivering, and administering of narcotics for medical purposes, 1939–63.

18 S.D. Stein, *International Diplomacy, State Administrators and Narcotics Control* (Aldershot, UK: Gower Publishers, 1985), 184.

19 A.W.K. de Jong, *Coca en de Extractie der Alkaloïden*, speech (13 December 1907), 9.

20 A.W.K. de Jong, "Coca," in *Dr. K.W. van Gorkum's Oost-Indische Cultures*, vol. III, second edition (Amsterdam: de Bussy pub., 1919) 277–302.

21 Emma Reens, *La Coca de Java, Monographie Historique, Botanique, Chimique et Pharmacologique* (Lons-le-Saunier: Ecole Superieure de Pharmacie, 1919), 15.

22 A.W.K. de Jong, "Coca," in C.J.J. van Hall and C. van de Koppel, *De Landbouw in de Indische Archipel, Volume IIA Voedingsgewassen en Geneesmiddelen* ('s-Gravenhage: Van Hoeve pub., 1948), 866–88.

23 de Jong, "Coca," (1948), 874.

24 E. Poulsson, "Cocaïne," *Wetenschappelijke Bladen* (1926), 98–109; *Pharmaceutisch Weekblad* (1912), 982.

25 Association of Coca Producers, Annual Report (1926), file 1643, 2.20.04, Archive: ARA II.

26 Association of Coca Producers, Annual Report (1927), file 1643, 2.20.04, Archive: ARA II.

27 Association of Coca Producers, Annual Report (1927), file 1643, 2.20.04, Archive: ARA II.

28 Association of Coca Producers, Annual Report (1928), file 1643, 2.20.04, Archive: ARA II.

29 Association of Coca Producers, Annual Report (1931), file 1643, 2.20.04, Archive: ARA II.

30 Association of Coca Producers, Annual Report (1950), file 1643, 2.20.04, Archive: ARA II.

31 John P. Gavit, *Opium* (London: Routledge, 1925), 45.

32 *Pharmaceutisch Weekblad* (1925), 269.

33 Nederlandsche Cocaïnefabriek to Ministry of Agriculture and Trade, 25 August 1914; Ministry of Labor to Ministry of War, 27 August 1914, files 1.450.00 and 2.06.01, Archive: ARA II.

34 Nederlandsche Cocaïnefabriek to State Public Health Inspectorate, 2 December 1929, box 1596, file 2.05.21, Archive: ARA II.

35 Report of E.D. van Walree, W.G. van Wettum, and J.B.M. Coebergh on the Limitation Conference, box 1596, file 2.05.21, Archive: ARA II.

36 *Pharmaceutisch Weekblad* (1925), 269.

37 Report of the Koloniale Bank, 29 November 1945 on the N.V. Nederlandsche Cocaïnefabriek, box 928, file 2.20.04, Archive: ARA II.

38 Report of the Koloniale Bank, 29 November 1945 on the N.V. Nederlandsche Cocaïnefabriek, box 928, file 2.20.04, Archive: ARA II.

39 Studies in English on the Dutch opium trade in the East Indies include: Frits Diehl, "The opium-tax farm on Java, 1813–1914: A quest for revenue by Government and Chinese tax farmers," *Conference on Indonesian Economic History in the Dutch Colonial Period* (Canberra: n.p., 1983); James R. Rush, *Opium to Java: Revenue Farming and Chinese Enterprise in Colonial Indonesia, 1860–1910* (Ithaca: Cornell University Press, 1990); Eric W. van Luijk, "A lesson from history on the issue of drug legalization: The case of the opiumregie in the Dutch East Indies (1890–1940)," *Law and Society Association Conference*

paper (Amsterdam, 1991); E.W. van Luijk and H.J.C. van Ours, *How to Control Drugs*, Serie Research Memoranda 1993 – 30, Faculteit der Economische Wetenschappen en Econometrie, Vrije Universiteit (Amsterdam, 1993).

40 Ewald Vanvugt, *Wettig Opium, 350 Jaar Nederlandse Opiumhandel in de Indische archipel* (Haarlem: In de Knipscheer Pub., 1985).

41 de Kort, *Tussen Patiënt en Delinquent*, (1995) 53.

42 S.K. Chatterjee, *Legal Aspects of International Drug Control* (the Hague: Nijhoff Pub., 1981).

43 Ministry of Labor to Ministry of Foreign Affairs, 22 July 1926, box 1467, file 2.05.21, Archive: ARA II.

44 Report by van Wettum on Geneva conferences, no. 1154, 20 May 1925, box 16569, file 2.05.21, Archive: ARA II.

45 Tan Tong Joe, *Het Internationale Opiumprobleem* ('s-Gravenhage: Gerretsen pub., 1929), 13–14.

46 van Wettum to Ministry of Foreign Affairs, 22 July 1926, box 1467, file 2.05.21, Archive: ARA II.

47 Chatterjee, *Legal Aspects* (1981), 201.

48 Edwin M. Schur and Hugo A. Bedau, *Victimless Crimes: Two Sides on a Controversy* (Englewood Cliffs: Prentice Hall, 1974).

49 Legation of United States to Ministry of Foreign Affairs, no. 170, 29 July 1932, inv. 16770. exh. 5911, file 2.09.22, Archive: ARA II.

50 Malcolm Delevingne, Home Office, London, to Ministry of Foreign Affairs, 30 July 1926, box 1534, file 2.05.21, Archive: ARA II; Terry M. Parssinen, *Secret Passions, Secret Remedies: Narcotic Drugs in British Society 1820–1930* (Philadelphia: Institute for the Study of Human Issues, 1983), 177.

51 Report of Rotterdam Police, A.No.436/1926, 18 February 1926, p. 15, box 1534, file 2.05.21, Archive: ARA II.

52 Report of Rotterdam Police, 15 September 1927, box 1570, file 2.05.21, Archive: ARA II.

53 See for example: Annual Report Nederlandsche Centrale tot bestrijding van den smokkelhandel in verdoovende middelen, 1938, no. 854, p. 1, box 1143, file 2.09.22, Archive: ARA II.

7 Japan and the cocaine industry of Southeast Asia, 1864–1944

Steven B. Karch, MD

I received instructions through military channels to provide opium for the Chinese people by establishing an opium suppression board.
(Harada Kumakichi, Japanese Military Attaché at Shanghai from 1937–9)[1]

[T]hey [German representatives at Geneva] don't understand action based on humanitarian motives and ... would understand it still less when called on to enact legislation to restrict German traders [cocaine manufacturers] in the legitimate business of poisoning Hindoos and Chinese.
(A British representative at the Hague Conference, 1912)[2]

Introduction

The Marqués de Cañete, the second Spanish viceroy in Peru in 1555, was the first Government official to enact a law requiring that alternate crops be substituted for coca. His attempts at limiting coca production in this fashion were utterly ineffective. His efforts were important, nonetheless, because they were the first example of what has now become the hallmark of government drug control programs everywhere: a preoccupation with production limitation. The difficulty with production limitation, at least in the case of coca, is that it can be grown anywhere. Coca has, in fact, been raised commercially in Nigeria, Sri Lanka, Malaysia, Indonesia, Taiwan, and Iwo Jima.[3] And because coca can be grown in many parts of the world, governments in many parts of the world have seized the opportunity to make money selling coca and refining cocaine. With so many potential players, and opportunities, schemes for production limitation have never worked particularly well.

The failure of production limitation was already apparent at the turn of this century. In 1910, Sir Edward Grey, the British Foreign Minister, wrote to the American Ambassador in London, warning that the "spread of morphia and the cocaine habit, is becoming an evil more serious and more deadly than opium smoking, and this evil is certain to increase." Sir Edward was correct. In 1910, total world production of refined cocaine amounted to less than ten tons. Drug Enforcement Agency analysts believe that as of 1995 South American production exceeded 740 tons.[4] Identifying which factors led to such explosive growth is a difficult, and perhaps impossible, undertaking. But whatever the explanation, part of the answer must have to do with the actual business practices involved in the making and selling of cocaine. The brief account that follows chronicles the rise and fall of the cocaine industry in Southeast Asia, with emphasis on the enabling technology and business practices.

How coca came to Southeast Asia

The Treaty of Tordesillas, signed on 7 June 1494, divided Africa and Latin America between Spain and Portugal. Spain got much of South America, along with the coca plant, and quinine. Spanish administrators were not exactly eager to share their discoveries with the rest of the Europe. After the treaty was signed, more than a hundred years passed before the rest of Europe learned much about New World plants, and even longer until significant numbers of Europeans got to see the plants first-hand. Cinchona was the first plant transported back to Europe. Malaria was rampant in both the New and Old World, and the medicinal benefits of "Jesuit bark" were immediately apparent.

At first, quinine was scarce, and very expensive. Administrators at the Royal Botanical Gardens at Kew, outside of London, changed that. They sent botanists Richard Spruce (1817–93) and Clement Markham (1830–1916) to South America where they succeeded in smuggling thousands of cinchona plants (the source of quinine) home to England. Once the seedlings recovered from their voyage, establishing new cinchona plantations in Ceylon and India was no great challenge. Dutch agriculturalists did exactly the same in Java. And they all made a great deal of money.[5] The same scenario was envisioned for coca. Coca seedlings arrived at Kew decades before anyone realized that cocaine could be used as a local anesthetic. Coca was of interest because the leaves were thought to relieve hunger and thirst, and to improve performance. Officials at Kew sensed an economic opportunity at hand.

Seeds of the coca plant are hardy, and were often sent via the regular mails, packed in a little moist soil. They were sent to the Botanical Gardens at Calcutta, to the Peradeniya Gardens in Ceylon, to the Agricultural Society of India, and to agricultural stations at Assam and Darjeeling. Seeds planted at the tea estates in Assam did very well, and coca remained a minor cash crop there for many years. Efforts at coca growing were very successful at the Botanical Gardens outside of Lagos, Nigeria, and also in Sierra Leone.[6] Attempts at coca cultivation in the Blue Mountains of Jamaica met with less success, and the fields were eventually planted with coffee.

The first coca seedlings were planted in Java in the 1850s. In 1854, a Dutch botanist named Hasskarl, who had helped the Indian government establish cinchona plantations, wrote a letter to the Dutch Colonial Office suggesting that coca cultivation might provide nearly as many opportunities as cinchona. Hasskarl described how coca chewing imparted energy and feelings of well-being, and he outlined in some detail his reasons for believing that coca plants were well adapted for growth in Java. However, his suggestions were rejected by both the chief of the Public Health Service, and the Head of the Department of Agriculture.

Dutch colonial officials were convinced that once the Javanese found out how good coca could make them feel, they would not be "morally strong enough to refrain from excessive use."[7] They also argued that there was really no need to start growing another dangerous stimulant. After all, coffee already grew in Java. Why risk the "moral health" of the country just for colonial revenue? In spite of the early decision not to pursue commercial coca development, the agricultural chief did decide to start a trial garden, just to raise enough coca for "chemical and physiological" studies.

Coca seedlings were planted at Buitenzorg, the Dutch Botanical Gardens, located in the highlands just southeast of Jakarta. The experimental coca garden still existed in 1876, when Herman Linden, a Belgian seed exporter located in Ghent, sent a different set of coca seedlings to Buitenzorg. Just where Linden got his seedlings is not known, but wherever they came from, they thrived in Java. Government botanists were soon providing seeds to growers throughout Java. By 1883, the year before the cocaine market exploded, modest quantities of coca leaf, mostly for use in the production of coca-based wines, were being exported from Madera and Sumatra for auction in Amsterdam.[8]

Government surveys taken in 1885 revealed that many tea growers planned on switching over to coca growing entirely. They were advised not to by a colonial office agriculturist, Professor van Gorkum. He wrote a newspaper article suggesting that the tea growers should only plant coca between rows of the tea bushes. He warned that if the growers planted too much coca, prices would go down, and coca cultivation would not be worth the effort. Leaf from Java finally began to appear in London's Mincing Lane auctions in 1889, but did not sell very well.[9]

Coca cultivars and coca chemistry

Not only did Linden's seedlings grow well, but their leaves contained a great deal of cocaine – far more than the leaves being grown commercially in South America. All cultivated coca comes from two closely related New World species: *Erythroxylum coca Lamarck*, and *Erythroxylum novogranatense* from Colombia, the former Spanish colony of New Granada. Each of the two species has two distinct varieties. The seeds that botanists at Kew Gardens sent around the world were, almost certainly *E. Coca novogranatense var. truxillense*. Unfortunately for the Kew administrators, that was not the variety most commonly grown in the Amazon basin, where *Erythroxylum coca Lamarck* was the preferred cultivar. The first seeds of *E. coca novogranatense* did not arrive at Kew until 1870. They had been collected from the vicinity of Huánuco (eastern Peru). Unfortunately, the seeds chosen for distribution by the Kew Gardens botanists produced leaves that contained only modest amounts of extractable cocaine.[10]

Coca leaves contain a number of other chemicals besides cocaine, and it took some time for the chemists of the nineteenth century to identify all of the different compounds. Growers took a more simplistic approach. They distinguished between "crystallized" and "uncrystallized" alkaloids. "Crystallizable" alkaloid is another word for cocaine. "Uncrystallized" alkaloid is another way of referring to all the other molecules, many closely related to cocaine, that are contained in coca leaves (mostly cinnamyl-cocaine). Leaves grown in Java contained much more "uncrystallized" alkaloid than leaves from South America. The total alkaloid content of *Erythroxylum coca Lamarck*, at least at the turn of the century, was usually in the range of 0.5 percent, nearly all of it crystallizable. The alkaloid content of *Novogranatense* varieties was between 1–2 percent, but only one-third was crystallizable. At first, most manufacturers felt that Southeast Asian coca leaf was not good for anything, except perhaps to make wine and beverages.[11]

The situation changed at the turn of the century. German chemists discovered how to convert uncrystallizable alkaloid to crystallizable cocaine. In 1898, a German chemical manufacturer patented a process that allowed drug manufacturers to convert all of the alkaloid in coca leaf into usable cocaine. The cinnamyl-cocaine in the leaves was first converted to ecgonine, and the ecgonine was then mixed with benzoic acid and methanol. All of the alkaloids were thereby converted into cocaine, giving a yield much higher than could be obtained from leaves grown in South America.[12] The only problem for the Dutch was that bulk coca leaf had to be shipped to Germany for processing. It remained therefore a perishable commodity, and the Dutch growers remained at the mercy of German importers.

The Netherlands and Germany did not sign a patent treaty until the 1920s, so there was nothing to prevent the Dutch Colonial Development Board, and coca growers in Java, from building their own coca refinery utilizing the patented German process. The Nederlandsche Cocainefabriek (NCF) opened in March of 1900 in Amsterdam. Even though Java leaf still had to be shipped halfway across the world, the presence of a second factory in Amsterdam broke Germany's stranglehold on the Indonesian market. The Dutch refinery was so successful, that a second floor was added to the factory in 1902. By 1910, the NCF claimed to be the largest cocaine manufacturer in the world, producing more than 1,500 kilograms per year of refined cocaine.[13] The NCF moved to new, even larger, premises that same year.

When the German patent expired in 1903, other German chemical makers began using the same process. In order to ensure adequate supplies, and to control costs, German manufacturers, such as E. Merck (Darmstadt), purchased their own plantations in Java. At the same time, privately owned Dutch factories opened and went into competition with the NCF. Another factory was established in nearby Bossum by a disgruntled NCF employee and another plant, called Brocades and Steehman, opened in Meppel. Coca exports from Java began increasing at a steady pace. Leaf exports rose from 45 tons in 1904, to 83 tons in 1906, and to 1,300 tons in 1913. Exports peaked at 1,650 tons in 1920.[14] Java leaf that was not shipped to Amsterdam was purchased by representatives of Japanese drug houses for their own cocaine refineries in

Tokyo. The Japanese had also mastered the German technique for refining Java coca. Dutch coca growers, unwisely, came to rely increasingly on exports to Japan.

Demise of the Dutch and rise of Japanese plantations

A number of factors combined to drive the Dutch out of the cocaine business. To begin with, the Netherlands ratified the 1925 Geneva Convention. Signatories to the Convention had to initiate import and export controls for coca and opium, and limit production of refined drugs to what could be justified by legitimate medical needs. Once the Dutch Government had signed the treaty, growers in Java and the management of the NCF in Amsterdam could no longer continue to produce cocaine on a massive scale and expect to find legitimate buyers for their product – a transformation explored by de Kort in Chapter 6.

Even without the treaty, the medical use of cocaine had already declined to negligible levels. Alternatives to cocaine anesthesia were developed during the early twentieth century, and there was simply no way to hide, or justify, the large amounts of cocaine being produced. The magnitude of the surplus production can be gauged from the fact that during the months leading up to the implementation of import certificate regulations, more than 220 tons of stored coca leaf were shipped from warehouses in the Netherlands.[15]

The other circumstance working against the Dutch was Japanese trade policy. Even as they continued to import coca leaf from Indonesia and South America, Tokyo drug companies also planted their own coca plantations in Taiwan, Iwo Jima, and Okinawa. By 1929, the plantations in Japan and its colonies were producing enough leaf to supply Japanese drug manufacturers. In 1929, the Japanese central Government simply stopped granting import permits for Java coca, unless, naturally, the leaves came from plantations owned by Japanese companies operating in Java. The Dutch Association of Coca Producers was understandably upset by this move. It filed a series of complaints with the Colonial Ministry's office in Amsterdam.[16] Japan ignored the complaints. By 1935, Java's exports of leaf fell to under 100 tons. Professor van Gorkum had been correct: coca proved an unreliable cash crop.

Taiwanese coca

When Japan took control of Taiwan (then Formosa) in 1895, agriculture and forestry were the basic industries on the island. The Japanese occupation did little to change those industries. But, by 1930, the effects of the depression in the United States were being felt as far away as Japan and its possessions. If anything, farmers in Japan suffered more than their counterparts in the United States. During the early 1930s, the average Japanese city dweller experienced a 35 percent decline in earnings. In the countryside, the earnings decline was closer to 60 percent. Peasant farmers were reduced to eating bark and selling their daughters to brothels. Starvation was a reality for many. A textile export boom fueled by devaluation of the yen from US $.50 to $.21 in November 1931, did little to improve overall conditions.[17] Overseas sales of sugar were particularly hard hit and slow to recover. Japan's entrance into the cocaine trade coincided with a steep decline in its sugar exports.

With sugar almost impossible to sell, some Formosan growers decided to explore other possibilities. The Home Office ordinances that governed Taiwan, initially contained no specific provisions relating to coca production or cocaine refining. In theory, going into business was easy. To start making refined cocaine, a drug company only had to get a business license (like any other business on the island), and submit quarterly statements of the raw material processed. No limitations were placed on the quantities produced or sold, no records or reports of sales were required and no inspections or audits were conducted.[18]

Coca production in Taiwan began in 1916. The first coca plantation on the island was developed by the *Ensuiko* Sugar Company of Formosa. Ensuiko held the monopoly to grow sugar cane and manufacture sugar in the Kagi area, which included the village of Sinei, where Ensuiko's sugar refinery was located.[19] During the early twentieth century Ensuiko was the fourth largest sugar producer on the island, processing nearly 10 tons of sugar each month. It also owned large sugar cane plantations in Java and regularly shipped large quantities of sugar cane back to Taiwan for refining.

In 1916, while the medical community still used cocaine, and legitimate profits were to be made in refining and selling pharmaceutical-grade cocaine, Taiwan's Governor General encouraged a plantation owner named Abe Konosuke to try planting coca. A cocaine refinery was built and coca seedlings were planted in different areas around the property. According to the British Consul in Taiwan, the cocaine refinery was a crude affair built a few yards away from the site of the original sugar refinery. Konosuke's efforts were not successful. Coca was not native to Taiwan and had never been grown there before; the planters knew a great deal more about growing sugar than coca.[20] Konosuke lost his business in 1922, and was forced to sell out to the Ensuiko Sugar Company.

When the demand for sugar exports declined, Ensuiko shares dropped precipitously. Ensuiko's Chief Director, Tetsu Maki, needed a white knight. A member of Ensuiko's Board of Directors, Norakata Takahashi, thought his father might be interested. Takahashi's father was not just any venture capitalist; in fact, he was Japan's Minister of Finance. Takahashi's father invested 100,000 yen. A friend of Takahashi's, Matasakau Shiobara, invested an additional 150,000 yen. After World War II, United States intelligence agents interviewed several sources who claimed Minister Takahashi was acting as a frontman for Mitsui's trading division, *Mitsui Gomei Kaisha* (MGK), the same company that was supplying opium to the government monopoly.[21]

Regardless of the source of the money, the new investors changed the name of the company from Ensuiko to *Taiwan Shoyaku*. They brought in new technical experts, streamlined operations, planted coca, and quickly reversed Ensuiko's downward slide. Takahashi, as the country's Finance Minister, was certainly in a position to steer military and government purchases towards his son's company, although no evidence for that practice was ever produced. By the fall of 1936, shares of Taiwan Shoyaku were trading at pre-depression levels. How much Taiwan Shoyaku's performance was bolstered by the Takahashi connection is difficult to say, but Shiobara's influence probably contributed to the success of the restructured company as much as Takahashi's did.

The legal system and Japan's drug industry

Opium smoking was unheard of under the old Tokugawa feudal system, and after diplomatic relations were established with the West, Japanese leaders took great pains to ensure that opium smoking never gained a foothold. In 1858, ten years before the Meiji Restoration and the end of feudal law, Japan signed treaties with the United States ("Treaty of Amity and Commerce") and England ("Regulations under which British Trade is to be Conducted in Japan"), which both specifically prohibited opium importation and imposed strict punishment on offenders.

After the Restoration, controls on drug use were tightened even further. In April 1868, Japan passed a new law that carried heavy penalties for opium users and sellers. Other laws controlling the medical use of opium were also passed in 1870 and even stricter sanctions were added to the criminal code in 1882. There simply were no Japanese opium smokers, at least none living in Japan. Not only was opium smoking unknown, the use of heroin and other narcotics was unthinkable. This, perhaps, explains a very peculiar anomaly in Japanese law: the criminal code only dealt with opium smoking.[22]

The same laws applied in Taiwan, then a Japanese colony, but the laws applied only to opium. Heroin and cocaine production were not specifically mentioned. Production and sales of other narcotics came under the Home Office ordinances, not the penal code. For all intents and purposes, regulations applicable to the production and sales of morphine, cocaine, and heroin were no different than the regulations that applied to the production of sugar or tobacco. As a consequence of this strange dichotomy, penalties for the violation of laws relating to narcotics other than opium were much more lenient than penalties for violations of the opium laws.[23] Conviction for opium-related offenses brought sentences of ten years' hard labor, but cocaine and heroin dealers could be sentenced to no more than three months. In most cases, Japanese offenders were simply fined, and the fines were not very large. In essence, the market was entirely unregulated.

The role of Hoshi Pharmaceuticals and Sankyo Pharmaceutical

Whatever the original intentions of the Diet, the existence of such large legal loopholes proved irresistible to the drug firms. Sankyo Pharmaceutical and Hoshi Pharmaceuticals were the biggest players, but there were many others. The Sankyo Pharmaceutical Company Ltd of Tokyo was one of only five companies in Japan licensed to process coca and produce cocaine from coca leaf. Sankyo Pharmaceutical also happened to be the largest pharmaceutical company in Japan. Its wholesale branch office in Taiwan had gross sales of more than a million yen per year.[24] As cocaine was added to the product lines of these companies, it was only natural that they would apply the lessons already learned marketing opiates.

Minister Takahashi's friend, Matasakau Shiobara, started Sankyo Pharmaceutical in 1899 to import and sell a digestive aid invented by an expatriate pharmacist, Jokichi Takamine (1854–1922). Takamine owned a private research laboratory in New York City, and had done contract work for Parke, Davis, which, along with Merck of Darmstadt, was one of the world's major producers of pharmaceutical cocaine. Takamine was, at first, unsuccessful in his attempts to sell his enzyme, but he did make a favorable impression on George Davis, who hired him as a consultant. Takamine remained in the United States for a number of years, working for Parke, Davis, which finally successfully marketed "Taka-Diastase" as a digestive aid.[25] Parke, Davis eventually was able to exploit another Takamine discovery: adrenaline. In 1894, researchers in London had discovered that, when given to animals, extracts of the adrenal gland raised blood pressure and heart rate. In 1901, Takamine and a second scientist named Thomas Aldrich, working independently, both managed to purify and isolate the compound: Takamine called it adrenaline.

Four years later, a German chemist, Friedrich Stolz (1860–1936), managed to synthesize adrenaline without using any animal extracts, and adrenaline became the first hormone to be isolated and synthesized artificially. Parke, Davis decided to manufacture adrenaline, and Takamine was placed in charge of setting up production. This is ironic because cocaine toxicity is partly the result of excessively high adrenaline and noradrenaline levels! In his position as a supervising industrial chemist at Parke, Davis, Takamine would certainly have been well acquainted with the latest techniques used by the company for making cocaine. And that knowledge almost certainly was of some use to Takamine when he returned to Japan, at the invitation of Matasaju Shiohara, the chairman of the board of Sankyo Pharmaceutical.

Sankyo Pharmaceutical had strong connections with the American chemical industry and held cross-licensing agreements with both Johnson & Johnson, and Parke, Davis. After World War I, Shiohara invited Takamine back to Japan and made him president of Sankyo Pharmaceutical, with Shiohara remaining as managing director. Partly because of the valuable training Takamine had received from North America's largest cocaine producer, Sankyo Pharmaceutical was able to produce more cocaine than either Emmanuel Merck or George Parke would ever have imagined possible.

In 1928, Sankyo Pharmaceutical signed a contract to purchase cocaine from Taiwan Shoyaku, the company partly owned by Shiohara and Takahashai (or Mitsui, if Allied allegations are true). Of course, Taiwan Shoyaku had other legitimate customers besides Sankyo Pharmaceutical. Its sales amounted to nearly 500 kilograms per month. Most of the semi-refined cocaine went to drug companies in Japan, including Koto Pharmaceutical, Takeda Pharmaceutical Industries, Sankyo Pharmaceutical, the Shinonogi Pharmaceutical Company Limited of Osaka and Hoshi Pharmaceuticals in Tokyo.[26]

The other important Taiwanese coca grower was Hoshi Pharmaceuticals. Hoshi Pharmaceuticals was founded by Hoshi Hajime who, like Takamine, had studied and worked in the United States. Hoshi even earned a Master's degree in Journalism from Columbia University in 1901. But instead of becoming a journalist, Hoshi returned to Japan and started a profitable business selling patent medicines.[27] In 1910, building on that base, he expanded into morphine production. The transition was facilitated by Japanese law; producing morphine for medical purposes was legal in Japan, but the government controlled opium imports. The government did not, however, regulate semi-refined morphine, a by-product produced when raw opium was converted to smoking opium. Hoshi went to Taiwan, cut a deal with the government-owned opium monopoly, and started buying their stocks of surplus semi-refined morphine. It was shipped back to his factory in Tokyo where it was, quite legally, converted to morphine and heroin.

Following a trend first begun by legitimate European manufacturers, Hoshi used his success in the morphine business to launch an equally successful expansion into the cocaine trade. Hoshi added cocaine to his product line in 1918. With the approval of both the Japanese Home Ministry and officials in Peru, Hoshi purchased a large coca tract in the Huallaga Valley – a trans-Pacific connection documented by Gootenberg in Chapter 3. At the same time, Hoshi began growing coca leaf in the Kagi district of Taiwan. Initially, the plantation covered 242 acres; by 1944, Hoshi had 392 acres (some documents put the number at 292) under cultivation in Taiwan. Whatever the actual number was, it was more than sufficient to supply Hoshi Pharmaceuticals with raw materials.[28] In the mid-1930s, Hoshi Pharmaceuticals was forced to sell off its lands in Peru, relying entirely on its Taiwan plant for raw materials. Hoshi Pharmaceuticals, at least, did its part for the environment, even if its motives were only for profit. During the 1930s, Hoshi Pharmaceuticals sold the residue of its leaves, which contained large amounts of nitrogen, to farmers for fertilizer. That practice was discontinued after ten years because the project was not very profitable. The extracted leaf was then used as fuel.

Creative cocaine accounting

Cocaine producers in Taiwan had three important advantages over their South American and European competitors: shipping costs were much lower, import permits could be had from the Foreign Office just for the asking, and, most importantly, Formosan coca contained more cocaine alkaloid than leaf grown in South America. Most of the cocaine and other narcotics produced by Japanese drug firms found their way on to the world's black markets and drug makers did little to hide this fact. Once the refined cocaine was produced in Tokyo, Japanese law made disposing of the cocaine an easy matter. Smugglers did not even bother to repackage the standard 700-gram packages of cocaine they purchased from the wholesalers. As a result, the brand names of the Japanese manufacturers, such as Hoshi Pharmaceuticals, Dai Nippon, and Sankyo Pharmaceutical, were as well known in Calcutta as they were in Tokyo, even though medicinal cocaine exports to India were nil. Black marketeers also bought the 1- and 5-gram packets of cocaine that were intended for sale to doctors' offices, repackaged the smaller containers into larger ones and then affixed their own brand name, for example, "Fujitsuru."[29] Even though there really was no company named Fujitsuru, customs inspectors around the world were all too familiar with the Fujitsuru-brand cocaine.

International treaties required Japan to file yearly reports on cocaine and narcotic production with the League of Nations. Officials at the League of Nations were apparently unaware of the differences between Southeast Asian and South American coca, and Japan was able to get away with understating its production figures with impunity. Between Taiwan Shoyaku and Hoshi Pharmaceuticals there were 684 acres under cultivation in Taiwan.[30] The average yield for South American coca is generally approximated as 0.6 ton per acre per harvest, with only three harvests per year. An area of 684 acres devoted to coca production in the Andes would be expected to yield 1,230 tons of leaves per year (684 acres × 0.6 tons per acre × 3 crops per year = 1,230 tons), which would give a total yield of refined cocaine of approximately 3 tons.

Yet official Japanese statistics for 1927 show total Taiwanese coca leaf production at 204,640 kilograms (i.e. 230 tons). This production number is hardly believable given that coca grown in Taiwan was presumably the same strain as that grown in Java, and Javanese coca was harvested four times a year. Leaf production in Taiwan should have been about 25 percent greater than for an equivalent area in the Andes; instead it was reported as 50 percent lower. And the coca leaf produced in Taiwan yielded twice as much cocaine as leaf grown in the Andes.

A general, and very rough, rule of thumb is that 400 pounds of South American leaf will yield a single kilogram of cocaine. For Southeast Asian cocaine, the number would be closer to 200 pounds of leaves to yield one kilogram of cocaine. Thus 230 tons of coca leaf grown in Taiwan should have yielded at least 2.3 tons of cocaine, even if there were only three harvests per year. A realistic estimate for Taiwanese coca production, based on production experience from Java, would be 1,500 tons of leaf per year from 684 acres, which (as Asian leaf) should have yielded nearly 7 tons of purified cocaine. Whatever the real figures were, they amounted to a great deal more than could ever be accounted for by legitimate medical use. The Health Committee of the League of Nations estimated that in countries possessing sophisticated medical care systems, the average annual cocaine requirement was 7 milligrams per person.[31]

Evidence subsequently developed by General MacArthur's intelligence staff subsequently revealed that Japanese bureaucrats routinely "cooked the books," adjusting production figures for opium and heroin production so that they agreed with the permissible values set by the League of Nations.[32] In the case of cocaine, a somewhat different approach was used. The Japanese imported coca leaf and crude cocaine not just from Taiwan, but also from coca plantations on Iwo Jima, Okinawa, and Java. During the 1920s, imports from Java averaged more than a million pounds a year.

The Ministry of Finance in Tokyo managed to hide all of these imports by lumping coca leaves together with other raw materials used to manufacture drugs. So when Japan's representative to the League of Nations' Opium Advisory Committee (OAC) stated that "The new policy of the Japanese Government would consist in reducing the output of cocaine," and that this reduction had been accomplished by "limiting the import of raw material," his claims were greeted with some skepticism. When asked by the Foreign Office for his opinion on the Japanese statements, G.P. Patton, the British Consul in Taiwan, wrote "How the import of raw material is to be limited without keeping an exact record of these imports transcends one's comprehension, though possibly to the statisticians in Japan it may not be so difficult."[33]

The role of the military

Over and above wholesale exchanges with black marketeers, large quantities of cocaine and heroin, far beyond any conceivable medical needs were sold to the Japanese armed forces. Onishi Takamatsu, an auditor with Sankyo Pharmaceutical until 1923, reported that when he was appointed Director of Taiwan Shoyaku's Tokyo branch, he had arranged sales of semi-refined cocaine to the Japanese army and navy. Sankyo Pharmaceutical, he said, acted as an intermediary. In 1938, Sankyo Pharmaceutical purchased 739 kilograms from Taiwan Shoyaku for direct sale to the army. From 1940–2, smaller quantities were brokered through other companies for delivery to the navy.[34]

At one point, the colonial Government of Taiwan took over partial control of Taiwan Shoyaku's factory and went so far as to supply special labels for the cocaine packages. During the early 1930s, packets of cocaine marked with the label "Taiwan Governor General, Central Laboratory" were regularly seized by customs agents in China and India. The Indian Government loudly complained to opium officials at the League of Nations, specifically mentioning the "Taiwan Governor General" brand by name. And for several years "Taiwan General" cocaine appeared to have completely replaced Tokyo-produced "Fujitsuru" as the most popular illegal brand of cocaine in India.

As the years went on, and the start of World War II approached, Japan's presentations to the League of Nations became ever more fanciful. Member countries were required to file yearly reports, detailing each country's production and sales of narcotic drugs. In 1930, Japan reported that it manufactured 320 kilograms of cocaine in the preceding year, claiming that only 28 kilograms had been produced in Taiwan.[35] Documents discovered after World War II show that Taiwan's cocaine refineries were producing more than that amount each day.

Of course, the other members of the OAC had a fairly good idea of what was going on and criticism of Japan became even more intense. Japan had quit the league in 1933, in response to condemnation over the occupation of Manchuria. However, even after Yosuke Matsuoka led Japan out of the League of Nations in 1933, Japanese representatives continued to attend OAC meetings for another six years. But finding legitimate buyers for excess Formosan cocaine was a problem. By 1920 the medical profession had pretty much abandoned the use of cocaine except for head and neck surgery, and the "legitimate" market for cocaine had almost disappeared.

Pharmaceutical companies in Europe and the United States were not interested in purchasing cocaine from Japan. Even if they had been, it would not have solved Japan's problem. Licit purchasers who could get export certificates would not pay anywhere close to the amount of money that smugglers were willing to pay. In 1938, the legal wholesale (factory) price of cocaine was only about 1,200 yen a kilogram (about $600 at then two yen to the dollar). Bulk shipments fetched almost twice that much on the Chinese black market.

Mitsui's trading division tried to help sell the surplus cocaine. They referred a representative of Taiwan Shoyaku to a Mitsui agent in Shanghai. Mitsui had a major presence in Shanghai and was already doing a profitable business supplying opium to the new opium monopoly. In July of 1939, Taiwan Shoyaku sent Chen Ching Po to Shanghai with instructions to set up a branch office there. Chen Ching Po made tentative marketing arrangements with the manager of the Sino-Japanese Chung Wah Motion Picture Company, and promised to send samples of cocaine as soon as he arrived back in Taiwan. While recruiting the movie producer, Ching Po boasted that he had the backing of the Japanese authorities, and that he could arrange shipment of the cocaine to Shanghai via Japanese warships.[36]

The claim was almost certainly true. Evidence presented at the Tokyo War Crimes Trials revealed that not only did State-owned shipping companies carry opium and other drugs for the government, but at times the Japanese navy also participated.[37] At one point, two destroyers of the Imperial Navy were dispatched to Ceylon to escort a tramp steamer laden with 80 tons of Iranian opium. The captain of the steamer was concerned about German submarines and refused to proceed any further without an escort. Naval concerns about the safety of the ship's cargo were understandable; at wholesale prices alone, the shipment was worth more than thirty million dollars. Transporting smaller quantities of cocaine certainly would have posed no great difficulties. Whether

Ching Po was successful is not known, but somehow a willing buyer was found. When Allied forces arrived in Taiwan, there was no cocaine left in the warehouse.

Conclusions

It would be wrong to suppose that cocaine was a vital product line for any of the major Japanese drug firms or, for that matter, to suppliers of raw materials such as Mitsui and Mitsubishi. Here, the cocaine trade was just not that important. And once World War II began there was simply not enough coca leaf available to meet black-market demands. Japanese interests then turned to heroin and the opium from which heroin is made. Opium was easier to procure, demand was high, and producing heroin was simpler than refining the kind of coca grown in Asia. It was all the same to the Japanese drug firms. Specialized drug sales, with one group selling cocaine and another heroin, were a phenomenon that only emerged after World War II. Before then, Japanese and some European manufacturers made whatever drug they could place on the market. Recent events in South America suggest a similar pattern: South American "cartels" now supply heroin *and* cocaine, not to mention methamphetamine and marijuana.

Four hundred years have elapsed since Europeans first heard about an exotic American plant called coca. During that time, a great deal has been learned about cocaine making and about cocaine producers, not to mention international cartels. It is hard to escape the conclusion that the attempts at solving the cocaine problem by controlling cocaine production, either of raw materials or finished product, have not worked very well. One reason they have not worked is that they rely on international co-operation between governments. Governments in need of revenue have been, and probably always will be, willing to allow sales of drugs to foreigners. Given that reality, there is no reason to expect "supply-side" drug-control strategies to be any more effective today than in the past.

Efforts at international narcotics control rely on the co-operation and good-will of participating nations. It is presumed that all member nations will recognize drug abuse as a dire threat and that all states will act for the common good – presumptions similar to those of international agreements to stem use of biological and nuclear weapons. Neither the Japanese Government nor Japanese drug firms shared any of these perceptions. Drug abuse was unheard of in Japan and the country's leaders did not view it as a menace to the Japanese people. So Japan entered the drug business; Japanese authorities at every level participated, producing quantities of drugs that had no conceivable medical use. As long as the drugs were not used at home or in Europe, manufacturers remained untroubled and the drug business continued on.

Primary sources: Japan and Southeast Asia

Botanists at London's Kew Gardens oversaw the distribution of coca plants around the world and documented the results in papers published in their *Bulletin of Miscellaneous Information*. The Botanical Gardens in Java had its own journal, *Tesymannia*, which details many early experiments growing coca in Java. Data on coca cultivation in Java can be obtained from various sources, including minutes of the League of Nations Opium Advisory Committee ("OC" documents, available in major depository libraries) and in a particularly useful Ph.D. thesis – Emma Reens, 'La Coca de Java' (1919) – of which only two copies are available in the United States: one in the National Library of Medicine, the other at Yale. Another vital site is the Netherlands National Archives in the Hague, and surprisingly many records dealing with the NCF and the Coca-Growers Cartel are in English. Japan's cocaine and drug trafficking is described, though not in detail, in trial transcripts from the Tokyo War Crimes Trials. The best source, however, is the recently declassified material from Harry J. Anslinger's old Bureau of Narcotics (FBN). Anslinger supplied drug intelligence officers to General Douglas MacArthur's occupation forces and archived copies of their reports. FBN records from the 1930s were taken over by the Drug Enforcement Agency and were still classified until I filed "Freedom of Information" requests in 1993. The most relevant documents are contained in RG 170, Records of the DEA, acc 71-A-3554, boxes 10–30. Many consider any information from Anslinger or his cohorts suspect, but much of the material they turned up for MacArthur has been substantiated by sources in Japanese archives. The recent book by John Jennings (*The Opium Empire: Japanese Imperialism and Drug Trafficking in Asia, 1895–1945*, Praeger, 1997) is based entirely on Japanese archival research and reaches substantially the same conclusion outlined here. Finally, interesting information is also to be found in the "SCAP" records (Supreme Commander Allied Pacific); the Public Health section deals with drug-related problems, though some files still remain classified. These records, along with DEA papers, are now found in the new United States National Archives in College Park, MD.

Notes

1 British Foreign Office (London, FO). Letter from Max Muller, FO 371/1076/461, 1912.
2 "Introduction" by B. Röling, in Bertram Röling and Charles F. Rüter, eds, *The Tokyo Judgement: The International Military Tribunal for the Far East (IMTFE), 29 April 1946–12 November 1948* (Amsterdam: APA University Press, 1977).
3 This chapter is based on my recent book, *A Brief History of Cocaine* (Boca Raton: CRC Press, 1998); Paul Gootenberg generously helped with organization of these notes. Joseph Gagliano, *Coca Prohibition in Peru: The Historical Debates* (Tucson: University of Arizona Press, 1994), ch. 2. For the issue of dispersion, see: Anon., "Erythroxylon coca," *Bulletin of Miscellaneous Information* (Royal Botanical Gardens, Kew), (hence: *BMI*) (1892), 72–3; "Cultivation of medicinal plants in India," *Chemist and Druggist* (London) (17 April 1886), 324; "Ceylon coca leaves," *BMI* (1890), 152–3; and James Holland, "The useful plants of Nigeria," *BMI*, additional series, IX, (1909), 116–21.
4 Quote: Sir Edward Grey to Whitelaw Reid, United States Department of State [British FO 33412], 1910. Louis Atzenwiler, "Prewar production and distribution of narcotic drugs and their raw materials." League of Nations, Permanent Central Opium Board (hence: PCOB), 1944; United States Office of National Drug Control Policy, *The National Drug Control Strategy*, Table 5-24, "Worldwide potential net

production, 1988–1995" (metric tons) (Washington, DC: National College of Justice, Publication NCJ 160086, 1996).

5   Mea Allan, *The Hookers of Kew, 1785–1911* (London: Michael Joseph, 1967); Emma Reens, "La coca de Java. Monographie historique, botanique, chimique et pharma-coligique," Doctoral thesis in Pharmacy, L'Université de Paris). Published in Paris by Ecole Superieure de Pharmacie, 1919.

6   "Erythroxylon coca," *BMI* (1892), 72–3; "Medicinal plants in India," *Chemist and Druggist* (17 April 1886); "Ceylon coca leaves," *BMI* (1890), 152–3.

7   "The cultivation of coca," *Chemist and Druggist* (12 January 1889), 122–4; "The coca plants in cultivation," *Pharmaceutical Journal and Transactions* (London), (hence: PJT) (2 April 1892), 817–19; Reens, "La coca de Java" (1919).

8   "Cultivation of coca," *Chemist and Druggist* (1889), 122–4; "Coca plants in cultivation," *PJT* (1892), 817–19.

9   Reens, "La coca de Java" (1919); "Cultivation of coca," *Chemist and Druggist* (1889).

10 "Coca plants in cultivation," *PJT* (1892), 817–19.

11 "Ceylon coca leaves," *BMI* (1890), 152–3.

12 Reens, "La coca de Java" (1919).

13 The Netherlands National Archives (the Hague), Colonial Bank, Report 29 on the Nederlandsche Cocainefabriek, Omslag 928, 2.20.04. Archief van de Cultuur-, Handels-, en Industriebank, later Cultuurbank, NV, ARA II, 1945.

14 "Jaarverslag Coca Producenten Vereeninging." Omslag 1643, 2.20.04; Archief van de Cultuur-, Handels-, en Industriebank, Cultuurbank NV, ARA II, 1928.

15 "Jaarverslag Coca Producenten Vereeninging." Omslag 1643, 2.20.04; Archief van de Cultuur-, Handels-, en Industriebank, Cultuurbank NV, ARA II, 1928.

16 "Jaarverslag Coca Producenten Vereeninging." Omslag 1643, 2.20.04; Archief van de Cultuur-, Handels-, en Industriebank, Cultuurbank NV, ARA II, 1928; William Feldwick, ed., *Present-Day Impressions of Japan* (London: Globe Encyclopedia, 1919), 1047–8.

17 W. Scott Morton, *Japan: Its History and Culture* (New York: McGraw-Hill, 1984).

18 League of Nations (LN), Traffic in Opium and Dangerous Drugs, "The control of narcotic drugs and of opium smoking and the drug situation in Formosa (Taiwan)." Note by the Drug Control Service of Secretariat, 1944.

19 Memo from United States Consulate, Taihoku, Taiwan, 5 May 1934, to Secretary of State, "Re: cocaine and coca production," 1934, RG 170 (United States National Archives, Records of the Drug Enforcement Administration), (hence: DEA), acc 71-A-3554, box 20, Japan Statistical Reports 1945–6, 1946; Feldwick, *Impressions of Japan* (1919), 1047–8.

20 British FO, Traffic in Dangerous Drugs, Enclosure 2 in Dispatch 43, from G. Patton, Consul in Tamsui, Formosa [F 471/469/87], 1929; W. Speer, "Information concerning narcotics in Taiwan," Report of Agent Speer to GH, Supreme Commander for the Allied Powers, (hence: SCAP), Public Health and Welfare Section, 1946.

21 R. Nicholson, "Formosan cocaine factory," Report of Treasury Attaché Nicholson; introduced as Exhibit 388, IMTFE, 3 September 1946; copy to J. Henry Anslinger, 1939, in RG 170 DEA, box 20.

22 "Japan and Narcotic Drugs," RG 170 DEA, acc 71-A-3554, box 20, Japan Statistical Reports 1945–6. Tokyo, Ministry of Foreign Affairs of Japan, 1950.

23 League of Nations (LN), Traffic in Opium and Dangerous Drugs, "The control of narcotic drugs and of opium smoking and the drug situation in Formosa (Taiwan)." Note by the Drug Control Service of the Secretariat, 1944.

24 "Survey of production, manufacture and distribution of narcotic drugs and preparations by the Sankyo Company, Limited (Sankyo Kabushiki Kaisha)," Reports of Joseph Bransky, Field Investigator for Office of Counter-Intelligence, Tokyo, RG 170 DEA, acc 71-A-3554, box 20, Japan Statistical Reports 1945–6, 1946.

25 Anon., *Parke Davis, 1866–1966: A Backward Glance* (Detroit: Parke-Davis, 1966); Feldwick, *Impressions of Japan* (1919), 1047–8.
26 "Survey of production, manufacture and distribution of narcotic drugs and preparations by the Sankyo Company, Limited," J. Bransky, RG 170 DEA, acc 71-A-3554, box 20, Japan Statistical Reports 1945–6, 1946.
27 John M. Jennings, *The Opium Empire: Japanese Imperialism and Drug Trafficking in Asia, 1895–1945* (Westport: Praeger Press, 1997), 42–3, 54–7.
28 British FO, Memorandum from A. Ovens, "On the production of dried coca leaves and drugs derived therefrom, in Formosa," Enclosure 2 in memo of British Ambassador (Tokyo) to Foreign Office [F 8/8/87], 1930; J. Bransky, Survey of Hoshi Pharmaceutical Co., RG 170 DEA, acc 71-A-3554, box 20, Japan Statistical Reports 1945–6, 1946.
29 "Organized bands of traffickers in cocaine from Japan to India," letter of British Representative, 11 July 1932, League of Nations, Advisory Committee on Traffic in Opium and Other Dangerous Drugs (ACTODD), 1932; ACTODD, Report to Council on Work of the 13th Session, Geneva, 30 January 1930; Speech by Sir John Campbell, India representative to Committee, 1930; Wayland Speer to Anslinger on origin of "Fujitsuru" brand, RG 170 DEA, acc 71-A-3554, box 20, Japan Statistical Reports (1946); British FO, "Fujitsuru brand cocaine seized in India port," Letter of Second Secretary at British Embassy (Tokyo), in despatch, J. Dormer to Sir Austen Chamberlain [F 1556/201/87], 2 April 1928.
30 British FO, memo, A. Owens, "On the production of dried coca leaves," in Enclosure 2, memo of Ambassador to FO [f 8/8/87], 1930.
31 Calculated from Reens, "La coca de Java" (1919); Atzenwiler, "Prewar production and distribution of narcotic drugs and their raw materials," LN, Permanent Central Opium Board (PCOB), 1944.
32 Y. Yasynu, "Translation of a written statement submitted by Yasumi relative to the fraudulent figures furnished to the League of Nations and the Manchurian affair," RG 170 DEA, acc 71-A-3554, box 20, Japan Statistical Reports, 1945–6.
33 British FO, Traffic in Dangerous Drugs, Enclosure 2 in Despatch 43, G. Patton, Consul in Tamsui, Formosa [F 471/469/87], 1929.
34 Bransky, "Survey of production, manufacture and distribution of narcotic drugs and preparations by the Sankyo Company," RG 170 DEA, acc 71-A-3554, box 20, Japan Statistical Reports 1945–6, 1946.
35 League of Nations, ACTODD, Report on Work of 13th Session, January 1930, Speech by Sir John Campbell, India representative to the Committee (1930); Speer, "Information concerning narcotics in Taiwan," SCAP, Public Health & Welfare Section, 1946.
36 Nicholson, "Formosan cocaine factory," Treasury Department, as Exhibit 388, IMTFE, 3 September 1946; Anslinger copies (1939) in RG 170 DEA, box 20.
37 International Military Tribunal for the Far East (IMTFE), April 1946–November 1948, "Office report for 1939 of the Third Section of the Treaty Bureau – Foreign Ministry: The internal opium problem." Doc. 1045, 1939, IMTFE Exhibit 427.

Part III

The new American nexus (Colombia, Mexico)

8 Colombia

Cocaine and the "miracle" of modernity in Medellín

Mary Roldán

Miss Panela

era la reina de no se que cosa cuando la vio por *tv* …
enamorado quedó en el instante juró que la iba a tener …
conquistar la reina fue sólo lo que pensó este mal amor lo obsesionó
dando malos pasos nuevo rico se volvió tanto billete lo confundió
no importo a quien por encima le pasó hasta que al fin la coronó

le siguieron el rastro y la *DEA* lo agarró esa mujer lo delató

ya tras las rejas el día de visitas nuestro hombre se perfumará
enamorada pero del billete ella lo exprimirá
probablemente esta *love story* con balas terminará

miss panela tiene carro casa y ropa nueva
miss panela una triste vida lleva

(Los Aterciopelados, c.1996)[1]

The scope of the essay

This essay focuses on the cultural impact and (sometimes unintended) political and social consequences of narcotics trafficking during the last three decades in one limited, albeit centrally important, Colombian city, Medellín. As other essays in this collection suggest, cocaine has functioned as a totem for broader concerns regarding social unrest, class conflict, and political change in Europe, its former colonies and the United States since the late nineteenth century. Exploring the history of the drug and the pathology that surrounds it can thus provide a point of entry for an examination of political and economic processes and the fears and reactions these elicit within a specific society at a particular moment in time. It is in the spirit of such an inquiry that the essay that follows was conceived. I examine the cocaine trade within the context of Medellín's twentieth-century history, exploring how and why a hierarchical and paternalistic social and political order was challenged and to some extent transformed by the advent of cocaine in the early 1970s. In the course of confronting such a challenge, I argue, cultural practices, beliefs, and values in Medellín were altered in fundamental and intimate ways, or if you will, cocaine – as *La Violencia* is said

to have done for other parts of Colombia in the decades of the 1940s and 1950s
– broke the city's and the region of Antioquía's history in two.

The early years of the cocaine trade

There is something of an irony in the fact that the country that has become
synonymous with cocaine production in the late twentieth century had only a
limited history of cocaine cultivation and use until relatively recently. Indigenous
communities have grown and consumed coca leaves and other mind-altering
plants from pre-Columbian times to the present, of course, but the reduced size
of Colombia's indigenous population when compared to that of either Peru or
Bolivia – where everyday coca consumption has historically constituted an
important sector of the domestic economy in selected regions – ensured that
indigenous consumption had little impact on Colombian society as a whole. A
study of national substance abuse (including alcohol and tobacco consumption)
conducted by the University of Antioquia in 1987 estimated that 0.8 percent of
all Colombians consumed cocaine, a number that had declined five years later
when a follow-up study was conducted by the Ministry of Health in 1992.[2] This
is not to say that narcotics consumption in Colombia was unheard of before the
1960s: in the late nineteenth century, morphine and opium were popular drugs
among some upper-class individuals and professionals, while small groups of
marijuana and cocaine consumers existed in cities such as Cali, Medellín, and
Barranquilla from the decade of the 1920s on. In the early 1950s when
Colombians were busy killing each other in the fratricidal conflict known as *La
Violencia*, for instance, Liberal guerrillas in Urrao Antioquia were rumored to
fortify themselves before engaging in conflict with the government's forces by
ingesting a concoction of marijuana and gunpowder – an elixir that proved
equally popular thirty years later among the youth assassins employed by
Medellín's narcotics dealers. Still, for many years, Colombian coca leaf
production remained minor when compared to either Bolivia's or Peru's output,
accounting for no more than 10–15 percent of all the coca leaf processed into
cocaine for export.[3] Indeed, if any drug could be considered a "menace" in
Colombia before the 1970s that drug was alcohol – either in the form of
fermented corn-based *chicha* (beer) in the highlands or as processed sugar cane
distilled into rum and *aguardiente* on the coast and in the interior. The value of the
latter was so great (and remains so) that its production is still organized in
regional monopolies from whence a large percentage of Colombia's departmen-
tal revenues are derived.

The production of cocaine and the advent of an organized international
narcotics trade to commercialize and export it is therefore a "modern"
phenomenon in Colombia, one that first made its formal appearance in 1972.
Fittingly, the new cocaine industry initially emerged in Medellín, the first city to
industrialize in Colombia and for many decades the nation's leading exporter of
other valuable commodities such as gold and coffee. The earliest members of
what would gradually become a cocaine "Mafia" honed their skills in the

contraband trade of whiskey, cigarettes, and other luxury goods, expanded into the trade in marijuana during the drug's boom on the north coast in the 1960s and then began to traffic in cocaine in response to an upsurge in demand from North American merchants and contrabandists based in Colón, Panama City, and Turbo in Urabá in 1970.[4] The most notable of these early contrabandists/drug traffickers was Pablo Escobar Gaviria, an ambitious young man from the outskirts of Medellín (Rionegro) who had already forged a successful career as a tombstone thief and dealer in stolen vehicles prior to venturing into the commercialization of cocaine. While other traffickers were still immersed in the possibilities of the coastal marijuana trade, Escobar and his associates established contacts with coca producers in Bolivia and Peru, and firmed up their expertise in refining and distribution. Cocaine was both easier to transport and more profitable than marijuana, thus, when trade in Colombian marijuana was eclipsed by the successful introduction of a seedless variety grown and controlled by North American producers in the early 1970s, Escobar and other contrabandists like him were uniquely positioned to substitute cocaine for marijuana as Colombia's premier illicit export commodity. By a happy coincidence, moreover, large numbers of Colombians – the majority of them *paisas* (i.e. inhabitants of Antioquia, the department in which Medellín is situated) – were migrating and settling in the United States during exactly these years (1965–75), a phenomenon that enabled Escobar and other Antioqueño traffickers to count on a ready-made international distribution network for their increasingly lucrative commodity.[5] In 1978 the DEA estimated that 85 percent of all the cocaine sold in the United States originated in Colombia and that the trade was worth some $4 billion dollars a year (three years later *Time* estimated that $30 billion dollars worth of cocaine was being traded on United States streets – an amount that rivaled the revenue of many multinational corporations.)[6]

The trade in cocaine expanded so rapidly that by 1976 the heads of large drug-trafficking clans (*capos*) began to organize industry-wide meetings to centralize production, distribution, and commercialization of the drug, and to establish large-scale transportation systems and routes. Those who succeeded in securing control of trade routes to the United States quickly consolidated themselves as the industry's monopolists.[7] Consolidation came at a price, however. The drug trade (including marijuana), which had not been notably violent before the mid-1970s, became increasingly characterized by the Colombian equivalent of drive-by shootings and Mafia-like executions as criminal organizations competed for control of the narcotics trade with the old contraband networks that had initially managed the export of cocaine. Feuds between rival groups gradually gave rise to the creation of what would be known as "*pistolocos*" or youth assassins on motorbikes hired by the narcotics bosses to eliminate competitors, undesirables, and perceived traitors.[8] In the decade of the 1980s when tensions between some narcotics dealers and the State came to a head, the *pistolocos* of the 1970s evolved into neighborhood gangs of "*sicarios*" whose lethal task it became to target uncooperative public officials for hefty pre-established rates (the execution of a lowly policeman commanding a price of a few hundred dollars while the politically charged murder of a state minister or politician might cost the drug bosses several hundred thousand). Regional differences among the various narcotics trade "families" began to emerge during these years as well. While Medellín's cocaine traders established a reputation as violent thugs who would stop at almost nothing to maintain their control of the market (including putting together a war chest to mount a campaign of terror against the Colombian State), Cali's narcotics traffickers were notably more low-key and refused at various points to either take part in a war against the State or to consolidate their control of the market through the use of widespread violence.[9]

While what would emerge as Medellín's most significant export item was being quietly organized, the city's other industries, most notably the textile industry, were struggling to restructure themselves to compete in the modern world and survive. The 1960s and early 1970s were bleak years in Medellín, a city that despite its considerable economic importance and early integration into an international market-place had remained a highly parochial place in which the bulk of its inhabitants were caught uncomfortably between an immediate, traditional rural past and an incomplete, fractured urban present. Before the advent of the cocaine trade Medellín was known for its business acumen, conservative politics, religious devotion, large families, and an exaggerated sense of regional pride. It was a city where despite the presence of a large and old working class there were hardly any unions and most of these were led by priests. On any Sunday – and even on certain weekdays – the city's churches were filled to capacity at every mass and the family that could not boast a priest or nun among its children or closest relatives was an anomaly. The wealthy drove VW bugs and an occasional Mercedes while the middle classes and the poor lined up patiently to ride buses to their places of work. On Saturdays at midday the city rolled up its sidewalks; stores closed at noon and the downtown area was abandoned. Those with *fincas* (estates) piled into the family Land Rover and headed out to the countryside while those without, well, who knows what they did, for the city boasted no discothèques, few restaurants, no malls to shop in, no public entertainment, and almost no nightlife. There were plenty of bars and corner stores, however, and men could be seen in every neighborhood drowning their sorrows in shot glasses of *aguardiente*.

Into this somnolent morass of provincial life, home to the Colombian version of Puritanism – a city modeled on the virtues of frugality, thrift, and enterprise, where money was worshiped but ostentation and conspicuous consumption were contemptuously looked down upon – cocaine erupted with an explosive force. The first casualties of the narcotics industry were beggars. A fixture of life on Medellín's streets, clustered on street corners, around the entrances of the city's churches, stationed along the city's banks and office buildings exhibiting nauseous wounds and astonishing deformities, they suddenly began to disappear. Petty thievery declined during the same period as the unemployed youth of the city's surrounding slums found more lucrative work in the emergent drug syndicate – as messengers, bodyguards, *mulas* (human transporters of the drug), assassins, enforcers, gun runners, and distributors. As the industry gained ground, moreover, and its profits became more visible and widespread, other shocking social changes took place. Upper-class women who had cultivated particular seamstresses, masseuses, and beauticians, and considered them practically part of their retinue suddenly found themselves jilted as it became far more profitable to cater to the needs of endless molls and would-be mistresses of the gangster underworld. Beauty queens who in the past might have expected to make a brilliant match with some up-and-coming businessman or politician were seen on the arms of gold-chain-bearing individuals garbed in garish shirts unbuttoned to the navel, sporting cowboy hats and accompanied by hordes of pistol-toting youths.

Medellín jolted alive. Discothèques sprang up in what were once empty overgrown lots along Las Palmas, the road leading to El Retiro and Rionegro where many of the city's well-heeled inhabitants kept their weekend estates. On Saturday nights, the rural quiet of Oriente would be shattered by the sound of fireworks as Mafiosi celebrated having "coronado," that is, having successfully shipped a large cargo of cocaine to the United States. The city's first malls opened and stores selling an unheard-of array of imported items proliferated. Along the main road to the upper-class neighborhood of El Poblado imported car dealerships mushroomed. Rumors abounded of Dionysian parties where coke and drink flowed freely, and where Medellín's pretty young things gathered like moths around the flame of money and power, their used-up nubile bodies sometimes found dead and violated after a particularly intense night of partying. It became usual to see the small grotto outside the crude little chapel of Sabaneta covered in expensive flowers and the field surrounding it crowded with late model BMWs, Mercedes Benz, and Montero jeeps as drug dealers and their wives and girlfriends paid their respects to the Virgin and expressed their gratitude for being alive. The business of holy stamps flourished and on particularly active weekends when a heavy shipment of cocaine was sent out, not a single one of those bearing the image of Saint Jude – the patron saint of desperate causes – could be found within the confines of the city.

I have my own personal memory of when Antioquia and Medellín seemed to split into before and after cocaine. My cousins had a farm in Barbosa about forty minutes from the city where for generations sugar cane for the production of molasses loaves had been cultivated and processed. The farm houses in the area were whitewashed adobe structures encircled by brightly painted verandahs whose columns were strangled by masses of brilliant fuchsia-colored bougainvillea. The road was unpaved and in the rainy season sometimes impassable. There were two phones in the entire hamlet, both of them at little stores where items like liquor, coffee, candy, and matches were sold at vastly inflated prices. Electric service was sporadic and poor, and most of the farms had their own generators to supplement it. Labor relations were still feudal. On pay day the tenants and mill workers would climb up the steep hillside from the sugar plantation and line up, hats in hand, heads hung in deference before the elaborate wooden window grill from whence my uncle and the administrator would consult a huge ledger where wages, advances, and loans were recorded in an even hand and each worker's weekly pay was calculated. Like the land, the workers had been part of the farm for generations and even in the late 1970s still expected that their children too would one day work for my uncle, the girls as maids until they married, the boys as mill-hands and sharecroppers. Sometime in the early 1980s, however, I became aware that this little corner of the Middle Ages was on the verge of disappearing. Nubia, the farm's young housekeeper began to recount tales that in retrospect sealed the fate of "traditional" Antioquía and the paternalistic and static relations and cultural values that had characterized it for more than a century. Young men were leaving, she confided, and soon there would be no one to work the farm or to marry the local girls. Several of the latter had already been left pregnant or abandoned at the altar and many of them were moving away to look for factory work in nearby Girardota and Bello. Where were the men going I asked? Matter-of-factly she informed me that they had left in search of better economic prospects in the drug trade.

Soon after that the landscape made physically manifest the transformation wrought by cocaine. The adobe farmhouses gave way to concrete bunkers surrounded by security cameras that swiveled menacingly day and night at guarded steel gates painted strident tones of orange and red. Haphazardly planted orchards were transformed into well-manicured lawns dotted with miniature golf courses and huge stadium-like lights that insured against intruders. The road that local property holders had struggled for more than a decade to have paved was suddenly a smooth ribbon of tar and gravel that did not flood in the rainy season. Overbearing sport utility vehicles and souped-up jeeps with tinted, bullet-proof windows in whose murky interiors one could just make out the silhouette of machine-gun-toting bodyguards sped past one in a cloud of threatening dust, the tips of guns just visible through half-open windows, as if to say, don't even think of honking, yelling, or complaining unless you want to die. And as if this were not enough, a bullring sprang up on land that had once been an empty field owned by a distant relative. Spanish bulls and bullfighters were shipped in and out by jet at huge expense for the pleasure of the local Mafiosi. These arrived decked out in a ludicrously expensive version of the regional folk garb – *aguadas* hat, poncho, *carriel*, and hand-tooled leather riding gear resurrected in recreation of a long-disappeared rural past – astride pure-bred horses valued at more than a million dollars. Telephone lines appeared as if by magic and it was suddenly possible to receive television signals where once the radio had been the only source of projected sound. It became a commonplace saying that no one knew how poor Medellín's rich really were until the arrival of the cocaine Mafia.

At first no one really paid attention to cocaine. In the early 1980s it wasn't being consumed domestically in significant quantities and what became the terrifying political and social effects of the drug trade had yet to be felt. There were no dead presidential candidates, roaming legions of paramilitaries, groups of social cleansers, or car bombs set to go off in broad daylight in densely populated zones. When dead bodies did appear these were attributed to squabbles within the drug business itself, a matter about which few people cared. To the city's traditional élite, *arriviste* narcotics dealers were vulgar thugs with a jarring sense of style, their *guayaberas* and white leather shoes striking a discordant note in normally staid Medellín, but they were not at first perceived as a threat. To the city's poor and to some of the members of its impoverished middle class, in contrast, the drug lords were modern heroes – employers, benefactors, the harbingers of prosperity. Pablo Escobar and men like him became cultural icons and their possessions and extravagant ways a source of widespread voyeuristic interest. Otherwise respectable people made day trips by car from Medellín to Escobar's Hacienda Nápoles in southeastern Antioquia on the shores of the Magdalena River where the drug lord kept exotic animals and where the Cesna twin-engine plane in which he'd made his first successful drug shipment to the States rested triumphantly atop the estate's elaborate entry gate. It became common for young men from even respectable families to risk transporting drugs to the United States either as a lark or as a quick route to financial success, and among the twenty-something crowd schooled in the monotony and suffocatingly restrictive cultural environment of pre-cocaine Medellín, the narcotics trade offered freedom and unheard-of excitement. Medellín became addicted – not to cocaine, but to the effects of cocaine – to the money, scandal, and power created by cocaine, to the novelty of consumption and the eruption of late twentieth-century capitalist culture made possible by cocaine. Cocaine wrought in Medellín what the Vietnam War and the cultural revolution of "the sixties" wrought in the United States – it ruptured tradition, transformed social mores, restructured morality, thought, and expectations. In the process it also gradually emerged as the greatest threat yet to élite hegemony and the avenue for rethinking the city's structure of power and social relations.

The demise of "traditional values": cocaine as catalyst for class struggle

It has become commonplace to dwell on the economic effects of cocaine and to focus on the conspicuous consumption to which the drug lords' billionaire fortunes gave rise. The profits from cocaine were indeed fabulous. By one estimate Colombia's foreign reserves nearly doubled in the space of two years from $262.7 million dollars in 1975 to $467.9 million in 1977 and a good chunk of this was derived from drug dollars laundered through "*la ventana siniestra*" of the *Banco de la República*.[10] When the United States began to impose tougher banking laws that made the direct export of cash profits to Colombia more difficult, narcotics profits made their way into other sectors of the economy. In addition to the financial sector and the expanded contraband of consumer items, money was laundered through fictitious export billing, construction, medium-sized industries, urban and rural real estate, service industries, and recreation.[11] Perhaps the greatest impact of the profits from cocaine, however, was on the distribution of land in Colombia. In 1992 narcotics traffickers were estimated to own nearly 13 million hectares (or 31.2 million acres) of excellent agricultural land worth about $300 million dollars not including improvements, machinery, or cattle.[12] No one as yet has calculated the impact of the narcotics trade on employment, but it was surely notable. Francisco Thoumi, for instance, has argued that in 1985 Colombia's underground economy accounted for more than 8.7 percent of the country's GDP and that it was growing at a faster rate than the licit economy and rapidly becoming Colombia's most dynamic and important economic sector.[13]

The economic impact of the cocaine trade was particularly felt in Medellín where the emergence of the narcotics trade coincided with a decline in traditional industries that had given rise to significant economic dislocation among the city's least well off. A study by the National Planning Department (Departamento Nacional de Planeación) commissioned in 1991 in response to a special presidential program created to address Medellín's alarmingly high rates of violence found that by the 1960s "two cities" had developed and that the city as a whole was characterized by a high level of "social, spatial, and economic inequality among residents."[14] This was reflected in statistics on urban housing and income distribution. Most of the rural migrants to Medellín in the 1950s, many of them refugees from *La Violencia*, for instance, had settled on geologically perilous slopes because the city's location in a valley meant that there was little available flat land on which to expand. Eighty percent of the housing settlements established twenty years earlier were still illegal in 1990; these amounted to 30 percent of all the city's housing (or 100,000 settlements).[15] The distribution of income in Medellín also contrasted sharply with tendencies in other Colombian cities during the same decades: whereas in the rest of Colombia income inequality had tended to decrease since the 1960s, in Medellín income inequality had increased to such a degree that the distribution of wealth was worse in 1989 than it had been in 1967. Of Colombia's four major urban centers Medellín exhibited the highest concentration of wealth.[16] Fifteen years after the cocaine trade's emergence when the State forced several of its most notable *capi* (among these Pablo Escobar and the Ochoa brothers) into jail cells and prompted the partial dismantling of a vast narcotics empire, the impact of the cocaine trade on employment became even more evident. The number of unemployed or "inactive" male youths between the ages of twelve and twenty-nine rose to become the highest in the nation: the 1991 National Planning Department study estimated that in 1990 17.6 percent or 64,000 male youths neither worked, nor studied, nor looked for employment in Medellín, whereas the average among Colombia's four major urban centers for the same age group was 12.2 percent.[17]

Indeed, Medellín was a city where the nearly unbridgeable gulf between the residents in the *comunas* (working-class neighborhoods and slums) and its wealthier inhabitants was drawn in stark spatial, moral, and political terms. The *comunas* (in local parlance, "rough parts") cling precariously to the hillsides that ring the city while the principal administrative, commercial, political, and cultural establishments are located down in the valley in the center of Medellín. The physical location of the poor and the better off, of the powerless and the seat of power, shaped a discursive construction of the city in pathological terms that narcotics dealers such as Escobar exploited with great success. This sense of a bifurcated urban consciousness in which half the population (over a million people) see themselves and are seen by others as carriers of moral contagion and "outsiders" is reflected in Víctor Gaviria's 1985 film, *Rodrigo D – No Futuro*.[18] In it the main protagonist, who lives on slopes a mere fifteen minutes from downtown Medellín, refers to the city as a distant place fraught with danger where people like him meet hostility and repudiation. To "descend into the city" requires traversing psychic as well as physical space. Shortly before the protagonist is overcome by his sense of alienation and anomie, and commits suicide, the perception that he is the bearer of moral disease is confirmed by the disgusted reaction of the elevator operator in the elegant building that he chooses to throw himself from in the heart of Medellín's financial district.

More ominously, Antonio, the gang leader in Alonso Salazar's 1992 inter-view-based study, *Born to Die in Medellín*, envisions the center of Medellín as a cannibal, a living organism ready to consume the slum dwellers on the hillside above.[19] "Take a good look at the buildings in the center," he warns: "You can see their long arms stretching out, trying to catch something. It's us they're trying to grab."[20] While *comuna* dwellers perceived the city as a place where the centrally settled, better-off inhabitants threatened to devour and extinguish them, the latter perceived the *comuneros* as the source and embodiment of violence in Medellín. *Comuna* dwellers were melded with *sicarios* (assassins), *milicianos* (militia members), and *pandilleros* (gang members) – predators who undermined the integrity and boundaries of propriety and social place. Stallybrass and White note how the bourgeoisie in nineteenth-century London imagined slums as filthy lungs, sewers, and wounds that opened up to emit thieves and prostitutes, dangerous elements that penetrated bourgeois suburbs and infected these.[21] In a similar vein, Medellín's wealthier inhabitants invoked tropes of invasion and contamination to describe their sense of being besieged by a ring of slum dwellers who increasingly transgressed the ideological and physical space separating civilization from barbarism.

It was the skewed balance of power represented in this pathological concep-tion of the city that the cocaine trade, and the poor's participation in it, ultimately affected. In the decades before 1960 when Medellín was relatively prosperous, exclusion from direct participation in the city's decision-making was partially offset by the promise of a better material life. Access to jobs, housing, education, and public-health facilities overshadowed the natural limitations of the paternalistic ethos that underwrote Medellín's urban development. But by the late 1960s and 1970s the poor neighborhoods were increasingly the site of emergent gangs, petty thieves, and turf wars between older working-class residents and newly arrived, unemployed, and dislocated survivors of *La Violencia*. When Escobar and other drug leaders such as the Ochoa brothers began to recruit troops for the narcotics trade they found a ready pool of unemployed and alienated youths in the *comunas*. More importantly, however, the internal structure and culture characteristic of the narcotics trade generated precisely that which bourgeois politicians had once promised the *comuna* dwellers and never completely fulfilled: access to economic opportunity and social services in exchange for loyalty and obedience to the "traditional values" that underwrote bourgeois hegemony in Medellín. The internal organization of the narcotics trade faithfully reproduced the central values of regional culture: a hierarchical organization of authority, a glorification of "hard work," loyalty, and capitalism, and a near-fanatical devotion to religion and the cult of Mary and the saints. Medellín's schools of assassins, moreover, provided the structure, discipline, solidarity, and authority missing in "legitimate" society.[22]

The emergence and growth of the drug economy, moreover, made possible for the first time the satisfaction of a regional ethos of economic success that had been closed off to the members of the *comuna* by structural impediments in Medellín's licit economy, and although it occurred at the margins of legitimate society, the drug economy permanently redefined and altered prevailing codes of taste, consumption, and behavior in Medellín, not only among *comuneros*, but among other sectors of society as well. A blurring of formal distinctions between social sectors increasingly occurred. In addition, once the drug trade in Medellín assumed a political character under the tutelage of Escobar, and it became imperative to train and deploy armed youths into the heart of what had once been areas off-limits to the poor, the last of the cultural barriers between sectors of the city disappeared. Areas of the city that had once seemed distant, unobtainable, forbidden, became familiar in the day-to-day labor of death. By achieving economic success while reproducing the elements of bourgeois order outside the boundaries of legality, the drug trade also sparked a rethinking of the way society and power within it was distributed. The aura of privilege, the sense that political and economic entitlement was limited to a select few, was breached. The cocaine trade and the increased availability of arms and cash enabled the inhabitants of the *comuna* to assert a presence and to sometimes dominate parts of the city from which they had previously been excluded.

From the perspective of Medellín's traditional élite the cocaine trade was to blame for making what they had once thought of as a "quiescent" city violent and unstable. They accused Pablo Escobar and his lower-class *comuna* minions of destroying the city's "traditional values" (i.e. of destroying deference and paternalism as a form of political control). But although the narcotics trade can hardly be said to have introduced violence in Medellín what it did do was make violence the vehicle for the city's least powerful to contest the distribution of urban political, social, and economic power in ways that threatened the primacy of a historically exclusionary system of political control and its hierarchical social order. The narcotics trade thus served to turn society upside down. This reversal of the order of things had many effects, but perhaps one of the most significant was that it permanently destroyed any remaining awe that might have inhibited poor urban inhabitants from challenging the structure and process of political expression and participation imposed from above.

Cocaine's lessons? Responses to Escobar's death and State repression

Pablo Escobar met an ignominious death atop a rooftop in a residential area of Medellín in December 1993. For days after the event the media ran gory shots of the dead drug dealer's bullet-riddled overweight body as élites and Government officials gloated that they had finally eliminated the individual whom they believed to be the author of all of Colombia's recent ills. But Medellín's *pueblo* responded in an entirely different manner. They remembered Escobar not as the fiendish mastermind of the many bombs that had ended innocent people's lives, nor as the author of an all-out war against the Colombian State, but as one of themselves who had made good, a hero who even when he achieved unheard-of material success never forgot his humble beginnings or the people who accompanied him on his scale to the top. To many of the inhabitants of the *comunas* Pablo Escobar would be remembered as the man who distributed cash and groceries when people lost their jobs, the man who built soccer fields in poor neighborhoods and gave out tennis shoes to adolescents, the individual who founded and led community organizations such as *Medellín Sin Tugurios* (Medellín without Slums) and the *Movimiento Civismo en Marcha* (Civic Movement on the March). Indeed, many of them refused to believe that *"el Doctor"* or *"el Patrón"* (as they reverentially called him) had truly died; hardened by years of official lies and betrayals, Escobar's death was interpreted by many as but the latest in a long list of attempts by the Central Government and regional authorities to divest the *pueblo* of its leaders, to make them believe they were orphans without defenders.

It was precisely in the turbulent years following Escobar's demise when the State unleashed an unprecedented wave of repression against *comuna* inhabitants that the long-term effects of cocaine on the city's history became fully apparent. Escobar's imprisonment in 1991 and then his death two years later had reintroduced a state of chronic unemployment in Medellín, a situation felt with particular acuity in the slums and poverty belt that ringed the city. Former bodyguards, messengers, assassins, and operatives increasingly turned to kidnapping, assault, and robbery as substitutes for lost earnings. Even those engaged in licit activities in poor neighborhoods suffered as the ready supply of cash that had kept the local economy bouyant increasingly dried up. Armed organizations proliferated within the *comunas* as the unemployed forces of the narcotics trade emerged in reorganized fashion. Although *comuna* inhabitants were hardly – as the élite believed – the exclusive source of urban violence, they were certainly its primary victims: every weekend between twenty and forty young men were found dead in the city's poorest zones, the victims of either death squads (sometimes made up of rogue policemen), turf wars between competing criminal bands, or simply as casualties caught between an unfortunate exchange of crossfire.

In response, young people within the *comunas* – some of whom had at one time or another been influenced by urban cells of Marxist guerrilla groups such as the M-19 or EPL,[23] others by Christian radicalism, and still others with no ideological formation – organized armed neighborhood groups to engage in "clean-up" campaigns to rid their neighborhoods of drug dealers, prostitutes, homosexuals, molesters, rapists, and thieves. In lieu of the State, *comuneros* created their own forms of private justice and accountability. Young men such as "El Loco Uribe," a militia leader in Villa del Socorro in Medellín, began to mediate complaints of speculation, robbery, and bullying, gradually coming to have more legitimacy than "the legally established" authorities.[24] The militias initially enjoyed widespread support because they were perceived to eliminate only those who constituted "a threat to the community."[25] The contrast between the swift justice meted out by the militias and the glacial, frequently inequitable process of the legally constituted justice system was stark, but so too was the increasingly autonomous and arbitrary power of local "self-defense" units. The power to regulate people's personal and social lives soon became too great; militia members interceded in the domestic sphere to ensure that parents were caring properly for their children, and they held "people's courts" in which any individual found guilty of "speculating, cheating or double dealing" was condemned to death.[26] By 1993 many militias had begun to "exceed" their locally imposed mandate and like those involved in the narcotics trade before them, began to prey upon their own neighbors. "The situation began to slip out of our hands … [as] self enrichment through kidnaping, assaults, extortion, and threats" replaced an earlier sense of community protection and loyalty.[27] Dissatisfaction both within the militias and among the neighborhoods supporting these gradually generated among certain groups a desire to negotiate new formulations of local power and access to services between the State and the *comunas.*

For decades, the *comunros* had been forced by the inactivity of the State, but also by their own distrust of the State's objectives, to envision and generate solutions to their day-to-day problems that deviated from the accepted forms of authority and power inscribed in the city's official culture. In the course of doing so, the *comunas* experimented with and articulated a different vision of demo-cratic and community participation, a different vision of legitimacy and authority, a participatory rather than merely representative form of political identity that has fundamentally altered the definition of "citizenship" in Medellín. Militia demands for putting down arms included the creation of locally manned police forces; the demand that the appointment of appropriate interlocutors and local authorities obey *comuna* rather than officially determined notions of "legitimacy"; increased social investment with community participa-tion in the determination of that investment; and the development of permanent mechanisms of integration and non-violent forms of negotiation and representa-tion.[28] Representatives of the central State and Medellín's local officials were at first reluctant to accept the demands of the *comuneros.* The assistant to the *Consejería de la Paz* (Peace Commission) at the time, Ana Lucía Sánchez, remembers how representatives sent from Bogotá to negotiate with slum dwellers refused to accept as legitimate the spokespeople named by *comuna* residents to represent their interests because they were ex-gang members, former killers, and, in the eyes of Bogotá's officials, "common delinquents."[29] But faced with empty neighborhood halls and no interlocutors to receive the ministers and advocates sent from the capital to impose order, the State gradually gave way and found itself forced to deal with individuals who had until recently not only been the enemies of the State, but who insisted on an unheard-of degree of participation in the negotiating process.

The demands of the *comuneros* and the response of particular Government representatives to these demands point to the significance of the cocaine trade in the transformation of perceptions of power among the Medellín poor. Whatever ills were created by the narcotics trade – and they were horrible and many – the business of cocaine and the chain of events that it unleashed had the unexpected consequence of eradicating the last vestiges of subservience that for decades prior to the emergence of cocaine had made Medellín's poor accomplices in an exclusionary and paternalistic political and social order. Cocaine had stripped the élite of its aura of unassailable authority, made them vulnerable, and revealed the hypocrisy that overlay social barriers to popular participation. The attitude of disdain with which Medellín's wealthy had initially greeted the emergence of "*los mágicos*" had, for instance, long since given way to the seduction of cocaine – they sold their properties to narcotics dealers at ludicrously inflated prices, acted as their lawyers, accountants, and political allies, turned a blind eye to the dubious legality of business deals promising unprecedented profit margins. In the long run, moreover, the cocaine trade *democratized* violence (by affecting the city's wealthy as well as the poor) and served as a lesson to the poor that violence could be an effective instrument through which they could inspire fear and give political meaning to their discontents, even when these were not always coherent or consistently articulated. The city's élite had been reduced to men; no longer believers, the *comuna* inhabitants demanded to deal with them as equals.

After signing a series of non-aggression pacts in which locals determined the appointment of "*veedores*" who would oversee the peace process, Medellín's Government acknowledged that "the State must make its presence in the community felt to satisfy a debt with the community which it had abandoned during many years."[30] It was time, Antioquia's ex-Attorney General insisted, for the State to treat the *comuneros* as equals, not as victims: "[the State] should not act with pity towards them, but rather by giving them responsibilities and opportunities that they may be people [*que sean gente*]."[31] The recognition that paternalism inhibits the emergence of an identity as "people" represented an important step in the direction of acknowledging the long-term limitations of a style of government and social organization in which a few made decisions for the many and in which the latter were permanently relegated to the status of minors, wards, or children. However, the implication that the *comuneros* were not yet people struck a discordant note in the efforts of Medellín's authorities to come to terms with popular demands for political recognition and social integration. Thus, despite significant success in forcing the State and local authorities to accept local interlocutors as valid and legitimate representatives of community interests, and forcing the state to financially support and accept locally run community centers such as the *Casas Juveniles El Parche*, the State's ambivalent attitude toward the *comuneros* implicit in the ex-Attorney General's comment has recently represented a retreat on the part of regional powers in their relation to *comuna* leaders.

In the last two years, *Convivirs* – parastatal rural security forces, financed and run by members of the private sector, with the support and legal sanction of the State – have proliferated throughout Antioquia and given birth to fourteen urban cells operating in Medellín.[32] In January and February of 1997 a series of bombings in downtown Medellín and assassinations of community youth leaders such as Giovanni Osorio Acevedo from the *comuna* Villa del Socorro have seemed to indicate that the State has once more opted for a repressive response to popular mobilizations within Medellín, and that the slim victories achieved by *comuna* inhabitants after a decade or more of violence represented but a transient historical anomaly.[33] It nonetheless remains ironic that after decades of prolonged, recurrent violence, it was the *comuna* dwellers who generated and embraced democratic forms of participation and new ways of envisioning the distribution and exercise of power in Medellín, and the city's forefathers who were unable to make the transition to the political and social realities of the late twentieth century. For a brief moment cocaine wrought the "miracle" that made Medellín's poor into the powerful "menace" that forced the State to come to terms with these and to recognize – however reluctantly – that the Medellín of the 1990s shared little with the sleepy provincial capital where everyone had known their place before the advent of cocaine.

Epilogue

On the surface it is hard to discern the violent traces of cocaine on Medellín. After the seemingly endless nightmare of assassinations, homicides, and urban terror to which the city's inhabitants became inured in the late 1980s and early 1990s the city now seems eerily calm. In a poll conducted in February 1997 by Colombia's largest circulation daily, *El Tiempo*, Colombians were asked which of the nation's cities they would prefer to live in and Medellín won by a considerable margin. It is consistently perceived to be cleaner, more efficiently managed, friendlier, and less corrupt than other parts of Colombia. When people of the region leave and come back they are inevitably greeted by the smug remark, "there's no place like Medellín, is there?" With a mixture of pity and incredulity they ask: "how can you stand to live in Bogotá (Cali, Bucaramanga, etc., etc.)?" Gone are the days when government functionaries would refuse to board planes for meetings in Medellín because they feared for their lives, or the days when admitting one's city of provenance met with suspicious and derisive remarks about thugs and assassins. *Medellínenses* are convinced that the rest of Colombia abandoned them to confront the threat of the narcotics industry alone, and they succeeded in surviving anyway. There is bustle everywhere – malls are filled to capacity, new restaurants and trendy bars (replacing the old ones that were bombed) spring up with astonishing regularity in El Poblado's *Zona Rosa* as youngsters zip around the city in brand new Chevrolet Blazers and Jeep Cherokees, garbed in Oakley sunglasses, their ears glued to cellular phones as they whip and wind through traffic. Pert models with bursting décolletages and reinforced rear ends touting everything from beer to lingerie intrude as constant reminders of the feminine ideal the cocaine trade fashioned into a societal norm from plastic surgery. In the last national beauty contest acrid accusations flew back and forth regarding just how much physical reconstruction was allowable before banning a contestant from participating (and, *sotto voce*, how much drug money was involved in launching the career of more than one beauty).

The local newspaper no longer reports massacres or homicides, car-jackings or gang rapes. It really does appear at first glance that, except for having completely internalized the trappings of late consumer capitalism introduced by cocaine, the city has returned to its "traditional values" and smug provincialism of yore. But scratch the glittery, upbeat surface just a little and you can still find the presence of cocaine affecting more than the city's consumer patterns. Cocaine still runs the show at the city's numerous "in" nightclubs where dropping a drink or refusing the advances of a surly *"traqueto"*[34] can mean instant death or, in the case of women, a vicious rape while the upper-class young men in whose company "good girls" flirt with the thrill of violence are forced to watch helplessly. Perhaps more disturbingly, cocaine and its salesmen are once more heroes – they represent manly values, a cowboy ruggedness attractively enveloped in power and easy money. Violence has become the drug of choice among wealthy young men in Medellín and the self-made, aggressive arrogance of cocaine CEOs their ideal. On the other side of town in the *comunas* – conveniently out of sight of boutique-ridden El Poblado – business is also as usual, only no one bothers to keep statistics of the weekend homicides that have in the last year and a half eliminated every single one of the community leaders who emerged in the aftermath of Escobar's death. Even the San Pedro cemetery where the majority of these young men are buried has stopped indicating the date of birth on the tombstones of the recently deceased – perhaps for fear of the shock it might create to know what a large percentage of the city's young male poor have disappeared. Indeed, while many Colombians have made clear their dissatisfaction with corruption and their repudiation of the violent ethos embraced by the drug trade, in cities such as Cali and Medellín, where it constituted a crucial source of employment and economic welfare, the recent passage of stricter sentencing and expropriation laws directed at reducing the wealth and influence of drug traffickers such as Cali's Rodríguez Orejuela brothers sparks little more than disdain and dismay from the urban poor. As one taxi driver succinctly put it to Santiago Montenegro (a *Banco de la República* board member in town for a high-powered summit on economic reform and employment policy) when asked what he thought might be the best way of reducing unemployment in the city, "take those guys out of jail. *Esos manes [those guys*, i.e. narcotics dealers] knew how to create employment."[35]

Primary sources: Colombia

The material for this essay was drawn from government documents and officially commissioned studies such as those published by the *Instituto de Desarrollo Económico de Antioquía* (IDEA) in the 1960s, Antioquía's (State) Governor's office in the 1980s and the Bogotá-based *Consejería Presidencial para Medellín y su Area Metropolitana* sponsored by the *Presidencia de la República* in the early 1990s. I have also relied on personal interviews with former judicial employees, *comuna* residents, and sectors of Medellín's élite and commercial communities who witnessed or took part in the heady years of the narcotics trade's emergence. Newspapers (especially Antioquia's major circulation daily, *El Colombiano*, and the Bogotá-based *El Espéctador*) are an excellent if sometimes subjective source of statistical and urban policy information. News magazines such as *Alternativa* and *Semana* are particularly useful for information on the emergence of militias, gangs, and paramilitary groups, as are the human rights reports published by the Commission of Andean Jurists. A source of rich insight into Medellín neighborhood life over the last forty years may be found in recorded interviews and research notes collected as part of an extensive oral-history project conducted by research associates of the *Instituto de Estudios Regionales* (INER) at the Universidad de Antioquia in Medellín.

Reliable economic data about the cocaine industry is much more difficult to obtain than other types of primary material. Roberto Steiner, an economist affiliated with Bogotá economic think-tank, Fedesarrollo, argues in a recent essay in *World Development* that official estimates of the impact of the drug trade on Colombia's economy present wildly divergent data.[36] Inconsistencies and unsubstantiated approximations of narcotics revenue, employment, and consumption patterns in both the United States and Colombia are commonly found even among data collected by government and independent agencies operating in the same country. That same essay, however, provides a good comparative perspective on differing estimates and sources on the economic impact of the narcotics trade, including data collected by the DEA, the United States Customs Office, Office of National Drug Control Policy, Federal Drug Seizure Program, and Congressional inquiries in addition to calculations made by Colombian economists such as Kalmonowitz, O'Byrne, and Reina. Finally, much of the social detail seen in the essay is the product of my own personal observation over a two-decade research relationship with Antioquia and from participation in an interdisciplinary seminar and consulting group of scholars studying varied aspects of urban violence sponsored by the Governor's office in Antioquia during the late 1980s and 1990s.

Notes

1 Translation: *She was the queen of who knows what when he saw her on tv ... he fell in love immediately and swore she would be his ... conquering the queen was his only thought, this ill-fated love obsessed him ... setting off on a bad path he became nouveau rich, so much money confused him, he cared not whom he stepped on until finally he got her ... the DEA tracked him down, that woman had betrayed him ... now behind bars on visitors' day our man bathes himself in aftershave, she's in love but with money and she'll wring him dry, this love story will probably end with bullets ... Miss Panela has a car, a house and new clothes, Miss Panela has a sad life.* "Miss Panela" from the album, *La Pipa de la Paz*, by Los Aterciopelados (a well-known Medellín rock band), 1996.

2 *Semana* (4 May 1993), 108.

3 This may soon change. In 1997 Colombia was estimated to have 79,200 hectares of land planted in poppies and coca, making it Latin America's leading narcotics cultivator (not just the leader in narcotics processing). *El Tiempo* (21 June 1998).

4 Dario Betancourt and Martha L. García, *Contrabandistas, Marimberos y Mafiosos: Historia Social de la Mafia Colombiana (1965–1992)* (Bogotá: Tercer Mundo Editores, 1994), 70.

5 Betancourt and García, *Contrabandistas* (1994), 70.

6 Alonso Salazar and Ana María Jaramillo, *Medellín: Las Subculturas del Narcotráfico*, Colección Sociedad y Conflicto (Bogotá: CINEP, 1992), 46, 51.

7 Salazar and Jaramillo, *Medellín* (1992), 42.

8 Salazar and Jaramillo, *Medellín* (1992), 43.

9 Salazar and Jaramillo, *Medellín* (1992), 53, 72.

10 Salazar and Jaramillo, *Medellín* (1992), 111. Meaning "left" or "back window" – i.e. "under the table."

11 Mario Arango, *Impacto del Narcotráfico en Antioquia* (Medellín: Editorial J.M. Arango, 1988), 78.

12 Betancourt and García, *Contrabandistas* (1994), 120.

13 Francisco Thoumi, *Economía Política y Narcotráfico* (Bogotá: Tercer Mundo Editores, 1994), ch. 5.

14 Presidencia de la República, Dirección Programa Presidencial para Medellín y el Area Metropolitana, Departamento Nacional de Planeación, *Medellín: Reencuentro con el Futuro* (Bogotá, 1991), 8.

15 *Medellín: Reencuentro con el Futuro* (1991), 20.

16 *Medellín: Reencuentro con el Futuro* (1991), 10. Medellín's Gini Coefficient was .516 compared to an average of .467 among the other three major urban centers and a national average coefficient of .474.

17 *Medellín: Reencuentro con el Futuro* (1991), 15. The possibilities for future employment were also bleaker in Medellín than in other urban areas. Whereas other Colombian metropolitan areas typically experienced an annual rate of employment growth of 2.5 percent, Medellín boasted a mere 1.5 percent growth in employment, and while total unemployment figures in other metropolitan areas fell from an average of 10.6 to 9.9 percent, the average number of unemployed increased in Medellín from 12.4 to 14 percent. It bears mentioning that these statistics reflect "official" unemployment figures; unofficial sources typically estimated the "real" level of unemployment in Medellín at closer to 30 percent during the same period.

18 The actors in the movie were all young *comuna* males, among them several ex-*sicarios* or youth assassins. By the time the movie had finished filming only the main protagonist was still alive in real life.

19 Alonso Salazar, *Born to Die in Medellín* (London: Verso, 1992).

20 Salazar, *Born to Die in Medellín* (1992), 32.

21 Peter Stallybrass and Allon White, *The Politics and Poetics of Transgression* (Ithaca: Cornell University Press, 1985), 133.

22 For a revealing discussion of the importance of order, discipline, and hierarchy among gang members, see interviews conducted with members of the Bloods and the Crips in Leon Bing, *Do or Die: The Bloods and the Crips Speak for Themselves* (New York: HarperCollins, 1989).

23 Typically, guerrilla groups had long abandoned the urban areas and individuals who had once been exposed to their teachings adapted them to the current situation of community disorder in the 1990s. In other words, groups embracing the ideological precepts of radical organizations were not directly operating here.

24 *El Espéctador*, "Diálogos en un país loco de violencias" (13 February 1994).

25 *El Espéctador*, "Diálogos" (1994).

26 *El Espéctador*, "Diálogos" (1994).

27 *El Espéctador*, "Diálogos" (1994).

28 It is interesting to compare demands made by Medellín *comuna* members with those articulated by members of the Bloods and the Crips in Los Angeles in the immediate aftermath of the Los Angeles riots; their demands were nearly identical (community policing; the creation of neighborhood associations with decision-making authority and say over urban projects; greater investment in small businesses, etc.). See Alexander Cockburn, "Beat the devil," *The Nation* (May 1991).

29 Interviews conducted by the author with Ana Lucía Sánchez, Medellín, 1992, 1994.

30 "Paz con las milicias está madura," *El Espéctador* (Bogotá) (13 February 1994).

31 "Paz con las milicias," *El Espéctador* (1994). An alternative translation is "as *if* they were people."

32 *El Tiempo* (Bogotá) (17 November 1996), 6A (and 30 January 1997). For a more complete look at the advance of the *Convivir* organizations, see *Espéctador* (27 October 1996 and 3 November 1996); and "Mano dura o tenaza militar?," *Alternativa* 5 (15 November–15 December 1996), 11–14.

33 *El Tiempo* (1 January 1997).

34 Slang for drug dealer.

35 Reported with shock in *El Tiempo* (15 February 1998).

36 Roberto Steiner, "Colombia's income from the drug trade," *World Development* 26(6) (1998), 1013–31.

9 Cocaine in Mexico

A prelude to "*los Narcos*"

Luis Astorga

(Translated by Paul Gootenberg)

Coca to cocaine, 1880s–1960s

Mexico's familiarity with cocaine began in the nineteenth century in medical usage. By 1889, in the view of one professor Francisco Solórzano Arriaga "use of coca has spread widely in Mexico, given its reputation as a digestive aid, calming agent and nutritive."[1] Little else was said about its actual users. His study dealt mainly with the coca plant itself, the cocaine alkaloid, and its therapeutic properties. As the essay closes, he observes: "I consider medical coca an herb to be included among the most vital of our therapeutic tools, and its active agent [cocaine] as an anesthetic of great value." Mexico's specialized journals reported on the applications of a variety of pharmaceuticals from across the world, their composition, means of preparation, suggested dosage, and practically all the latest novelties in the field. For example: intravenous injections of cocaine against cholera in Hamburg (1893); "wafers" of cocaine and caffeine to ward off migraines; elixirs of cola nut, coca, and glyceric-phosphates of calcium, and the like. Ads even showed up in Porfirian-era (1877–1910) agricultural journals to promote Mexican cultivation of coca as a *hacienda*-style export crop (fruitlessly it seems).[2] Coca remained well-ensconced in the Pharmacopeia of Mexico into the 1940s.

There were of course the coca wines. Among the typical brands of the era, inspired by the success of *vin Mariani*, we must mention Mariani's wine itself: "The best tonic and restorative. It's a delicious Bordeaux with Coca of Peru."[3] Plus *San Germán, Dinamógeno, Désiles*, Nutritious Tonic Wine, *San Julián*, etc. The second was touted as a remedy against female anemia as well as for children and the aged – against arthritis, paralysis, and senility. They also insisted its use would rejuvenate and prolong life. It was recommended for all ages, in all seasons, and all climes. In Mazatlán (state of Sinaloa), one could find this item at the Italian Pharmacy of L.B. Canobbio;[4] in México, the country's capital, one could buy it from the drug wholesaler, José Uihlein, his branches, and surely elsewhere. In 1939 there was still advertising for this product. The third brand was claimed as a powerful "restorative" free of poisons or bitterness; even children could take it without disgust or danger. It was indicated against anemia, neurasthenia (chronic nerve disease), debilitation, exhaustion, vertigo, neuralgia, Saint Vito's sickness (Parkinson's), in lactation, and so on. All of this potency was packed in a 225-gram bottle costing a mere 75 *centavos*. The fourth medicine above made claims for strengthening the lungs, regularizing heart rate, and activating good digestion. Regular use of this "cordial" was the suggestion for very active people.[5]

Around 1920, Mexican health officials decided to institute their growing eugenic concerns, echoing the criminalizing (prohibitionist) spirit of the international conferences beginning at Shanghai in 1909. They forcibly establish throughout the country "Regulations around products tending towards the spread of vices that degenerate the race and on the cultivation of plants useful to similar ends" – i.e. that prohibited growing and selling of marijuana. Opium poppies were still allowed, along with their by-products, as well as the importation of prepared opium, morphine, heroin, cocaine, and preparations from these substances for pharmaceutical use, always with the corresponding permits of the Department of Health. On 8 January 1925, President Plutarco Calles signs a decree to establish the procedures for said importation of opium, morphine, cocaine, and the like, abrogating those of 1923. In the new regulations, products are enumerated whose imports will be subject to permits of the Department of Public Health, and those that can be freely imported in small quantities, for example: 2 percent solutions of opium, 1 percent extracts of opium, 0.2 percent morphine, 20 percent coca leaf solutions, 2 percent coca extracts, etc. Furthermore, "strictly forbidden are the importation of smoking opium, marihuana in any form and heroin, its salts and its derivatives." In 1926, the prohibition that began against cultivation and sale of marijuana is extended to opiates as well.[6]

The scale of consumption of medications like morphine, heroin, marijuana, and cocaine outside of therapeutic control provoked the concern of doctors and pharmacists. There was worry about the "clandestine and illicit use" of these substances, which could be acquired in *cantinas* (Mexico's popular-class bars), cabarets, houses of prostitution, "and other dens of iniquity" for "criminal demand." There were calls for vigilance, halting production and for pursuit and punishment of such "public poisoners." If unheeded, such substances "would end up turning the entire world into a mass lunatic asylum." In Mazatlán, it was said that cocaine enjoyed its greatest demand among the "good folk" (i.e. regional élites) and that it easily could be found in bars and whorehouses. The quantities mentioned would hardly shock us today, but then were presented as "frightening facts": a little over a kilo of cocaine and less than 16 of opium confiscated "in just a short space of time." Moreover, the source of such facts suggested that while less than a kilo of cocaine and 2 of morphine were enough to satisfy the annual demand of a typical drugstore of Veracruz, "a few days ago I saw sold in a neighborhood pharmacy a kilo of cocaine in less than a fortnight." If still referred to as "heroic drugs," other terms invoked approach current concepts: "For patriotism, morality, and even personal survival, we must fight this shocking vice."[7] In a work published in 1927, Jesús Galindo y Villa remarked that the abuses of heroic drugs and narcotics, among them opium, morphine, heroin, cocaine, and marijuana "is a factor in our depopulation and degeneration."[8]

By the 1930s, a drug traffic existed in such cities as Mazatlán, Monterrey, Puebla, Nuevo Laredo, Tijuana, Ciudad Juárez, and Veracruz, among others. The amounts confiscated were generally counted in grams, except for one case in the port of Veracruz (12 kilograms of heroin) and another in Mexico City (1 or 10 kilos of cocaine, depending on the account). Home deliveries or through the post were already part of the seller's stratagem. The bribing or complicity of high officials and the police, as well as charges of trafficking or the protection thereof – against the Honorary Consul of Greece in Mexico, James Page or Dimistri Psihas, and against the Governor of Chihuahua, General Rodrigo Quevedo – were heard during the decade. Throughout the early 1930s, officials of the FBN (the United States Federal Bureau of Narcotics) also warned against an ongoing retail border trade in vials of French medicinal cocaine, marked "Pharmacie Ferdinand Roques, Paris" – all from one errant 1920s shipment to Mexico.[9]

From the 1940s through the 1970s cocaine rarely surfaces in the press. According to Felipe Bustamante in the newspaper, *Novedades*, that which circulated in Mexico in the 1960s arrived from Europe, Panama, Buenos Aires, and above all Cuba, as well as directly up from Peru itself. The "White Bride" – or *la novia blanca* as it was dubbed – entered Mexico via the ports of Salina Cruz, Acapulco, and Veracruz. Among the known spots of consumption in Mexico City were a few luxury houses of sin. For example, one was located at number 33 Pennsylvania Street (in the plush new neighborhood of Nápoles), run by the brothers César and Luis Ríos; another found on Melchor Ocampo, under the thumb of "Pepa la Gachupina" (Tricky the Spic, roughly translated), who also managed various apartments for drug dealing "frequented by the filthy rich and politicians." In such dens, as well as those of Esther, Estela, Liliana, La Malinche, Marta, Ruth, and so on, a gram of coke fetched 500 *pesos*, some ten times the authorized price of pharmaceutical cocaine. Among smugglers of the drug one hears of ships' crews and airline employees.

George Asaf Bala, José Mawayek Mayer, and Manuel Sharfen Pérez, Mexicans of Middle Eastern extraction, were regarded by Mexican authorities as the main supply sources for both heroin and cocaine. Asaf, known as the "Mexican Al Capone," and whose open profession was clothing sales, allegedly obtained his cocaine from Peruvian diplomats. James Attie, an American undercover agent, also noted the name of J.A. Couttolenc, a shipowner, smuggler of diamonds, and additionally of cocaine, which he would ship from Peru. He was apparently well connected with Mexican politicians. According to Agent Attie, Coronel Héctor Hernández Tello, Deputy Commander of the Federal Judicial Police, told him that Mexico possessed clandestine laboratories for producing heroin and cocaine. One of them, apparently for cocaine, was discovered in Mexico City in late June of 1960, thanks to leads provided by informant José López to American anti-drug agents working in Havana (Cuba), who then alerted the Mexican Federal Police. Four Cubans, a Mexican, and one

Ecuadorean were rounded up. According to the records of United States authorities, 7 kilos of refined cocaine were confiscated, along with seven more of cocaine paste.[10] Another cocaine-processing lab was discovered in Cuernavaca (Morelos), when it rather conspicuously blew up, on 19 November 1960! Among those held responsible were six Cuban nationals and a Mexican. However, only 74.5 grams of cocaine could be recovered at the scene. Harry J. Anslinger (veteran chief of the FBN) explained that at the start of the 1960s world consumption of cocaine was still quite minimal – except in Cuba, where according to him, more users could be found than on the rest of the planet combined.[11]

Rise of the Sinaloan *Narcos*, 1970–

A reporter murdered in Sinaloa in the 1970s had broached in his articles that as far as drug trafficking went, there existed a "silent complicity in Sinaloan society." Besides being "one of the leading producers of marijuana and heroin," Sinaloa served as a "permanent corridor" of cocaine. By then a qualitative change is noticeable, for example, in the data from confiscations, destruction or incineration of drugs: at the start of the decade (1962) cocaine was routinely included among opium, heroin and morphine, but at the end of the decade it mysteriously disappears from the lists. Sinaloa had distinguished itself, since the United States Prohibition era of the 1920s, as an important site in the production and traffic of (alcohol-substituting) drugs. From here would emerge the great majority of Mexico's most powerful traffickers, who profited from several generations of accumulated experience in the cultivation of poppies and marijuana, and in sales of opium, and heroin. In the 1970s, they were to diversify their exporting skills and added cocaine to their list of merchandise.

Between 1949 and 1958, in the entire country only 417 grams of cocaine were confiscated. Between 1960 and 1970, 29.5 kilograms of cocaine were captured across Mexico. From 1970 to 1976 that total soared to 1,089 kilos. Still, the Sinaloans mentioned in relation to drug possession almost never carried more than a few kilos. The largest cache, some 13 kilos, was confiscated from a Colombian in the Mexico City airport in 1976. But as the 1970s opened, even the non-initiated recognized the sound of the "pericazos" (cocaine snorting) in the bathrooms of the nightspots of Culiacán. Legends were inevitably spun around the erotic uses of cocaine. In 1975, the price of a kilogram in Sinaloa was estimated at around 1.5 million *pesos* (still at 12.5 to the dollar).[12]

Between January 1989 and October 1993, the amount of confiscated cocaine hit 215.5 tons, with annual lows and highs fluctuating between 37 tons in 1993 and 50.2 tons in 1991. From December 1994 to December 1996 the estimates reach 46.9 tons. Between December of 1988 and July of 1993, only the states of Aguascalientes, Hidalgo, and Tlaxcala saw no drug busts. In seven of the states the quantities seized exceeded 10 tons – for example, 25.05 in Chihuahua and 10.7 in Chiapas, for 60 percent of the total. In only three zones – the Federal District (Mexico City), Querétero, and San Luis Potosí – were these quantities less than a ton. In 1995, Mexican states with the largest confiscations were (from first to last): Quintana Roo, Sinaloa, Chiapas, Baja California, Sonora, and the Federal District. In 1996 the ranking was Tamaulipas, Baja California, Veracruz, Durango, Baja California Sur, and Chihuahua.[13]

In 1984, Carlos Aguilar Garza, the ex-co-ordinator of the anti-drug campaign of the 1970s in the northeast, was detained with 6 kilos of heroin and cocaine in Tamaulipas. In 1989, he was nabbed in Texas as an alleged "drug kingpin" (*Narcotraficante*) and handed over to Mexico's federal judiciary; he was assassinated in 1993. Cases like these of functionaries and ex-police officials enmeshed with drug trafficking, along with *políticos*, have been an integral part of this Mexican saga since the 1910s – as an immediate effect of the United States Harrison Narcotic Act (1914). The Mexican trade would be managed from political posts and through coercive pacts. It has proved a most practical business for men whose social positions enjoy high degrees of impunity.

The "primitive accumulation" of the Mexican traffickers was largely built upon opium smuggling and later marijuana. This capital was reinvested in the 1970s by the Sinaloan dealers in order to enter the cocaine bonanza in league with the Colombians – around the same time as the definitive displacement of the Cuban pioneers of this field. In 1976, a warrant was issued in Tijuana against the Sinaloan, Miguel Angel Félix Gallardo, for alleged traffic in heroin and cocaine. Nothing would happen – according to the DEA – because he enjoyed the support of Jaime Torres Espinoza, then an assistant director of the Mexican anti-drug campaign. In 1979, Félix Gallardo was named to the board of the Banco Somex in Chihuahua, along with his "lieutenant," Tomás Valles Corral. The bank's general manager between 1976 and 1982 was (the well-known politician) Mario Ramón Beteta. Until at least 1982, Félix Gallardo was a major bank stockholder and a nationally distinguished client. In late May of 1983, a photo was published in the society page of the Culiacán newspaper, *El Sol de Sinaloa*, where Félix Gallardo appears as the best man at the wedding of Rodolfo Sánchez Duarte, along with his father, the ex-governor of the State of Sinaloa, Leopoldo Sánchez Celis, who years before had served as best man at Félix Gallardo's own wedding. And in January 1985 he appears in another pose inaugurating an automobile dealership with his partner and godson, Sánchez Duarte. This burgeoning career soon became public knowledge far outside his place of origins. He had been an agent of the State judicial police of Sinaloa and later a member of the personal security guard of Governor Sánchez Celis during his term of office. Suspicions arose that his rise in the world of drug trafficking was not unrelated to his personal connections to the ex-governor.

Miguel Angel Félix Gallardo was formally accused of possession and trafficking of cocaine, maintaining a personal arms cache, and bribery. Since 1971, there appeared at least fourteen arrest warrants against him. Enrique Alvarez del Castillo, the head of the Mexican FBI (*Procuraduría General de la República* or PGR) was governor of Jalisco when Félix Gallardo operated there, and has dubbed him "*el número uno* of the international traffickers." Born in 1946 in Bellavista, a ranch on the outskirts of Culiacán, Félix Gallardo attended high school and studied business in the Sinaloan capital. Working in small businesses from his youth, in his twenties he joined the State judicial police and hence the governor's mansion assignment as a bodyguard for the children of Governor Sánchez Celis – who would then become his protector and "Godfather." Other biographical details suggest that his start in the drug business came through links to Eduardo "Lalo" Fernández – the legendary "capo" (Mexican Mafia chief) of the 1960s and 1970s.

After his ultimate capture in 1989, Félix Gallardo was described as a man of "skill, vision, discretion, refined, and surprisingly austere ... a friend of politicians of all stripes, with connections to commerce, agriculture, ranching, the press, and even in the university." His discretionary talents had won him "success as the public-relations specialist of the *narco*-political world ... avoiding scandals with the instincts of a cat."[14] Curiously, during almost two decades as "the world's most wanted man" (in the words of the PGR), Félix Gallardo operated openly as a businessman and nonchalantly circulated in Sinaloa's economic, political, and social circles, as elsewhere. His personal fortune was estimated at fifty million dollars in cash and real estate. He claimed ignorance of types like Caro, Fonseca, and even the Honduran, Matta Ballesteros, connected to the infamous Camarena case (the DEA agent assassinated in Guadalajara in 1985). He said that he had signed his first confession about this case under pressure and pointed to his signs of torture. According to the DEA, Matta was the pipeline to the Colombian traffickers and partner of the Cuban-born trafficker, Alberto Sicilia Falcón, a pioneer in the routing of South American cocaine to the United States via Mexico, who was apprehended by Mexican police in 1975. Matta was also Félix Gallardo's partner in cocaine starting in 1975, when the Mexicans first began dealing in cocaine on a grand scale and sought control in a business where Cuban-based traffickers had much experience. But these Cubans were few; nor could they rely on the army of "mules," networks of transport and distribution in both Mexico and the United States, nor the political or police protection afforded for decades to the Mexicans. By the mid-1980s, it is said that Félix Gallardo was moving a ton and a half monthly – mainly to one Pablo Acosta, who oversaw the passage of five tons of cocaine every month across his personal border territory of Ojinaga, Chihuahua, when annual United States consumption was calculated at close to 100 tons. Indeed, the estimated aggregate production of Peruvian, Bolivian, and Colombian cocaine for this era (1984 to 1986) is 251.9, 321, and 380.2 tons, respectively. Not until May of 1994 – during the bilateral talks between the Mexico and the United States attended by then Secretary of State Warren Christopher – was Félix Gallardo finally sentenced in the Camarena affair. He got forty years' time.

In the eyes of the DEA, the genuine kingpins – those involved mainly in heroin and cocaine trades rather than just marijuana – were not those apprehended for the 1985 killing. Instead, political meddling – particularly from the head of the PGR itself, Sergio García Ramírez – led to deception and cover-ups, effectively painting the case as a local police affair. Edward Heath, the DEA operations chief in Mexico, has said that Kiki Camarena was murdered as a result of pursuing their so-called "Operation Padrino," which naturally touched upon Félix Gallardo.

After his arrest, various groups emerged out of Félix Gallardo's network, quickly becoming as, or more, powerful than the original organization. The ongoing older Sinaloan oligopoly of traffickers assumed control of the principal trans-shipment and producing zones of the country – with the exception of the northeast, reserved for the group now headed by the Tamaulipan, Juan García Abrego. His rise and fall coincided with the *sexenio* (six-year term) of ex-President Salinas, whose elder brother Raúl is suspected of shielding him. "Raúl," of course, is still imprisoned accused of "illicit enrichment" (that most Mexican of crimes) and of masterminding the elimination of his ex-brother-in-law, Francisco Ruiz Massieu, then-president of the PRI (Mexico's official ruling party).[15]

At the start of the 1990s another Sinaloan boss arose, Amado Carrillo Fuentes, born near Culiacán. He had been dispatched the decade before by the Félix Gallardo organization to Ojinaga to work with Pablo Acosta, innovating methods of smuggling wholesale cocaine in larger aircraft. His group, based in border-town Ciudad Juárez, soon appeared as *número uno* on the wanted lists of United States authorities after the successful 1996 extradition of García Abrego. At the same time, the Arellano Félix brothers, presumptive relatives of Féliz Gallardo (and also of Culiacán), with their Tijuana-based network, moved into first place when Carrillo officially ended his days after complications from "aesthetic surgery" – on the ironically staged date of the fourth of July (1997). Within months, this version of events had even been questioned by Mexican soap operas (especially *Demasiado Corazón*, "Too Much Heart," famous for its frank depiction of the lives of *Narcos*).

None of these groups has relied exclusively on cocaine, but this is the drug behind their rapid accumulation of riches. The latest gossip about (a still-alive) Carrillo – seemingly the most entrepreneurial and cosmopolitan of the lot – suggests that with the recent break-up of his Morelos lair he has ventured several times to South America searching for a new base of operations, with free-market Chile best fitting his specifications. The unstated goal is to establish direct control, without Colombian intermediaries, over processes of Andean cocaine production and distribution, and to open up new routes and markets across Europe and the Pacific to boot.

In sum, cocaine in Mexico as elsewhere made its debut via nineteenth-century medical usage. Although its prohibition was on the books by the 1920s, Mexican authorities were mainly concerned about the opiates and marijuana. The consumption of cocaine locally has never come close to that seen in the United States, not even today. For that reason, commerce in cocaine had since its start a specific aim: to satisfy the demands of our neighbor to the north. The most prominent of traffickers after prohibitions have come from the Mexican northwest, an area that has long cultivated illicit substances. Their transformation and diversification in the 1970s – towards non-national products like cocaine – was due to clear geographic advantages, the relative profitability of cocaine, decades of prior experience in local drug smuggling, and to the established networks of political protection, transport, and distribution in both countries. To the Colombian traffickers, mounting obstacles to funneling cocaine through their time-honored Florida route became sufficient cause to reach mutually beneficial accords with their Mexican counterparts. This was a union of comparative advantages. The motley fortunes made in the process are considered by United States authorities to be the most dramatic in the global world of drugs. Nonetheless, the ways in which Mexico and Colombia have historically and structurally absorbed the politics and economy of drugs have proved considerably different. That, though, is another story.

Primary sources: Mexico

Among the most important sources for study of cocaine and other prohibited drugs in Mexico one must underline the United States National Archives, in College Park, MD, especially its Record Group 170 of the Drug Enforcement Agency (DEA). These were declassified in 1997–8, under the categories "Subject files of the Bureau of Narcotics and Dangerous Drugs, 1916–70" (boxes 3, 10, 22, 28, and 29) and "Office of Enforcement Policy, 1932–67" (boxes 10 and 13).

These papers allow one to appreciate the relative importance of cocaine in the Mexican drug market over time and the geographic relevance of Mexico as a transit point for cocaine to the United States. They are based on the vigilance, pursuits, observations, trials, and investigations of anti-drug agents and United States officials in Mexico, and communications with their Mexican counterparts. Official documents classified as "confidential" or "restricted use" from other eras often seem like signs of bureaucratic paranoia, weakly supported or simply exaggerated by academic standards. In many cases, the sources indicated by agents and officials are newspaper notes that mention suspects – above all *políticos* – and anonymous tips or named ones. The influence of such data depends on the level of authority that gives it credibility, independent of any basis in research. The most detailed reports, if less frequent, are those penned by United States anti-drug agents stationed in Mexico.

Besides United States archives, I have perused many old local newspapers from my home state of Sinaloa, medical and pharmacy journals from Mexico City (best preserved in the National University's specialized "Hemeroteca"), and the gamut of current Mexican political magazines and official documentation, however spotty or slanted, as well as, mentioned before, a few continuing national soap operas.

Notes

I thank Paul Gootenberg for suggestions and comments for the final version of this chapter and for clues on the existence of bibliographic rarities and other facets of the Mexican case. And Abel Barajas for help locating these in the *Hemeroteca Nacional*.

1 Francisco Solórzano Arriaga, "Apuntes relativos a la coca y la cocaína," in *Memorias de la Sociedad Científica "Antonio Alzate,"* vol. III (México: Imprenta del Gobierno Federal, 1889).
2 Oral communication, Paul Gootenberg, 1997.
3 See *La Semana Ilustrada* (México) (15 May 1912).
4 *El Correo de la Tarde* (Mazatlán) (27 January, 28 July 1898).
5 *El Correo de la Tarde* (20 November 1900).
6 *Diario Oficial* (28 July 1923; 15 January 1925). *La Farmacia* (June 1926).

7 See *La Farmacia*, vols V, X (1923); *El Demócrata Sinaloense* (7 June 1927).

8 Jesús Galindo y Villa, *Geografía de la República Mexicana*, vol. II (México: Librería Franco-Americana, 1927), 324–5, 327–8. Underlining in original.

9 United States Department of Treasury, Federal Bureau of Narcotics, "Report by the Government of the United States of America for the year 1931 on the traffic in opium and other dangerous drugs" (Washington, DC, 1932), 11–12. The problem started in 1922 with "2 lots" sold in Mexico with "25,344" quarter-ounce bottles, some 900 later seized in the United States. FBN officials alluded to this throughout the 1930s.

10 *Excélsior* (1–2 July 1960); *Ultimas Noticias* (1–2, 5 July 1960). C.A. Emerick, Deputy Commissioner, to Ralph Kelly, Commissioner of Customs, "Seizure of cocaine in Mexico City on information furnished by customs informer" (5 July 1960); Kelly to Harry J. Anslinger, Commissioner of Narcotics, "Seizure of Cocaine in Mexico City" (6 July 1960). Anslinger to Oscar Rabasa, Mexican Ambassador (Washington) (13 July 1960). RG 170/SF/FBNDD, box 29, 1957–60. The press versions are quite contradictory. The cocaine-processing laboratory was transformed, without explanation, into a lab for morphine and heroin. Neither were United States officials terribly precise: Anslinger in his note to Rabasa never mentions the lab. He simply mentions the confiscation of 14 kilos of "narcotics," and refers to cocaine in the following terms: "This case again illustrates the enormous diversions of cocaine that are now occurring in Peru and Bolivia."

11 Anslinger to Amb. Rabasa, 22 January 1960, RG 170 SF/FBNDD, box 29, 1957–60.

12 *La Voz de Sinaloa* (Culiacán) (16 April 1973; 9 March 1976); *El Sol de Sinaloa* (12 November 1975); *El Debate* (Culiacán) (11 November 1975). Olga Cárdenas de Ojeda, *Toximanía y Narcotráfico: Aspectos Legales* (México: Fondo de Cultura Económica, 1974), 137 and Table VII.6.

13 See Mario Ruiz Massieu, *El Marco Jurídico para el Combate de Narcotráfico* (México: Fondo de Cultura Económica, 1994), 146–7, 152, 156–7, and Tables 2, 3, 4. Secretaría de Relaciones Exteriores (Mexico), *México y Estados Unidos ante el Problema de las Drogas: Estudio-diagnóstico Conjunto* (México: Formación Gráfica, 1977), 99.

14 *El Proceso* 650 (17 April 1989).

15 *La Jornada* (México) (25 November 1995); *El Financiero* (México) (13 June 1995).

Bibliography

Major secondary sources

Adams, Samuel Hopkins, *The Great American Fraud*, Chicago: American Medical Association Press, 1912.

Albornoz, Mariano Martín, *Breves Apuntes sobre las Regiones Amazónicas*, Lima: Imprenta de el Progreso, 1885.

Aldrich, Michael R. and Robert W. Barker, "Historical aspects of cocaine use and abuse," in S.J. Mule, ed., *Cocaine: Chemical, Biological, Clinical, Social, and Treatment Aspects*, Cleveland: CRC Press, 1976, 1–13.

Allan, Mea, *The Hookers of Kew, 1785–1911*, London: Michael Joseph, 1967.

Allen, Catherine J., *The Hold Life Has: Coca and Cultural Identity in an Andean Community*, Washington, DC: Smithsonian Institution, 1988.

American Medical Association, *Nostrums and Quackery*, second edition, Chicago: AMA, 1912.

Andrews, George and David Solomon, *The Coca Leaf and Cocaine Papers*, New York: Harcourt Brace Jovanovich, 1975.

Anglin, Lise, *Cocaine: A Selection of Annotated Papers from 1880 to 1894 Concerning Health Effects*, Toronto: Addiction Research Foundation, 1985.

Anslinger, Harry J. and William F. Tompkins, *The Traffic in Narcotics*, New York: Funk & Wagnalls, 1953.

Arango, Mario, *Impacto del Narcotrafico en Antioquia*, Medellín: Editorial J.M. Arango, 1988.

—— *Los Funerales de Antioiquía la Grande*, Medellín: Editorial J.M. Arango, 1990.

Aschenbrandt, Theodor, "Die psysiologische Wirkung und Bedeutung des Cocain. muriat. auf den menschlichen Organismus," *Deutsche Medicinische Wochenschrift* 50 (12 December 1883), 730–2.

Ashley, Richard, *Cocaine: Its History, Uses and Effects*, New York: St Martin's, 1975.

Astorga, Luis A, *Mitología del "Narcotraficante" en México*, Mexico: Plaza y Valdés, 1995.

—— *El Siglo de las Drogas: Usos, Percepciones, Personajes*, Mexico: Espasa-Hoy Mexicana, 1996.

Baumohl, Jim, "The 'dope fiend's paradise' revisited: Notes from research in progress on drug law enforcement in San Francisco, 1875–1915," *The Surveyor* 24 (1992), 3–12.

Becker, Howard S, *Outsiders: Studies in the Sociology of Deviance*, New York: The Free Press, 1963.

Benjamin, Ludy T., Jr, Anne M. Rogers, and Angela Rosenbaum, "Coca-Cola, caffeine, and mental deficiency: Harry Holingworth and the Chattanooga trial of 1911," *Journal of the History of the Behavioral Sciences* 27 (1991), 42–55.

Berger, Cyril V., *La "Coco," Poison Moderne*, Paris: n.p., 1924.

Berridge, Virginia, "Opium over the counter in nineteenth-century England," *Pharmacy in History* 20 (1978), 91–100.

—— "War conditions and narcotics control: The passing of Defence of the Realm Act Regulation 40B," *Journal of Social Policy* 7 (1978), 285–304.

—— "Drugs and social policy: The establishment of drug control in Britain, 1900–30," *British Journal of Addiction* 79 (1984), 17–29.

—— "The origins of the English drug 'Scene,' 1890–1930," *Medical History* 32 (1988), 51–64.

Berridge, Virginia and Griffith Edwards, *Opium and the People: Opiate Use in Nineteenth-Century England*, London: Yale University Press, 1987.

Bertram, Eva, H. Blachman, K. Sharpe, and P. Andreas, *Drug War Politics: The Price of Denial*, Berkeley: University of California Press, 1996.

Bessel, Richard, "Policing, professionalism and politics in Weimar Germany," in Clive Emsley and B. Weinberger, eds, *Policing in Western Europe: Politics, Professionalism and Public Order, 1850–1940*, Westport, CT: Greenwood Press, 1991, 187–218.

Betancourt, Dario and Martha L. García, *Contrabandistas, Marimberos y Mafiosos: Historia Social de la Mafia Colombiana (1965–1992)*, Bogotá: Tercer Mundo Editores, 1994.

Binda A., Dante, "La cocaína: problema industrial en el Perú," *Actas y Trabajos del Segundo Congreso Peruano de Química* (Lima), vol. 1 (1943), 375–79.

Bing, Leon, *Do or Die: The Bloods and the Crips Speak for Themselves*, New York: HarperCollins, 1989.

Bitter Jz., Hendrik, *Experimenteele Oonderzoekingen over Bestrijding van Cocaïnevergiftiging door Inademing van Amylnitrie*, Helder: De Boer pub., 1888.

Block, Alan A., "European drug traffic and traffickers between the wars: The policy of suppression and its consequences," *Journal of Social History* 23 (1989), 314–37.

Boldó i Climent, Joan, ed., *La Coca Andina: Visión Indígena de una Planta Satanizada*, Mexico: Instituto Indígena Interamericana, 1986.

Bolten, G.C., "Over cocaïne-intoxicatie," *Nederlandsch Tijdschrift voor Geneeskunde* (1904), 673–87.

—— "Geschiedkundige bijzonderheden aangaande morphinisme en cocaïnisme," *Nederlandsch Tijdschrift voor Geneeskunde* II (1923), 1670–3.

Bourgois, Phillipe, *In Search of Respect: Selling Crack in El Barrio*. Cambridge: Cambridge University Press, 1995.

Brecher, Edward M. and the Editors of *Consumer Reports*, *Licit and Illicit Drugs*, Boston: Little, Brown & Co., 1972.

Buder, Johannes, *Die Reorganisation des Preussischen Polizei 1918–1923*, Frankfort: Peter Lang, 1986.

Bües, C., *La Coca: Apuntes Sobre la Planta, Beneficio, Enfermidades e Aplicación*, Lima: Ministerio de Fomento, 1911.

Burnham, John C., *Bad Habits: Drinking, Smoking, Taking Drugs, Gambling, Sexual Misbehavior, and Swearing in American History*, New York: New York University Press, 1993.

Byck, Robert, ed., *The Cocaine Papers by Sigmund Freud*, New York: Stonehill Publishing, 1974.

Cabieses, Fernando, *La Coca: ¿Dilema Trágico?* Lima: ENACO, 1993?.

Cámara de Comercio de Lima, *Guía Comercial e Industrial del Perú*, Lima: La Unión, 1921.

Camporesi, Piero, *Bread of Dreams: Food and Fantasy in Early Modern Europe*, orig. 1980, trans. D. Gentilcore, Chicago: University of Chicago Press, 1989.

Cárdenas de Ojega, Olga, *Toximanía y Narcotráfico: Aspectos Legales*, Mexico: Fondo de Cultura Económica, 1974.

Carter, William E. and M. Mamani P., *Coca en Bolivia*, La Paz: Librería Ed. Juventud, 1986.

Castillo, Fabio, *Los Jinetes de la Cocaína*, Bogotá: Editorial Documentos Periodísticos, 1987.

Chase, Paul W., "The politics of morality in Weimar Germany: Public controversy and parliamentary debate over changes in moral behavior in the twenties," unpublished Ph.D. dissertation in History, SUNY-Stony Brook, 1992.

Chatterjee, Syamal K., *Legal Aspects of International Drug Control*, the Hague: Nijhoff Pub., 1981.

Chester, Francis, *Shot Full: The Autobiography of a Drug Addict*, London: Methuen, 1938.

Conroy, Mary Schaeffer, "Abuse of drugs other than alcohol and tobacco in the Soviet Union," *Soviet Studies* 42 (1990), 447–80.

Corporación Región, ed., *Ser Joven en Medellín: Seis Ensayos*, second edition, Medellín: Corporación Región, 1993.

Courtwright, David T., *Dark Paradise: Opiate Addiction in America Before 1940*, Cambridge: Harvard University Press, 1982.

—— "The hidden epidemic: Opiate addiction and cocaine use in the South, 1860–1920," *Journal of Southern History* 49 (1983), 57–72.

—— "The rise and fall of cocaine in the United States," in J. Goodman, P. Lovejoy, and A. Sherratt, eds, *Consuming Habits: Drugs in History and Anthropology*, London: Routledge, 1995, ch. 10.

Cribb, Robert, "Opium and the Indonesian revolution," *Modern Asian Studies* 22(4) (1988), 701–22.

Cueto, Marcos, "Andean biology in Peru: Scientific styles on the periphery," *Isis* 80 (1989), 640–58.

—— *Excelencia Científica en la Periferia: Actividades e Investigaciones Biomédica en el Perú, 1890–1950*, Lima: Instituto de Estudios Peruanos, 1989.

Curtin, Philip D., *Cross-Cultural Trade in World History*, New York: Cambridge University Press, 1984.

Derdak, Thomas, *International Directory of Company Histories*, vol. 1, Chicago: St James Press, 1988.

Derteano, M.A. "Informe que presenta el Consul que suscribre sobre la coca en la isla de Java," *Boletin de Ministerio de Relaciones Exteriores del Perú* 15 (1918), 347–58.

Diehl, Frits, "The opium-tax farm on Java, 1813–1914: A quest for revenue by government and Chinese tax farmers," in *Conference on Indonesian Economic History in the Dutch Colonial Period*, Canberra: n.p., 1983.

Dingelstad, David, R. Gosden, B. Martin, and N. Vakas, "The social construction of drug debates," *Social Science Medicine* 43(12) (1996), 1829–38.

Douglas, Mary, *Purity and Danger: An Analysis of the Concepts of Pollution and Taboo*, orig. 1966, London: Routledge, 1991.

Durand, Juan E., *Ferrocarril de Lima a Yurimaguas a orillas del Huallaga*, Lima: Cámara de Diputados, 1903.

Eisewirth, Nancy, David E. Smith, and Donald Wesson, "Current perspectives on cocaine use in America," *Journal of Psychedelic Drugs* 5(2) (1972), 153–7.

Escohotado, Antonio, *Historia de las drogas*, 3 vols, Madrid: Alianza Editorial, 1989.

Estes, J. Worth, "The pharmacology of nineteenth-century patent medicines," *Pharmacy in History* 30 (1988), 3–18.

Esteves, Luis, *Apuntes para la Historia Económica del Perú*, Lima: Imprenta Huallaga, 1882.

Feldwick, William, ed., *Present-Day Impressions of Japan*, London: Globe Encyclopedia, 1919.

Flexner, Abraham, *Prostitution In Europe*, New York: Century Publishers, 1914.

Flynn, John C., *Cocaine: An In-Depth Look at the Facts, Science, History and Future of the World's Most Addictive Drug*, New York: Birch Lane Press, 1991.

Fosdick, Raymond B., *European Police Systems*, New York: The Century Company, 1915.

Freidson, E., *Profession of Medicine: A Study of the Sociology of Applied Knowledge*, New York: Dodd and Mead, 1970.

Freud, Sigmund, "Beiträge über die Anwendung des Cocain (Contribututions about the applications of cocaine)," *Weiner Medizinische Wochenschrift* 28 (9 July 1887), 929–32. Translated and reprinted in R. Byck, ed., *Cocaine Papers by Sigmund Freud*, New York: Stonehill Publishing, 1974, 171–6.

—— "Über Coca," translated and reprinted in R. Byck, ed., *Cocaine Papers by Sigmund Freud*, New York: Stonehill Publishing, 1974, 48–73.

Friman, H. Richard, *NarcoDiplomacy: Exporting the U.S. War on Drugs*, Ithaca: Cornell University Press, 1996.

Gagliano, Joseph, *Coca Prohibition in Peru: The Historical Debates*, Tucson: University of Arizona Press, 1994.

Galindo y Villa, Jesús, *Geografía de la República Méxicana*, 2 vols, Mexico: Librería Franco-Americana, 1927.

Garland, Alejandro, *Las Industrias en el Perú*, Lima: Imprenta del Estado, 1896.

—— *El Perú en 1906*, Lima: Imprenta la Industria, 1907.

Gay, George, C. Sheppard, D. Inaba, and J. Newmeyer, "Cocaine in perspective: 'Gift of the sun' to 'the rich man's drug,' " *Drug Forum* 2(4) (1973), 409–31.

Gereffi, Gary and Miguel Korzeniewicz, eds, *Commodity Chains and Global Capitalism*, Westport, CT: Greenwood Press, 1994.

Gilse, P.H.G. van, E. Laqueur, A.J. Steenhauer, and F.K. Wolff, *De cocaïne en hare vervangmiddelen als oppervlakte anaesthetica*, Leiden: A.W. Sijthoff Pubs., 1929.

Ginzburg, Carlo, *Ecstacies: Deciphering the Witches Sabbath*, orig. 1989, trans. R. Rosenthal, New York: Penguin, 1991.

Glaserfeld, Bruno, "Über das gehäufte Auftreten des Kokainismus in Berlin," *Deutsche Medizinische Wochenschrift* 46 (1920), 185.

Goode, Erich and Nachman Ben-Yehuda, *Moral Panics: The Social Construction of Deviance*, Oxford: Blackwell, 1994.

Goodman, Jordan, *Tobacco in History: The Cultures of Dependence*, London: Routledge, 1993.

Goodman, Jordan, P. Lovejoy, and A. Sheratt, eds, *Consuming Habits: Drugs in History and Anthropology*, London: Routledge, 1995.

Gootenberg, Paul, *Imagining Development: Economic Ideas in Peru's "Fictitious Prosperity" of Guano, 1840–1880*, Berkeley: University of California Press, 1993.

Grinspoon, Lester and James B. Bakalar, *Cocaine: A Drug and its Social Evolution*, New York: Basic Books, 1976.

—— "Coca and cocaine as medicines: An historical review," *Journal of Ethnopharmacology* 3 (1981), 149–51.

Guía Lascano: Gran Guía General del Comercio y de la Industria, 13 editions, Lima: O. Lascano, 1928–51.

Gusfield, Joseph R., *Contested Meanings: The Construction of Alcohol Problems*, Madison: University of Wisconsin Press, 1996.

Gutiérrez, Carlos and Vicente Zapata Ortiz, *Estudios Sobre la Coca y la Cocaína en el Perú*, Lima: Dirección de Educación, 1947.

Guttmacher, H., "Neue Artzmittel and Heilmethoden, über die verschiedenen Cocäin-Präparate und deren Wirkung," *Weiner Medizinische Presse* (9 August 1885). Translated and reprinted in R. Byck, ed., *Cocaine Papers by Sigmund Freud*, New York: Stonehill Publishing, 1974, 121–5.

Hamowy, Ronald, ed., *Dealing With Drugs: Consequences of Government Control*, Lexington, MA: Lexington Books, 1987.

Harnoy, Geoffrey, *Opiate Addiction, Morality and Medicine: From Moral Illness to Pathological Disease*, London: Macmillan, 1988.

Heather, Nick, A. Wodak, E. Nadelmann, and P. O'Hare, eds, *Psychoactive Drugs and Harm Reduction: From Faith to Science*, London: Whurr Publishers, 1993.

Helfand, William H., "Vin Mariani," *Pharmacy in History* 22(1) (1980), 11–19.

Helms, Dennis, T. Lesscault, and A. Smith, "Cocaine: Some observations on its history, legal classification, and pharmacology," *Contemporary Drug Problems* 4(2) (1975), 195–216.

Henman, Anthony ("Antonil"), *Mama Coca*, London: Hassle Free Press, 1978.

Hickel, Erika, "Das Kaiserliche Gesundheitsamt (Imperial Health Office) and the chemical industry in Germany during the Second Empire: Partners or adversaries?," in Roy Porter and M. Teich, eds, *Drugs and Narcotics in History*, Cambridge: Cambridge University Press, 1995, 97–113.

Higginson, Eduardo, "Memoria del Consul-General del Perú en Nueva York," *Boletín de Ministerio de Relaciones Exteriores del Perú* 9 (1912), 110–11.

Hirschmüller, Albrecht, "E. Merck und das Kokain: Zu Sigmund Freuds Kokainstudien und ihren Beziehungen zu der Darmstädter Firma," *Gesnerus* 52 (1995), 116–32.

Hissink, Coen, *Cocaïne, Berlijnsch Zedenbeeld*, Amsterdam: Antwerpen, 1928.

Hobsbawn, Eric, *Age of Extremes: The Short Twentieth Century, 1914–1991*, London: Michael Joseph, 1994.

Hohagen, Jorge, *Sumario de Informaciones Sobre Exportación del Perú*, Lima: Casa de Moneda, 1927.

Holmstedt, Bo and Arne Fredga, "Sundry episodes in the history of coca and cocaine," *Journal of Ethnopharmacology* 3 (1981), 113–47.

Instituto de Desarrollo Económico de Antioquia (IDEA), 11 August 1969, vol. II, Medellín, 1969.

Jennings, John M., *The Opium Empire: Japanese Imperialism and Drug Trafficking in Asia, 1895–1945*, Westport, CT: Praeger Press, 1997.

Joël, Ernst and F. Fränkel, *Der Cocainismus: Ein Beitrag zur Geschichte und Psychopathologie des Rauschgifte*, Berlin: Julius Springer, 1924.

Johnson, Bruce, "Righteousness before revenue: The forgotten moral crusade against the Indo-Chinese opium trade," *Journal of Drug Issues* 5 (1975), 307–16.

Jong, A.W.K. de, "Coca en de Extractie der Alkaloïden," voordracht gehouden ter gelegenheid van het Koffie-congres te Soerabaia op, 13 December 1907.

—— "Coca," in *Dr. K.W. van Gorkum's Oost-Indische Cultures, Derde Deel*, Amsterdam: Van Hoeve Pub., 1919, 277–302.

—— "Coca," in C.J.J. van Hall and C.van de Koppel, (eds) *De landbouw in de Indische Archipel, Deel IIA Voedingsgewassen en Geneesmiddelen*, 's-Gravenhage: van Hoeve, 1948, 866–88.

Jonnes, Jill, *Hep-Cats, Narcs, and Pipe-Dreams: A History of America's Romance with Illegal Drugs*, New York: Scribner, 1996.

Kalant, Oriana Josseau, *Maier's Cocaine Addiction (Der Kokainismus)* [translated excerpts], Toronto: Addiction Research Foundation, 1987.

Kaplan, Amy and Donald Pease, eds, *Cultures of United States Imperialism*, Durham: Duke University Press, 1993.

Karch, Steven B., *The Pathology of Drug Abuse*, second edition, New York: CRC Press, 1996.

—— *A Brief History of Cocaine*, Boca Raton: CRC Press, 1998.

Kawell, JoAnn, "The 'essentially Peruvian' industry: Legal cocaine production in the 19th Century," MS, "From Miracle to Menace," Russell Sage Foundation, New York, 1997.

—— *Going to the Source*, MS, Berkeley, 1997.

Kennedy, Joseph, *Coca Exotica: The Illustrated History of Cocaine*, New York: Cornwall Books, 1985.

Kinder, Douglas C. and William Walker III, "Stable force in a storm: Harry J. Anslinger and United States narcotic foreign policy, 1930–1962," *The Journal of American History* 72(4) (1986), 908–27.

King, Monroe Martin, "Dr. John S. Pemberton: Originator of Coca Cola," *Pharmacy in History* 29 (1987), 85–9.

Kohn, Marek, *Narcomania: On Heroin*, London: Faber & Faber, 1987.

—— *The Dope Girls: The Birth of the British Drug Underground*, London: Lawrence & Wishart, 1992.

Kolb, Eberhard, *The Weimar Republic*, trans. P.S. Falla, London: Unwin Hyman, 1988.

Kolko, Gabriel *The Triumph of Conservatism: A Reinterpretation of American History, 1900–1916*, New York: The Free Press, 1963.

Köller, Karl, "On the use of cocaine for producing an anesthesia in the eye," *The Lancet* (6 December 1884), 990–2.

Korf, Dirk and Marcel de Kort, "NV de Witte Waan, de Geschiedenis van de Nederlandsche Cocaïnefabriek," *NRC Handelsblad* 13 (5) (1989), Zaterdags Bijvoegsel, 5.

—— *Drugshandel en Drugsbestrijding*, Amsterdam: Verloren Pub., 1990.

Kort, Marcel de, "Drug policy: Medical or crime control? Medicalization and criminalization of drug use, and shifting drug policies," in Hans Binneveld and Rudolf Dekker, eds, *Curing and Insuring, Essays on Illness in Past Times: The Netherlands, Belgium, England and Italy, 16th–20th centuries*, Hilversum: Veloren Pub., 1993, 203–18.

—— "A short history of drugs in the Netherlands," in Ed Leuw and I. Haen Marshall, eds, *Between Prohibition and Legalization: The Dutch Experiment in Drug Policy*, Amsterdam/New York: Kugler Publications, 1994, 3–22.

—— "The Dutch cannabis debate 1968–1976," *Journal of Drug Issues* 24 (3) (1994), 417–27.

—— *Tussen Patiënt en Delinquent. Geschiedenis van het Nederlandse Drugsbeleid*, Hilversum: Verloren Pub., 1995.

Kort, Marcel de and Dirk-Jan Korf, "Hollandse prioriteiten, de ontwikkeling van de drugshandel en de opkomst van de narcoticabestrijding in Nederland," *TvC* 1 (1990), 13–31.

—— "The development of drug trade and drug control in the Netherlands, an historical perspective," *Crime, Law and Social Change* 17(1) (1992), 123–44.

Krauss, Melvyn B. and Edward P. Lazear, eds, *Searching for Alternatives: Drug Control Policy in the United States*, Stanford: Hoover Institution Press, 1991.

Laqueur, Walter, *Weimar: A Cultural History*, New York: Putnam, 1974.

Lausent-Herrera, Isabel, "La presencia japonesa en el eje Huánuco-Pucallpa entre 1918 y 1982," *Revista Geográfica* (Mexico) 107 (January–June 1988), 93–118.

League of Nations, Opium Advisory Committee, *Traffic in Opium and Other Dangerous Drugs* (OC series), Geneva: 1922–1940.

Lema, Ana María, "La coca de las Americas: Partido renido entre la Sociedad de las Propietarios de Yungas y la Sociedad de Naciones," in *I Coloquio Cocayapu*, La Paz: Cocayapu, 1992, 1–12.

Lewin, Louis, *Phantastica: Die Betäubenden und Erregenden Genussmittel*, Berlin: Georg Stilke, 1924. Translation: *Phantastica: Narcotic and Stimulating Drugs, Their Use and Abuse*, reprinted edition, New York: E.P. Dutton, 1964.

Liang, Hsi-Huey, *The Berlin Police Force in the Weimar Republic*, Berkeley: University of California Press, 1970.

Liebenau, Jonathan, *Medical Science and Medical Industry: The Formation of the American Pharmaceutical Industry*, Baltimore: the Johns Hopkins University Press, 1987.

Lissón, Carlos, *Breves Apuntes sobre la Sociología del Perú en 1886*, Lima: Imprenta Gil, 1887.

Lloyd, John Uri, *A Treatise on Coca (Erythroxylon Coca): The Divine Plant of the Incas*, Cincinnati: Lloyd Brothers, 1913.

Loynd, Harry, "Parke Davis: The never ending search for better medicines," *Addresses: The Newcomen Society in North America*, no. 4, New York: Princeton University Press, 1957, 12–15.

Luijk, Eric W. van, "A lesson from history on the issue of drug legalisation: The case of the opiumregie in the Dutch East Indies (1890–1940)," *Law and Society Association Conference*, Amsterdam, 1991.

Luijk E.W. van and J.C. van Ours, *How to Control Drugs. Serie research Memoranda 1993 – 30*, Faculteit der Economische Wetenschappen en Econometrie, Vrije Universiteit, Amsterdam, 1993.

Lutz, Tom, *American Nervousness, 1903: An Anecdotal History*, Ithaca: Cornell University Press, 1991.

Luzio A., Federico, "Tecnología: La fabricación de cocaína en Huánuco," *Agronomía* (La Molina) III(15) (1938), 44–55.

Lynch, A. Martín, "Factores que determinan la riqueza de cocaína de las hojas de cocaína," *La Riqueza Agrícola* (Lima) 7(1)0 (1912), 388–90.

McAllister, William B., "Conflicts of interest in the international drug control system," in William Walker III, ed., *Drug Control Policy: Essays in Historical and Comparative Perspective*, University Park: Penn State Press, 1992, 143–66.

—— "A limited enterprise: The history of international efforts to control addicting substances in the twentieth century," Ph.D. in History, University of Virginia, 1996.

MacDonagh, Michael, *In London During the Great War*, London: Eyre & Spottiswoode, 1935.

McWilliams, John C., "Through the past darkly: The politics and policies of America's drug war," in William Walker III, ed., *Drug Control Policy: Essays in Historical and Comparative Perspective*, University Park: Penn State Press, 1992, 5–41.

Maier, Hans W., *Der Kokainismus, Geschichte, Pathologie, Medizinische und Behördliche Bekämpfund*, Leipzig: Georg Thieme Verlag, 1926. Reprint: *Der Kokainismus*, trans. Oriana Josseau Kalant, Toronto: Addiction Research Foundation, 1987.

Manderson, Desmond, *From Mr. Sin to Mr. Big: A History of Australian Drug Laws*, Oxford: Oxford University Press, 1992.

—— "Metamorphosis: Clashing symbols in the social construction of drugs," *Journal of Drug Issues* 23(4) (1995), 799–816.

Mann, John, *Murder, Magic and Medicine*, New York: Oxford University Press, 1992.

Mannheim, Hermann, *Social Aspects of Crime In England between the Wars*, London: Allen & Unwin, 1940.

Mariani, Angelo, *Coca Erythroxylon (Vin Mariani): Its Uses in the Treatment of Disease*, fourth edition, New York: Mariani and Co., 1886.

—— *Coca and its Therapeutic Applications*, sec. edition, New York: J.N. Jaros, 1892.

Marshall, Jonathan, "Opium, tungsten and the search for national security," in William Walker III, ed., *Drug Control Policy: Essays in Historical and Comparative Perspective*, University Park: Penn State Press, 1992, 89–116.

Martindale, William, *Coca and Cocaine: Their History, Medical and Economic Uses, and Medicinal Preparations*, third edition, London: H.K. Lewis, 1894.

Merck, E., "Cocain und seine Salze," *Klinishe Monatsblätter für Augenheilkunde* 22 (November 1884), translated as "Cocaine and its salts," *Chicago Medical Journal and Examiner* 50 (February 1855), 157–63. Reprinted in Robert Byck, ed., *Cocaine Papers by Sigmund Freud*, New York: Stonehill Publishing, 1974, 77–81.

Mexico, Secretaria de Relaciones Exteriores, *México y Estados Unidos ante el Problema de las Drogas*, Mexico: Formación Gráfica, SA, 1997.

Mintz, Sidney W., *Sweetness and Power: The Place of Sugar in Modern History*, New York: Viking Penguin, 1985.

—— *Tasting Food, Tasting Freedom: Excursions into Eating, Culture, and the Past*, Boston: Beacon Press, 1996.

Morales, Edmundo, *Cocaine: White Gold Rush in Peru*, Tucson: University of Arizona Press, 1989.

Moreno y Maíz, Tomás, *Recherches Chimiques et Physiologiques sur L'erthoxlyum Coca du Pérou et la Cocaine*, Paris: L. Leclerc, 1868.

Morgan, H. Wayne, *Yesterday's Addicts: American Society and Drug Abuse, 1865–1920*, Norman: University of Oklahoma Press, 1974.

—— *Drugs in America: A Social History, 1800–1980*, Syracuse: Syracuse University Press, 1981.

Mortimer, W. Golden, *History of Coca, "The Divine Plant" of the Incas*, New York: J.H. Vail & Company, 1901. Reprinted San Francisco: F.H. Ludlow Library, 1974.

Morton, W. Scott, *Japan: Its History and Culture*, New York: McGraw-Hill, 1984.

Moscowitz, Milton, Michael Katz, and Robert Levering, eds, *Everybody's Business: An Almanac*, San Francisco: Harper & Rowe, 1900.

Musto, David F., *The American Disease: Origins of Narcotic Control*, New York: Oxford University Press, 1973, expanded edition, 1987.

—— "Lessons of the first cocaine epidemic," *Wall Street Journal* (11 June 1986), 11.

—— "America's first cocaine epidemic," *Wilson Quarterly* (Summer 1989), 59–64.

—— "Illicit price of cocaine in two eras: 1908–14 and 1982–89," *Connecticut Medicine* 54 (1990), 321–6.

—— "Opium, cocaine and marihuana in American history," *Scientific American* (July 1991), 40–7.

—— "International traffic in coca through the early 20th century," *Drug and Alcohol Dependence* 49 (1998), 145–56.

Nadelmann, Ethan A., "Global prohibition regimes: The evolution of norms in international society," *International Organization* 44(4) (1990), 479–526.

—— *Cops Across Borders: The Internationalization of U.S. Criminal Law Enforcement*, University Park: Penn State Press, 1993.

Office of National Drug Control Policy (United States), *The National Drug Control Strategy,*. Washington, DC: National College of Justice, 1996.

Pacini, Deborah and Christine Franquemont, eds, *Coca and Cocaine: Effects on People and Policy in Latin America*, Ithaca: Cultural Survival, 1986.

Parke, Davis & Company, *The Pharmacology of the Newer Materia Medica*, Detroit: George S. Davis, 1892.

—— *Seventy-five Years of Service to Medicine and Pharmacy: The Story of Parke, Davis & Company*, Detroit: Parke-Davis & Company, 1941?.

—— *Parke-Davis, 1866–1966: A Backward Glance*, Detroit: Parke-Davis, 1966.

Parssinen, Terry M., *Secret Passions, Secret Remedies: Narcotic Drugs in British Society 1820–1930*, Philadelphia: Institute for the Study of Human Issues, 1983.

Parssinen, Terry M. and Kathryn Meyer, "America and the world market for narcotic drugs, 1919–1939," paper presented to Organization of American Historians, 1990.

Paz Soldán, Carlos Enrique, "El problema médico-social de la coca en el Perú," *El Mercurio Peruano* 19 (1929), 584–603.

—— "La coca peruana y su futuro régimen político," *La Reforma Médica* (Lima) (January–February 1934), 69–77, 98–9.

—— *La Coca Peruana: Memorandum sobre su Situación Actual*, Lima: Sociedad Nacional Agraria, 1936.

—— "Luchamos contra la esclavitud del cocaísmo indígena: Sugestiones para una acción nacional," *La Reforma Médica* (1 January 1939), 19–24.

Pendergrast, Mark, *For God, Country, and Coca-Cola: The Unauthorized History of the Great American Soft-Drink and the Company that Makes It*, New York: Scribner, 1993.

Peru, Caja de Depósitos y Consignaciones (ENACO), *Memoria del Estanco de la Coca*, Lima: ENACO, 1955–60.

Peru, Comisión Peruana para el Estudio del Problema de la Coca [Dr Carlos Monge], *Contraréplica de la Comisión Peruana para el Estudio de la Coca a la Comisión de Encuestra de las Naciones Unidas sobre las Hojas de Coca*, Lima: Ministerio de Salud Pública y Asistencia Social, 1951.

Peru, Ministerio de Agricultura, *La Acción Oficial en el Desarrollo Agropecuario de la Colonización de Tingo María, Años 1942–46*, Lima: Dirección de Colonización, 1947.

Perú Indígena, Special Issue III (7–8) (December 1952).

"Peru: The White Goddess," *Time* (11 April 1949).

Phillips, Joel L. and Ronald W. Wynne, *Cocaine: The Mystique and the Reality*, New York: Avon Books, 1980.

Poppa, Terrence E., *El Zar de la droga*, Mexico: Editorial Selector, 1990.

Porter, Dorothy, "Social medicine and the new society: Medicine and scientific humanism in mid-twentieth century Britain," *Journal of Historical Sociology* 9(2) (1996), 168–87.

Porter, Roy and Mikuláš Teich, eds, *Drugs and Narcotics in History*, Cambridge: Cambridge University Press, 1995.

Poulsson, E., "Cocaïne," *Wetenschappelijke Bladen* (1926), 98–109.

Pozzi-Escot, E.M.M., "Recherches sur l'industrie de la cocaine au Pérou," *Bolletin des Sciences Pharmacologiques* (Paris) 20 (1913), 608–17.

Presidencia de la República (Colombia), Consejería Presidencial para Medellín y su Area Metropolitana, *II Seminario Alternativas de Futuro: Antioquia Hacia un Pacto Social*, first edition, Bogotá, 1993.

—— Dirección Programa Presidencial para Medellín y el Area Metropolitana, Departamento Nacional de Planeación, *Medellín: Reencuentro con el futuro*, Bogotá, 1991.

Rabines, Alfredo, "The production of cocaine in Peru," *Peru Today* (Lima) 3 (1911), 31–3.

Reens, Emma, *La coca de Java: Monographie Historique, Botanique, Chimique et Pharmacologique* (Doctoral thesis in Pharmacy, l'Université de Paris). Paris: Lons-le-Saunier, 1919.

Reid, William, *Coca: A Plant of the Andes*, Washington, DC: Pan American Union, Commodities of Commerce, 1918 (reprinted 1928, 1938).

Reinarman, Craig and Harry G. Levin, *Crack in America: Demon Drugs and Social Justice* Berkeley: University of California Press, 1997.

Renoz, Charles, *Le Pérou: Histoire-Description Physique et Politique: Productions-commerce, Immigration et Colonisation*, Brussels: P. Wensenbruch, 1897.

Ricketts, Carlos A., *Ensayos de Legislación Pro-indígena*, Arequipa: Tip. Cuadros, 1936.

Rodríguez, José, *Estudios Económicos-financieros y Ojeada sobre la Hacienda Pública del Perú*, Lima: Imprenta Gil, 1895.

Römer, J.A., *Hydrochloras Cocaini*, Leiden: Van Doesburgh Pub., 1885.

Rubio Correa, Marcial, comp., *Legislación Peruana sobre Drogas a partir de 1920*, Lima: CEDRO, Monografía de Investigación 2, 1988.

Rudgely, Richard, *Essential Substances: A Cultural History of Intoxicants in Society*, New York: Kodansha International, 1994.

Ruiz Massieu, Mario, *El Marco Jurídico para el Combate al Narcotráfico*, Mexico: Fondo de Cultura Económica, 1994.

Rush, James R., *Opium to Java: Revenue Farming and Chinese Enterprise in Colonial Indonesia, 1860–1910*, Ithaca: Cornell University Press, 1990.

Sainz, Luís, *La Coca: Estudio Médico-social de la Gran Toximanía Peruana*, Lima: Guardía Civil y Policía, 1938.

Salazar, Alonso, *Born to Die in Medellín*, London: Verso, 1992.

Salazar, Alonso and Ana María Jaramillo, *Medellín, Las Subculturas del Narcotráfico*, Colección Sociedad y Conflicto, Bogotá: Cinep, 1992.

Scheerer, Sebastian, *Die Genese der Betäubungsmittelgesetze in der Bundesrepublik Deutschland und in den Niederlanden*, Göttingen: Otto Schwartz & Co., 1982.

—— "Emergence of an international prohibition regime: The case of cocaine," MS, Law and Society Association Conference, Amsterdam, 1991.

Schivelbusch, Wolfgang, *Tastes of Paradise: A Social History of Spices, Stimulants and Intoxicants*, orig. 1980, New York: Vintage Press, 1992.

Schultze, Hermann, *Die Entwicklung der Chemischen Industrie in Deutschland seit dem Jahre 1875*, Halle a. S.: Tausch & Grosse, 1908.

Schur, Edwin M. and Hugo A. Bedau, *Victimless Crime: Two Sides on a Controversy*, Englewood Cliffs: Prentice-Hall, 1974.

Shannon, Elaine, *Desperados: Latin Drug Lords, U.S. Lawmen and the War America Can't Win*, New York: Viking Penguin, 1988.

Shultz, Carl B., "Statutory classification of cocaine as a narcotic: An illogical anachronism," *American Journal of Law and Medicine* 9(3) (1983), 225–45.

Siegal, Ronald K., "Cocaine and the privileged class: A review of historical and contemporary images," *Advances in Alcohol and Substance Abuse* (1984), 37–49.

Sijp, J.W.C.M. van der, "Cocaïne," Utrecht: Ph.D. thesis in Medicine, 1885.

Smith, David and Don Wesson, "Cocaine," *Journal of Ethnopharmacology* 10(4) (1978), 351–60.

Solórzano Arriaga, Francisco, "Apuntes relativos a la coca y la cocaína," *Memorias de la Sociedad Científica "Antonio Alzate"*, Mexico: Imprenta del Gobierno Federal, vol. III (1889).

Spencer, Elaine Glovka, *Police and the Social Order in the German Cities*, DeKalb: Northern Illinois University Press, 1992.

Spillane, Joseph F., *Cocaine: From Medical Marvel to Modern Menace in the United States, 1884–1920*, Baltimore: Johns Hopkins University Press, 1999.

—— "Did drug prohibition work? Reflections on the end of the first cocaine experience in the United States, 1910–45," *Journal of Drug Issues* 28(2) (1998), 517–38.

Stallybrass, Peter and Allon White, *The Politics and Poetics of Transgression*, Ithaca: Cornell University Press, 1985.

Stares, Paul B., *Global Habit: The Drug Problem in a Borderless World*, Washington, DC: Brookings Institute, 1996.

Starks, Michael, *Cocaine Fiends and Reefer Madness: An Illustrated History of Drugs in the Movies*, New York: Cornwall Books, 1982.

Starr, Paul, *The Social Transformation of American Medicine*, New York: Basic Books, 1982.

Stein, S.D., *International Diplomacy, State Administrators and Narcotics Control: The Origins of a Social Problem*, Aldershot, UK: Gower Publishers, 1985.

Steiner, Roberto, "Colombia's income from the drug trade," *World Development* 26(6) (1998), 1013–31.

Stepan, Nancy Leys, *"The Hour of Eugenics": Race, Gender, and Nation in Latin America*, Ithaca: Cornell University Press, 1991.

Strausbaugh, John and Donald Blaise, comps., *The Drug User: Documents 1840–1960*, New York: Blast Books, 1991.

Swann, John P., *Academic Scientists and the Pharmaceutical Industry: Cooperative Research in Twentieth-Century America*, Baltimore: Johns Hopkins University Press, 1988.

Szasz, Thomas, *Ceremonial Chemistry: The Ritual Persecution of Drugs, Addicts, and Pushers*, Garden City, NY: Anchor Press, 1974.

Tamayo, Augusto E., *Informe sobre las Colonias de Oxapampa y Pozuzo y los Ríos Palcuzu y Pichis*, Lima: Ministerio de Fomento, 1904.

Tan, Tong Joe, *Het internationale opiumprobleem*, Amsterdam: Gerretsen Pubs., 1929.

Täschner, Karl-Ludwig and Werner Richtberg, *Koka und Kokain: Konsum und Wirkung*, Köln: Deutscher Ärte-Verlag, 1988.

Taylor, Arnold H., *American Diplomacy and the Narcotics Trade, 1900–1939: A Study in International Humanitarian Reform*, Durham: Duke University Press, 1969.

Thamm, Berndt Georg, *Andenschnee: Die lange Linie des Kokain*, Basel: Sphinx Verlag, 1986.

—— *Drogen Report: Und nun auch noch Crack?*, Bergisch Gladbach: Gustav Lübbe, 1988.

Thoumi, Francisco, *Economía, Política y Narcotráfico*, Bogotá: Tercer Mundo Editores, 1994.

United Nations, Commission on Narcotic Drugs, "Peru: Annual Report for 1950," in *Annual Reports of Governments* (E/NR 1950), New York: ESC, 1952.

United Nations, Economic and Social Council, 5th year, 12th Session, *Report of the Commission of Enquiry on the Coca Leaf*, Lake Success, NY: ESC, 1950.

United States, Treasury Department, Federal Bureau of Narcotics, "Traffic in opium and other dangerous drugs," annual report, 1930–60, Washington, DC: United States Government Printing Office, 1930–60.

Van Dyke, Craig and Robert Byck. "Cocaine use in man," *Advances in Substance Abuse* 3 (1983), 1–2.

Vanvugt, Ewald, *Wettig Opium, 350 jaar Nederlandse Opiumhandel in de Indische Archipel*, Haarlem: In de Knipscheer Pubs., 1985.

Varallanos, José, *Historia de Huánuco: Introducción para el Estudio de la Vida Social de una Región del Perú*, Buenos Aires: Imprenta López, 1959.

Vershofen, Wilhelm, *Wirtschaftsgeschichte der Chemisch-Pharmazeutischen Industrie, Dritter Band, 1870–1914*, Aulendorf: Editio Cantor KG, 1958.

Vinelli, Manuel, "Contribución al estudio de la coca," Ph.D. thesis (published), Ciencias Naturales, Universidad Nacional Autónoma del San Marcos, Lima, 1918.

Waldorf, Dan, C. Reinarman, and S. Murphy, *Cocaine Changes: The Experience of Using and Quiting*, Philadelphia: Temple University Press, 1991.

Walker, William III, *Drug Control in the Americas*, Albuquerque: University of New Mexico Press, 1981.

—— *Opium and Foreign Policy: The Anglo-American Search for Order in Asia, 1912–1954*, Chapel Hill: University of North Carolina Press, 1991.

—— ed., *Drug Control Policy: Essays in Historical and Comparative Perspective*, University Park: Pennsylvania State University Press, 1992.

—— comp., *Drugs in the Western Hemisphere: An Odyssey of Cultures in Conflict*, Wilmington: Scholarly Resources, 1996.

Wallerstein, Immanuel, *Unthinking Social Science: The Limits of Nineteenth-Century Paradigms*, Cambridge, UK: Polity Press, 1991.

Warner, John Harley, *The Therapeutic Perspective: Medical Practice, Knowledge, and Identity in America, 1820–1885*, Cambridge: Harvard University Press, 1986.

Warner, Nicholas O., *Spirits of America: Intoxication in Nineteenth-Century American Literature*, Norman: University of Oklahoma Press, 1997.

Weil, Andrew, *The Natural Mind: An Investigation of Drugs and the Higher Consciousness*, Boston: Houghton Mifflin Co., 1972.

Weinstein, James, *The Corporate Ideal in the Liberal State 1900–1918*, New York: Beacon Press, 1968.

Willoughby, Westel W., *Opium as an International Problem: The Geneva Conferences*, Baltimore: Johns Hopkins University Press, 1925.

Wissler, Albert, *Die Opiumfrage: Eine Studie zur weltwirtschaftlichen und weltpolitischen Lage der Gegenwart*, Jena: Gustav Fischer, 1931.

Wolf, Eric R., *Europe and the People Without History*, Berkeley: University of California Press, 1982.

Wright, Hamilton, "The International Opium Conference," *American Journal of International Law* (October 1912).

Young, James Harvey, *The Toadstool Millionaires: A Social History of Patent Medicines in America before Federal Regulation*, Princeton: Princeton University Press, 1961.

—— *Pure Food: Securing the Federal Food and Drugs Act of 1906*, Princeton: Princeton University Press, 1990.

—— *American Health Quackery: Collected Essays by James Harvey Young*, Princeton: Princeton University Press, 1992.

Zimring, Franklin E. and Gordon Hawkins, *The Search for Rational Drug Control*, New York: Cambridge University Press, 1992.

Zinberg, Norman I., *Drug, Set and Setting*, New Haven: Yale University Press, 1984.

Index

Lightning Source UK Ltd.
Milton Keynes UK
UKOW06f1807190116

266701UK00003B/173/P